Sunburn

Also by James Felton

52 Times Britain was a Bellend

Sunburn

JAMES FELTON

THE UNOFFICIAL HISTORY OF THE *SUN* NEWSPAPER IN 99 HEADLINES

sphere

SPHERE

First published in Great Britain in 2020 by Sphere

3 5 7 9 10 8 6 4 2

Copyright © James Felton 2020
Illustrator © Emanuel Santos 2020

A CIP catalogue record for this book is available from the British Library.

ISBN 978-0-7515-8078-5

Typeset in Caslon by M Rules
Printed and bound in Great Britain by Clays Ltd, Elcograf S.p.A.

Papers used by Sphere are from well-managed forests
and other responsible sources.

Sphere
An imprint of
Little, Brown Book Group
Carmelite House
50 Victoria Embankment
London EC4Y 0DZ

An Hachette UK Company
www.hachette.co.uk

www.littlebrown.co.uk

For Katie, Hugo and Dylan

CONTENTS

INTRODUCTION

In 1969, Rupert Murdoch bought the struggling *Sun* broadsheet paper and turned it into a number-one bestselling tabloid that would also carry the nickname 'The Scum'.

Having inherited a newspaper from his father in Australia (as you do) and made it more profitable, Murdoch turned his attention to the UK, where he bought Sunday newspaper the *News of the World*, which you might know from such hits as hacking the phone of a murdered teenager and a name-and-shame campaign against paedophiles which led to vigilante attacks on a paediatrician's house (paedophile, paediatrician – tomay-to, tom-paedo). But the *Sun* was the real beginning of an empire that would spread across the pond and give Murdoch the ear of the President of the United States – both literally on the phone and because Donald Trump will frothily regurgitate in tweet form whatever he has just seen on Murdoch's Fox News.

But back to the *Sun*. Through it, Murdoch arguably revolutionised the media landscape by creating a paper more interested in desperately entertaining and gaining readers than anything trivial like getting your facts 100 per cent in order, and showing other proprietors that – in terms of profit – it's one hell of a business model.

The *Sun* has claimed to win elections and appeared to have influence over politicians and politics well beyond what a boob pamphlet might merit. Editors of the *Sun* have been seen going in and out of Downing Street in a way you just don't see with the people who run *Jugs*.

If you haven't ever read the *Sun* (and I truly envy you), while the *Guardian* is like the slightly pious guy in your sociology seminar who's done all the reading and really wants you to know it, and the *Daily Mail* is like your cantankerous elderly neighbour who almost certainly has Nazi memorabilia hidden away in her attic, the *Sun* is like your friend's friend who's fun to be around at first but ruins every night out at about 3 a.m. by ranting about 'poofs' (a term the *Sun* used constantly throughout the eighties). And though he's always good with celebrity gossip and chats about which football team are kicking balls the best this year, you wish he'd stick to those topics rather than poisoning the mind of your friend with long rants about groups of people he reckons we should be 'sending back'.

For those who don't buy the paper, the *Sun* and its sister paper the *News of the World* have had a reputation for sleazy, sensationalist and questionable stories that they've thoroughly earned throughout the years. I imagine they'd rather people forget how ardently they stuck to this line in stories such as *'Eastbenders'* – written by Piers Morgan – about the first gay kiss on *EastEnders* – and 'The Truth' (arguably their most infamous story) in which they smeared the victims of the Hillsborough disaster with claims that they had pissed on the dead. But if the *Sun* think it's OK to air other people's dirty laundry, then I think it's fair that they have theirs aired in return. Because despite declining circulation figures they've still felt pushily relevant in the Brexit referendum and recent general elections, in the junior doctors' strikes and in their obsession with an actress called Meghan Markle and her unemployed husband.

So whilst I've been fanning their skid-marked pages, I've been asking myself these questions:

Are they really the all-powerful newspaper they think they are? Do they really win elections, or just choose to back the people who are obviously going to win, like a weedy kid sucking up to the school bully in the hope that he won't get the crap kicked out of him during the bully's next monopoly commission? Do they influence their readers, or merely attempt to spell out what they're thinking in order to appeal to them and sell more papers? In short, are they more like a sewage factory pumping out human waste, polluting an otherwise basically clean sea, or like a mirror placed above a toilet, reflecting shit?

A few notes to readers and/or lawyers:

- The book will mostly focus on the *Sun* but will – where relevant – briefly stray into the now-defunct *News of the World*.
- The book is not just a factual account of stories covered by the *Sun*, it also contains a lot of my opinion. A ridiculous amount of it, in fact. If something has happened, there's a good chance I've had an opinion about it that I'm about to bore you with at length.
- I've picked ninety-nine stories from across the last fifty years because ninety-nine is as good a number as any and too many books have '101' written on them, the amateurs. I've arranged stories in categories rather than listing them chronologically, so you can get a sense of the *Sun*'s principles across its lifespan – and because nothing says 'humour book' like chapters called 'Misogyny' and 'Prejudice'.
- Along with the facts, there are some comic exaggerations. Fortunately, they're so obvious that if you can't spot them you're likely incapable of reading sentences. For instance, if I was to say the *News of the World* hired a private detective who hacked Milly Dowler's phone whilst she was missing and before her body was found, that would be a factual statement. If I was to say that there's nothing they love more than a missing kid and probably ring the office missing-child bell, punch the air with excitement and sing 'We're in the Money' the moment a white one goes missing, that would be hyperbole. It's a buzzer not a bell.
- A lot of the *Sun*'s coverage over the years has been awful, but I'm of the opinion that that doesn't mean a book about it should be entirely serious and self-important. If you're looking for a complex dive into media theory that cites Baudrillard at every available opportunity I'd highly recommend Baudrillard, the absolute narcissist. But if you're looking for a fun and at times horrible overview of the scandalous history of the *Sun* that I expect they'd rather you didn't see, then you're in the right place. Brace yourself, read on, and above all else don't buy the *Sun*.

GLOSSARY

For those of you unfamiliar with the *Sun*'s ways, here is a run-down of the key parts.

Sun Says

The 'Sun Says' section of the paper is the editorial or leader: it states an opinion on the news as opposed to neutrally reporting the facts like the rest of the paper also doesn't do. This is the section that makes clear the editorial stance of the paper, and often sounds like the reasonable common-sense talk of an especially gobby racist barfly boring the Wetherspoons staff at 11 a.m. on a Tuesday.

Page 3

This is the tabloid tradition of putting a woman with her boobs out on page 3 of the paper every day. This practice was started by the *Sun* in 1970, before being copied by other papers who noticed that the people-who-want-to-read-the-news demographic overlaps quite a lot with the people-who-are-horny demographic. The BBC like to pitch themselves as impartial, the *Guardian* as rigorous, and the *Sun* as here for you if you can't decide whether you'd like to find out about today's events or if you've got the horn.

Page 3, while called Page 3, could sometimes be pushed back to any of the odd numbers up to and including 9, depending on what tragic news was taking place that day. The readers didn't seem to mind as long as the boob count within the paper was some multiple of two.

Wardrobe malfunction

A mainstay of the *Sun* has been the wardrobe malfunction, where some celebrity has accidentally shown a body part that was meant to be in their shirt and/or pants. Why pay a professional model when, occasionally, a celebrity's skirt will catch a gust of wind and – if you happen to be at a low enough angle outside the taxi with the right telephoto lens – you can accidentally get a photograph of her bum.

The term 'wardrobe malfunction' makes it sound like a tailor has fucked up and done some sloppy sewing, leading to the bum or boob slip, when really it's more about the paparazzi following celebs on beaches like a pervert Jaws who prays to Satan that a wave knocks off their victim's bikini.

Nip slip

See **Wardrobe malfunction**, but for some reason the nipples have their own special terminology.

Bingo

Unlike broadsheets, tabloids like the *Sun* don't stick to trying to win over readers by being readable. As well as the generous serving of boobies, they like to run bingo competitions that keep the readers coming back, the theory being that whilst you might skip a newspaper every few days, you won't if there's a chance you might win thousands of pounds by buying it.

You the Jury

The *Sun* likes to ask questions of their readers in a section called 'You the Jury' (as though whatever decision readers come to is the final say in the matter), a bit like a toddler tugging at your shirt and asking 'Why is the sky blue?' Except they're an adult asking 'Should we bring back hanging?' and other questions that – had your kid asked them – would make you start to wonder if they might be the Antichrist.

If I had to rename it, a good candidate would be 'Crowbarring Open the Overton Window' or 'Let's Frame Questions in a Way that Keeps Debate Quite Fucking Right Wing Indeed, Please'.

Front page

Going to take a stab in the dark and guess you know what a front page is, but just to reiterate for when you're reading stories like 'Orville in sex romp' or an exposé on the secret lives of the Teletubbies, bear in mind that this page is to highlight what the *Sun* think are the most important stories in the world that day, and the surrounding smaller stories are the things they think will entice readers to buy a copy.

MISOGYNY

'SAM, 16, QUITS A-LEVELS FOR OOH-LEVELS'

17 November 1970

For a paper that likes to name and shame paedophiles, the *Sun* sure did like to feature images of the breasts of sixteen- to seventeen-year-old girls.

OK, going to level with you here: this is not the sentence I'd like to have started my book with. It's probably the last sentence I ever wanted to start any book with, and not just because it's distasteful. Bestsellers tend to start with something like 'Harry was a wizard' or 'Christian Grey and Anastasia Steele were porking again', not 'Hey, you know who used to love to publish what we'd now call indecent pictures of a child?'

But I felt that if I had to talk about Page 3 it would be somewhat odd to do it on page 9. So, like the *Sun* making everyone on a train see boobs the second an old pervert opens a paper, I'm going to throw you right into the Page 3 material.

Alright, here we go.

Exactly a year after the *Sun* relaunched as a tabloid under new management, they showed everyone what kind of paper they'd like to become by printing their first boobs. Breasts had appeared in newspapers before – in articles about health, or when talking about nudist beaches – but the new innovation from the *Sun* was they would just show you naked women for no reason at all. Here are some nipples, no I'm not going to justify it, just enjoy looking at them on the train whilst surrounded by possibly uncomfortable commuters, you honking great pervert.

German model Stephanie Rahn was pictured in a field, shot from the side: the *Sun* dipped their toes into the water by only showing the one boob. The move – as they'd probably expected – stirred up controversy, which Larry Lamb (real name Albert, and the editor at the time) used to his advantage. When the paper was banned from libraries and there were anti-pornography marches against it, it merely intrigued more people to buy it. By the following year, daily circulation had swelled from 1.5 million to 2.1 million and Page 3's erection has long been attributed as a factor. (Nope, I'm not even sorry.)

Throughout the seventies, the paper stuck to a reasonably tasteful tone to pictures. Journalists allege the Page 3 editors would show the images to female members of staff to check that they weren't too slimy, a strange and rarely heard-of version of 'feminism' where thrusting images of half-naked ladies in your employees' faces and asking 'Is this *too* dirty?' is somehow OK.

But in the eighties, the paper upped the sleaze and began making stars of their models. Not all of them could buy pints.

Sixteen-year-old Samantha Fox would go on to be probably the *Sun*'s most famous glamour model. She was first pictured topless under the title 'Sam, 16, Quits A-Levels for Ooh-Levels'. I'd argue it's no age to have to deal with creeps, and creeps did come a-creeping. On 30 January 1984, for instance, one man wrote in to the *Sun* to say that he'd built up a collection of photos of Samantha Fox but his mum had burned them (my guess would be because she'd rightly deduced collecting naked photos of a sixteen-year-old is the behaviour of a serial killer). He asked the paper to print more pictures of her for his stash and they obliged, printing quotes from the man like 'She would go down a treat if she ever came down here. She has a lovely body' and 'I'm thinking of emigrating to Australia and I'd love to take Sam with me' – sentences that should only really be read in a court transcript.

The models were so young they hadn't done much in their lives by this point to talk about, so the pictures would be accompanied by captions about how 'Laura, 17, has just passed an NVQ in the meat industry. But she's also a prime bit of rump-ty herself' (26 August 1996). And 'Zoe, 16, from Bristol, has been swotting up all term and has just finished taking nine GCSE exams. But now it's our turn for a bit of study. It was never this fun at school!' (5 July 1989).

In fairness to the *Sun*, fellow tabloid the *Daily Sport* went further – counting down the days until a model's sixteenth birthday, when it could legally photograph her topless. ('I think if you check the date in her passport you'll find we're not technically nonces, officer.') The *Sun* is obviously not responsible for what the *Daily Sport* did, but you could argue that they at least paved the way by being the first to market, creating a ready readership who expected news with a side of nipple.

Use of younger Page 3 girls became less frequent in the nineties and eventually the *Sun* was forced to stop photographing sixteen-year-old girls with their breasts out altogether when parliament passed the Sexual Offences Act 2003, which made it illegal. It's never great when the passing of something called the Sexual Offences Act stops you from doing something that you might otherwise continue to do.

'Had to make a few changes to the job lately.'

'Oh yeah, why's that?'

'Oh, because the new Sexual Offences Act reclassified what I was doing as child pornography.'

'Right.'

'Can't do anything these days—'

'I'll be honest, I'm dialling 999 in my pocket.'

THE SEXY CONFESSIONS OF AA MAN IN RAPE CASE

2 May 1979

In 1979, the *Sun* published the headline 'THE SEXY CONFESSIONS OF AA MAN IN RAPE CASE', about a man who would go on to be convicted of rape, like those were perfectly ordinary phrases you just jam together in a sentence, like 'elegant soirée' or 'multiple stab wounds'.

Historically, the *Sun* has had a problem of reporting sexual crimes, including rape, in a way that's quite jarring to modern eyes. I'd summarise this as quite a niche condition, where you can't stop seeing the word 'sexy' when the word is actually just 'sex', like how Boris Johnson sees 'another job well done, big boy' when it's just a graph showing the worst coronavirus death toll in Europe.

Some years later, on 15 March 1985, a doctor was taken to a disciplinary hearing for alleged sexual assaults on several patients, including a rape that resulted in the birth of a child. The *Sun* went with the headline 'SEXY DOC'S BLACK BABY SHOCK'. Little journalism tip: there are virtually no circumstances in which it's necessary to relay how fuckable you find an alleged rapist, least of all as your main title.

The next day – under the headline 'SEXY DOC SEIZED MY BOOBS' – they covered the allegations of a woman who said she was assaulted whilst seeking treatment for an itchy nose. They did so in unnecessary detail: 'Miss Y, wearing a grey sweater and smart green tartan skirt shook with emotion as she told the inquiry of an assault when she was 14 years old . . . and how a man had sucked her nipples' and 'he took hold of my nipples, one in each hand – and started twisting with his fingers for a couple of seconds. He then leaned over and started licking my breasts one at a time.' Which are the details you need to give during an inquiry to establish the facts, but not exactly stuff you need to report. Unless, of course, your main concern in writing the piece is entertaining and mildly titillating an audience in a two-page spread – then by all means crack on.

These crude headlines have spanned the years of the paper, growing even more creepy when dealing with statutory rape. 'SIR'S BABY OIL SEX ROMP WITH GIRL OF 15' read one from 3 November 1990, about a man being jailed for 'unlawful sexual intercourse and indecent assault'. Their hot take was that the man had been 'jailed over lessons in love' and the article made reference to how 'well developed and streetwise' the victim was, as well as describing the encounters as 'steamy'.

Another report of underage sex ran under the headline 'DISHY DAVID TAUGHT ME HOW TO LOVE' (1 March 1985), which was about a man who had allegedly had sex with an underage girl of fifteen. So why not include pictures of the girl in her bikini next to the headline, as well as on the front page, like a housemate saying 'You don't want to know what some pervert's gone and done in the toilet' before demanding you march in there to take a peek?

If you're thinking, sure it's bad, but the twentieth century was a different time, then 1) I won't be inviting you round for dinner; and 2) here's a headline just for you from 25 March 2003: 'NUDE NURSE RAN THROUGH HOTEL "TO FLEE RANDY VET"', neatly demonstrating how the *Sun* was still willing to use alleged sexual harassment for entertainment.

The 'SEXY CONFESSIONS OF AA MAN IN RAPE CASE' – with its quotes about conquests told by the (later jailed) defendant during the trial to bolster his defence that the encounter was consensual – is included here not for how shocking it is, but for how surprisingly ordinary it was for a paper that has at times seemed to see rape cases as just another way of entertaining their audience.

'I've got a story about someone who's confessed to seventeen rapes,' editor Kelvin MacKenzie allegedly said during his tenure. 'If it's a record, I want it on the front page.'

COP'S SEXY SNAPS
SEDUCED KATHY, 15

7 September 1988

THE CASE OF THE COP AND THE MINOR – MAKE SURE TO COVER THAT SENSITIVELY.

AND BY SENSITIVELY, YOU MEAN WITH REGARDS TO THE COP RIGHT?

The *Sun* seems to have a small subgenre of crime I'd categorise as 'cop might be a sex offender, but the *Sun* thinks he's a bit of a lad'.

'RANDY motorcycle cop Peter West took sexy snaps of an under-age beauty – then made her his mistress, a court heard yesterday,' one such article began on 7 September 1988. 'The married policeman photographed 15-year-old Kathy [NAME REDACTED BY ME] pouting in a skimpy dress and suspenders as she straddled his powerful bike.' Odd to throw in the detail about the bike – this is the story of a man getting convicted for a sex crime, not *Top Gear* – but OK.

The story continued in this weird tone, giving a lot of space to the convicted officer to explain how it was all fine. This would be like having a ten-minute slot at the end of *The Texas Chain Saw Massacre* for Leatherface to explain how, in the long run, needlessly chainsawing endless victims was good for carbon emissions.

'Girls grow up very quickly these days, she knew what she was letting herself in for,' was amongst other choice quotes. It was also made clear how the officer had been a credit to the force, other than that slight blip where he broke the law by repeatedly having sex with an underage girl.

The man now wanted to make a career as a photographer: presumably it could be a boost to his career to say 'Whilst it's not exactly an exhibition, they were once named "Exhibit B" when my photographs were used as evidence against me in court.'

There are a lot of words you can use to describe a thirty-one-year-old man photographing and then having unlawful sex with a fifteen-year-old but 'steamy' and 'sex romps' aren't among them. Unless you're the *Sun* in the eighties, of course; then that's totally legit.

Unbelievably, they then printed the pictures the cop was fired for, which I *guess* you could argue was done out of newsworthiness. But they were captioned 'Tantalising ... lovely Kathy' and 'Stunner ... Kathy's provocative pose' and 'sultry ... Kathy pictured by her lover' while she was casually described throughout the article as 'the schoolgirl stunner', 'his lovely Lolita', 'leggy'.

This is not the only article that appears to have been written by a prisoner on day release from a nonce wing. A teacher who was jailed after 'unlawful sex' with his fourteen-year-old student was described as giving her 'lessons in love' on 23 April 1977. Another, titled 'SEXY SECRETS OF RUFUS'S HAYLOFT', from 27 January 1978 invites you to think from the title 'hmm, sounds horny' before they hit you with the fact that it's a police matter. The 'sexy' secret the sixty-eight-year-old farmer was alleged to be hiding was a 'sex syndicate' (the *Sun*'s words) involving thirteen- to sixteen-year-old girls that allegedly met in his hayloft. The *Sun* somewhat bafflingly chose to describe the girls as 'a "hard core" of ten good-time pupils'. I'm youngish, though, so maybe that was the preferred term for 'victims of a paedophile gang' in the seventies.

NEWS IN BRIEFS

14 January 2003

After its introduction back in 1970, Page 3 rumbled along as it always had, educating the minds of its readers into thinking it was perfectly acceptable for women to be naked alongside their morning coffees. Then in 2003, Rebekah Wade (later Rebekah Brooks) became editor, succeeding David Yelland. According to the *Guardian*, some media pundits had speculated that she might put an end to Page 3.

However, that turned out to be wronger than Marmite yoghurt. On her first day at the paper, on 14 January 2003, she turned up wearing an actual 'I love Page 3' badge and had a model on page 3 as usual, under the title 'Rebekah from Wapping' (Wapping was where the *Sun* was printed at the time), just to make her feelings clear. Then, during her reign, a new feature was added: News in Briefs. The topless photos were accompanied by quotes from the models. Which sounds like a good idea at first, until you realise what they were 'saying'.

'Sam is pleased British Gas plans to freeze its prices but thinks it should go further. She said: "Surely after a winter of huge profits, British Gas could cut them. It should remember the words of US writer Denis Waitley, 'You must consider the bottom line, but make it integrity before profits.'"' (14 May 2013).

And:

'RUTH welcomed tougher laws on paedophiles – but she is incredibly suspicious that Home Secretary John Reid unveiled them just before retiring to the backbenches' (14 June 2007).

Another, from 3 February 2004, said, 'Zoe is 29 and here are her breasts. She endorses the war on Iraq and thinks they should use more Scud missiles to target war orphans.' OK, it didn't, but I'm only exaggerating slightly. It actually read:

'Zoe is certain Tony Blair was right to take Britain into the war with Iraq. She said: "You don't need to be an international diplomat to realise the world is better off without Saddam. We should be proud of what has been achieved."'

The aim of this mind-numbing and unsexy new feature is not clear. Were readers meant to find it arousing that the model echoed their opinion on gas prices, or was it meant to add an extra layer of difficulty to them climaxing, now that at the back of their mind they were thinking about the Iraq War? It's also suspicious just how closely the quotes echoed the editorial line, such as 'Melanie wants the government to get tough on benefits cheats' (16 August 2004), and it would be interesting from a scientific perspective to find out if sentences like 'Melanie thinks the poor should be left to die' made it more or less difficult for *Sun* readers to crank one out.

People say that pornography these days gives kids unrealistic expectations with regards to sex, but picture what it would have been like if your first introduction to women being naked was News in Briefs. 'I see you've got your top off, Michelle. Before we get down to business, I expect you'd like to tell me which group of immigrants you reckon should go home.'

Other models were quoted reciting obscure philosophical quotes, or world leaders, to back up their points. One woman, hands on her head, nipples pointed at the reader, reeled off a line from Gandhi, and I've spent far too much time wondering what he'd make of it if he knew.

'Danni says: "I've often wondered how quarks and other subatomic particles gain mass. So I was relieved to hear of the discovery of a new sub-atomic particle",' one sciency News in Briefs read on 8 July 2012. '"We can now say with certainty that a form of Higgs Boson 'sticks' to fundamental particles of matter. That's one less thing for me to worry about."'

Now, Danni could easily have been a university student studying physics, but I'd hazard a guess that this line was actually written by the same journo who thought it was funny to give models lines from philosophers. The (crap and misogynistic) joke being 'hahaha they're pretty, they can't be smart too'.

'FAT, JEALOUS' CLARE
BRANDS PAGE 3 PORN

14 January 2004

In 2004, the *Sun* spliced the MP Clare Short's head onto a Page 3 model's body because she had the audacity to say she didn't like the page as a concept.

Short had called for a ban in 1987, introducing a parliamentary bill for it to be outlawed. Her complaint wasn't from a place of puritanism. Personally – and I don't want to sound like a prude – if you're going to look at naked bodies I strongly feel like you should do it within the confines of a confession booth before doing a whole buttload of penance, but that wasn't her objection. She didn't support a separate bill to remove obscenity from the media and other published works (including sexual imagery, sexual language and images of graphic violence); what she wanted was legislation to 'remove the degrading images of women as available sex objects that were circulated in the mainstream of society through the tabloid press'.

The bill failed – it was, to be fair to it, a shit bill and would have seen medical textbooks being thrown in the same skips as hardcore pornography – and seventeen years went by. Then, in 2004, at a Westminster lunch reported by the *Guardian*, Short said she'd still love to ban it, and to 'take the pornography out of our press'.

The *Sun* reacted in a completely normal and not at all batshit fashion, sending a busload of Page 3 models to Short's house, where she lived with her elderly mother. The models were tasked with getting a photo with Short, but ended up only being able to get a photo with her door. The paper then ran several pages about the 'story', even though Short was a backbencher with limited opportunities to implement any kind of ban, having resigned from the government in 2003.

In an article titled '"FAT, JEALOUS CLARE" BRANDS PAGE 3 PORN' – with quotes from *Sun* models calling her a 'killjoy' as well as 'jealous and fat' – it placed her head on top of a topless model. Because nothing screams 'we do not objectify women' like taking a naked woman, cutting off her head but keeping her breasts, and replacing her head with that of another woman, who you're calling fat while attempting to humiliate for having thoughts.

One of the far too many pages declared 'SHORT ON LOOKS SHORT ON BRAINS'. On another were eight models with their breasts out under the title 'THIS ONE'S FOR YOU, CLARE'. An accompanying 'News in Briefs Special' said that 'Clare Short has built up her career by slagging off us Page Three girls' – she hadn't – 'well it's time for us to have our say', going on to call Page 3 empowering for models and telling Short to 'put a sock in it'. Bear in mind that there are eight of them on this page, apparently talking in unison like the Borg, and it all comes across quite threatening.

Whether or not it's empowering for the models themselves (sorry, reader, I am not going to solve this debate in the word count), it missed Short's point entirely, which was that she felt it was damaging to society to have these images circulated in the mainstream media where they could be easily viewed in public.

All in all, the *Sun* got a long line-up of Page 3 models, plus sleazy night-club owner Peter Stringfellow, MPs and people who just liked pornography to have a go at Short. The message was clear. Step out of line, MPs and public figures, and we will hound you.

In 2014, Rebekah Brooks would tell the phone-hacking trial that she regretted the 'cruel and harsh' attack on Short that day. But, really hammering it home, the 'Sun Says' section had reiterated that models had called Short 'fat and ugly', adding 'Who are we to disagree with their verdict?'

BBQ DAD KILLED 6 OVER WIFE'S AFFAIR

13 August 2012

Occasionally, the media will look at the case of a guy bludgeoning his family to death with a spade and think, the wife is to blame for this somehow, I'll bet.

Take, for example, Damian Rzeszowski, who in 2011 killed his wife and children, and his wife's friends, at a family barbecue. The *Sun* wrote that he 'slaughtered six people at a family barbecue after he flipped over his wife's affair' (15 January 2011), implying that his wife had some sort of partial culpability. In a later article, from 16 August 2011, he was described as a 'doting dad' and a 'great father'.

While a photo of the children had the simple and blameless caption 'so innocent', his wife received the explanation 'just six weeks earlier Rzeszowski had learned Izabela, 30, was cheating on him'.

In an article from 15 February 2011 about a separate killing, and as later highlighted in a study by the University of Hertfordshire on how the media portrays domestic violence, the *Sun* made it sound an awful lot like they were blaming the victim of murder for her own murder because her job paid too well.

'The carnage is thought to have been triggered by a long-running dispute between Bluestone and high-flying administrator Jill, his second wife, over her yearning to move nearer her job,' they wrote. 'She earned £40,000 as the head of Basildon District Council's policy and performance unit. And she faced rush-hour car journeys of up to two hours to reach her office in Essex. Karl earned £25,000 as part of a special police team tackling crime.'

So who is the real monster here? No, wait, it's the guy who killed his wife.

The same study found 'evidence aplenty of perpetrator responsibility for abuse receding from view', including an article from 2002 which, well, just read:

'Lawyer Les Humes stabbed his wife to death in front of their children after she told him she was cheating on him ... Humes worked long hours to provide his family with a comfortable lifestyle and a beautiful home.'

Kudos, Mr Humes, for providing a pretty house in which you could stab your wife.

An article from 15 February 2011 quoted a neighbour of a man who murdered his kids, saying how committed he was to his family, while 'all his wife' – who didn't murder her kids – 'did was sleep and go to work', the MONSTER.

Murdered but haven't cheated on the murderer or earned a salary? No problem – you can still get the blame for your own death if you're a woman who drinks alcohol. In 2016, the *Sun* came under fire for an article about a rape and murder victim which they put out on Twitter under the caption 'Woman "drank six Jagerbombs in ten minutes on the night she was raped and murdered"', as if the amount she'd drunk on a night out made her in some way responsible for her own murder.

So if you don't want to be portrayed as partly to blame for your own murder, then try not to cheat – even if it turns out to be on some kind of murderous arsehole, that's no excuse – not provide enough money or earn slightly *too much money*, and for fuck's sake, don't enjoy yourself on a night out. Is that too much to ask?

PAGE 3 V BREAST CANCER

4 March 2014

In 2014, the *Sun* was facing more and more pressure from protest group No More Page 3 to stop with the softcore pornography already. The campaign had begun in August 2012 when Lucy Anne Holmes noticed that, despite all the success of athletes at the London Olympic Games, the most prominent image of a woman in the paper was on page 3. She founded No More Page 3, which went on to lobby companies, such as Lego, not to advertise in the *Sun*. People were starting to find it weird and anachronistic to have stories of war and murder and terrorism and then some tits and then straight back to some more killing. (Yes, it's weird that it took until the 2010s for this to get some attention but you have to understand – those generations were too busy with Tamagotchis and cornering the property market so that no future generation could ever dream of owning a home to notice all the rampant misogyny.) Universities began boycotting the paper, calling for the page to be removed.

Before Page 3 was finally ended in 2015, the *Sun* genuinely tried to do some good with the format – or tried to get a bit of good publicity for it, depending on how cynical you are.

They launched a 'Check 'em Tuesday' campaign in conjunction with the breast cancer charity CoppaFeel!, which featured topless models holding their breasts (as per) but also encouraged women to check their own for lumps. The tone was odd, asking women to name their breasts ('Lacey has Ant & Dec! What do you call yours? Check 'em Tuesday urges you to name your boobs') and having models licking their lips while looking down at their breasts (in promotion of the campaign online). Which, correct me if I'm wrong, is not a classic way of performing a breast exam. But nevertheless, the campaign tried to raise awareness in women about getting to know their own breasts and what to look for when inspecting them. However, it's a fair bet that it wasn't women who were looking at the campaign anyway.

While many welcomed it, a lot of others saw it as a shield the *Sun* could use whenever Page 3 was criticised, along the lines of 'Well, our campaign with all those breasts you so despise helped save lives. I suppose you'd prefer it if they all died of cancer, would you?' They didn't exactly help themselves when the front page of 4 March 2014 read 'PAGE 3 V BREAST CANCER' like if you weren't backing Page 3 you were actively siding with cancer, the only two options available.

For their trouble, End Violence Against Women named the editor of the paper 'Sexist of the Year 2014', making special mention of the campaign.

'Our warmest congratulations to David Dinsmore for his valiant persistence in peddling pornography under the guise of "news",' they said in their announcement. 'Mr Dinsmore no doubt provoked more nominations than any other sexist this year for his additional daring in creating a cancer prevention campaign as a blatant cover for continued daily sexual objectification of women. Transparent!'

A *Sun* spokesperson hit back: 'On a day in which 150 women were executed by the Islamic State for refusing to marry IS militants' – which isn't a great start to a defence; it's like if your boss said 'Hmmm, these spreadsheets are a little off' and you reacted by telling them how many people were killed on 9/11 – 'to target a newspaper that has run high-profile campaigns against domestic violence and supported the causes of rape victims and victims of serial abuse is both absurd and ridiculous . . . At least four female *Sun* readers have said they owe their lives to the *Sun*'s Check 'em Tuesday campaign, which only the most closed-minded would deny is a great outcome.'

And it's true. Several readers, splashed across the front pages, had found lumps after seeing the *Sun*'s campaign. It probably genuinely saved lives. It's just amazing that even when they try to do something good they end up having to defend their misogynistic default setting and casually have to throw in 'OH COME ON, WE'RE MUCH BETTER THAN ISIS'.

It might be naive of me to think that the campaign was anything other than a PR stunt, but on this occasion, I don't think I'm going to come down on the side of 'they're no heroes, they just wanted to print pictures of breasts'. They had got away with printing the pictures for forty-four years: why suddenly, desperately try to justify it like this? I think they probably just tried to do something good but, with no self-awareness of how damaging their history of misogyny was to their reputation, they did it with all the grace and dignity of a tranquillised newborn foal trying to tap dance on jelly.

The *Sun* eventually dropped Page 3 in January 2015, but not before being dicks about it. They printed an edition with no topless Page 3 girl, and newspapers covered the end of the era widely. Then, just like James Cameron announcing an *Avatar* sequel for no fathomable or justifiable reason at all, they brought it back a few days later, on 22 January, writing 'Further to recent reports in all other media outlets, we would like to clarify that this is Page 3 and this is a picture of Nicole, 22, from Bournemouth. We would like to apologise on behalf of the print and broadcast journalists who have spent the last two days talking and writing about us.'

CELEBRITY

FREDDIE STARR ATE MY HAMSTER

13 March 1986

For those unfamiliar, Freddie Starr was a comedian and impressionist who was very popular in the seventies. He was also, thanks to a notorious newspaper story, an alleged consumer of rodent sandwiches.

On 13 March 1986, the *Sun* ran the headline 'Freddie Starr Ate My Hamster'. The story alleged that the comedian went to stay at a friend's house after a gig, whereupon he demanded a sandwich from his friend's girlfriend – twenty-three-year-old model Lea La Salle – like he'd mistaken her for a branch of Pret.

When no sandwich was forthcoming, the *Sun* wrote, Freddie naturally grabbed her pet hamster, named Supersonic, and proceeded to put it between two slices of bread and start crunching it down before you could even recommend adding mayo.

'It's something I'll never forget,' La Salle allegedly told the paper (though a later account from her would claim that she never said this). 'He put my hamster between two slices of bread and started eating it. He thought it was hilarious. He just fell about laughing. I was sick and horrified. He killed my pet.'

To give you a sense of the level of scandal we're talking here, it would be like if the *Daily Mail* revealed tomorrow that Michael McIntyre made a chihuahua into a broth.

Having been approached by the paper with the story and the fact they were going to run it, this left Freddie – a man who insisted he had never eaten a hamster – with two options: deny eating a hamster, which gives people the opportunity to run stories like 'Why's he denying eating hamsters? That makes me feel like there's some truth in there' or ignore it and run the risk of further 'Freddie Starr is *refusing to deny eating hamsters, the SHIT*' headlines.

Freddie chose to deny the story (correctly identifying it as the slightly better of the two options), which you'll be shocked to learn didn't help much. When you see something on the front page of a newspaper, people tend to think there must be *some* truth to it.

The story had a huge impact on his life. After a brief boost to his career – don't deny it, if I asked you to see a random comedian you weren't sure about but then said 'Oh, by the way, he eats hamsters' you'd be curious – he was hounded by the accusation right up until his death, and hated it.

Years after he allegedly crunched down the rodent like a pasty, he would tell interviewers 'I'm fed up of people shouting out "Did you eat that hamster, Freddie?" Now I say, give me £1 and I'll tell you. Then if they give me £1, I say "No" and walk away.' In his autobiography he even felt the need to clarify: 'I have never eaten or even nibbled a live hamster, gerbil, guinea pig, mouse, shrew, vole or any other small mammal', which only adds to my suspicions, if I'm honest. Why's he bringing up voles?

Lea later told the *Leicester Mercury* that 'There was nobody more shocked than me when that headline came out.' In reality, Starr had joked about eating the hamster, then bit into the bread 'but not the hamster' and the most harm that came of it was 'I was upset because the hamster was covered in butter which took two days for it to lick off.'

Why this got twisted into the story it became is unclear, though Starr's manager, Max Clifford, later claimed it was his attempt to boost his client's status – against Starr's own wishes.

'This was the way tabloids worked in the great old days,' Kelvin MacKenzie, who had been editor of the *Sun* at the time, told *Good Morning Britain* after Starr's death. 'I was in a bar in Fleet Street when the mistress of the managing director of the *Sun* and the *News of the World* said this is what had happened to a model friend of hers. And being a tabloid guttersnipe, I rushed back to the office and it was a very quiet day and so we led on that. The Berlin Wall and various other wars seemed less interesting than Freddie Starr eating somebody's hamster.'

And just like that, because there wasn't enough news and Freddie Starr's agent wasn't known for his scruples, a man was hounded for the rest of his life by accusations that he was a consumer of beloved rodents.

After he was finally freed from the rumours by being dead, the *Sun* covered his death by writing 'Freddie Starr Joins *His* Hamster' (10 May 2019), bringing up the story again while his family were mourning their hamster-eating son.

ELTON IN VICE BOYS SCANDAL

25 February 1987

> IT'S BEEN ALMOST A YEAR AND THERE HAVE BEEN *ZERO* NEW FAKE CASES OF CELEBRITIES EATING HAMSTERS.

> FAKE CASES OF HAMSTER EATING ARE SO 1986. IT'S ALL ABOUT FAKE CASES OF RENT BOYS AND PIMPS CALLED GRAHAM NOW.

'In retrospect, it was always only a matter of time until the *Sun* came after me,' Elton John wrote in his autobiography, *Me*. 'I was gay, I was successful, I was opinionated, which in the *Sun*'s eyes made me fair game for a vendetta.'

He was not kidding. The *Sun* pursued Elton like he'd written 'The Bitch is Back' about their mum. When he first shot to fame in the seventies he was largely left alone by the paper, even when he announced he was bisexual in 1976. In terms of the *Sun*, this was during the time of editor Larry Lamb, when such a detail might get mentioned in passing in an article about his music, rather than be a reason to hound him and call him a 'poof', which was much more the style of Kelvin MacKenzie throughout the eighties.

The first *Sun* exclusive about Elton alleged that he was in a 'shocking drugs and vice scandal involving teenage "rent boys"', based on the incredibly detailed accusations of a 'pimp' going by the pseudonym of 'Graham'.

The story continued on pages 4 and 5 under the headline 'ELTON'S LUST FOR BONDAGE'. Because when you're printing made-up dirt on a celebrity who'll sue, why not go the whole hog? It alleged that Elton John had been involved in a number of drug-fuelled orgies at the mansion of Rod Stewart's manager, after meeting Graham at the house while dressed in 'skimpy leather shorts', 'looking like Cleopatra and twirling a sex aid between his fingers'.

It's all very specific, isn't it? Maybe that's why the *Sun* weren't sceptical enough of the story, which would end up getting them sued. Someone tells you they've been having sex with Elton John, you go 'Nah, fuck off', but if they tell you 'On the fourth day of our cocaine binge at the house of the manager of the guy who sings "Do Ya Think I'm Sexy?" he said he wanted to "tie me up in the woods" and "make love to me" while twirling a butt plug like a fidget spinner' you think, well now hold on, that's quite specific, there might be something in this.

Elton was mortified by the accusations, as well as the historical inaccuracies.

'Ah, of course, Cleopatra,' he wrote in his autobiography. 'Last ruler of the Ptolemaic dynasty, lover of Julius Caesar and Mark Antony, and history's most celebrated dildo-twirler and wearer of leather shorts.'

As well as the sordid parts of the tale (the *Sun* printed allegations that he had a 'box of tricks' that they brought out, which contained leather whips and restraints), they also had some mundane stuff that should have set some alarm bells ringing. For instance, Graham recalled how Elton would get tired from all the orgies: 'I remember Elton sat in some jockey-shorts in the kitchen with his head in his hands going "phew, phew",' which is how tired people behave if they're in a Popeye cartoon.

As well as being humiliating, the accusations were pretty serious, as they involved men under the age of consent (which for gay men at the time was twenty-one). Fortunately for Elton, he had proof that it wasn't true, including hotel bills, restaurant receipts and plane tickets.

MYSTERY OF ELTON'S SILENT DOGS

28 September 1987

Most papers hit with a lawsuit by a millionaire who had receipts to prove he wasn't where you'd said he was might tone it down a notch or at least not go and harass him over the course of several months. The *Sun* isn't like most newspapers, and operates more like Captain Ahab desperately trying to seek vengeance on a whale who refused to just die already.

Following Elton's denial of Graham's dildo-twirling orgy claims, the *Sun* led with more 'revelations'. 'ELTON'S KINKY KICKS' read the front page on 26 February 1987. They'd proudly subtitled this with the words 'the story they're suing over', which (as they would go on to admit, they had the story wrong) is a bit like confessing 'we really fucked up, lads' on page 1.

This time, they printed claims that Elton had 'demanded the young male prostitutes found for him should also be drugged with vast amounts of coke before they were brought to his bed', making it sound like he was using some sort of *Pizza Express* for prostitutes where you can specify the toppings.

This was the second in a list of stories that the *Sun* would throw at Elton as they attempted to dig up more dirt – any dirt – to see what would stick. When Elton defended himself, they ran 'Graham's' accusation that Elton was a liar. They printed claims from people who declared 'I RAN COKE FOR ELTON – he tore at drug pack with his teeth' like a mad puppy with a Class-A chew toy. 'ELTON'S 5-DAY ORGY' on the same day (16 April 1987) got its own two-page spread, presumably because it had beaten Elton's previous completely made up four-day orgy by a whole extra day of orgying.

It then turned more sinister. Polaroids were unearthed of him having sex with a man. Though humiliating to have photos of him with former lovers splashed around the newspaper, as he put it: 'Gay man sucks penis: It's not exactly a Pulitzer-winning scoop.' Yet the prying into his love life continued.

The *Sun*'s weird blood feud with a man who was suing them (again, rightly, as they would later admit) was even at the expense of sales. When stories of Elton were printed, sales of the paper would dive. It's not clear whether this was because *Sun* readers just liked Elton (he was very popular – he's Elton John) or they were just plain bored of the story. I suspect it was probably the latter. Sometimes – and I'm sorry to any friends reading this – it's quite dull to hear about a row they're having with a co-worker. Here the *Sun* were printing weekly updates about a vendetta they were having with a pen pal to an audience who had mainly signed up to hear about and/or see boobs.

What was it about this unashamedly gay man that they didn't like so much? How odd, very odd. Thankfully, in a Sun Says piece from 16 April 1987 they made themselves quite clear, not as to why they'd started the claims, but why they'd carried on for so long.

'The *Sun* has no hard feelings towards Elton John,' they wrote. 'We wish him no ill. Certainly we shall never pursue him maliciously. But he must stop telling LIES about the *Sun*.

'In return, we shall stop telling the TRUTH about him.'

He needed to drop his lawsuits, or they'd continue to bore the crap out of their own audience until he did. Fortunately, for Elton and readers of the *Sun*, the paper was about to misreport on Elton's pet dogs so badly it would all come to a (really strange and expensive) humiliating end.

You'd think if someone told you something as completely batshit as 'Oh, Elton John's been removing dogs' voice boxes' you'd check. Especially if you were already being sued for libel by said Elton John. Nevertheless, on 28 September 1987 the *Sun* printed a front-page story saying the much-loved pop star had his pets' 'bark removed'.

'VICIOUS rottweiler dogs guarding pop star Elton John have been silenced by a horrific operation to stop them barking, it was claimed yesterday,' the story went. 'Their voice boxes have been sliced through, said one of the millionaire singer's workers.'

I probably don't need to tell you this, but Elton John did not own any rottweilers. The *Sun* soon learned this by trying to photograph them the next day – just a little tip, but if you're going to publish something like this, the best day to get photographic evidence is not the day after you've published – where they found loud Alsatians. You know the type: fluffy, with those little intact voice boxes they are famed for.

The *Sun* had seriously messed up, and damaged their own court case beyond repair. The case would no longer involve Elton just being on the stand talking about sex and would instead be closer to him pointing at a picture of his dogs, maybe playing a little video of them saying woof, before a quick gavelling* and Elton being handed a massive cheque.

The *Sun* settled instead, and Elton received £1 million from the paper, which also printed a full front-page story titled 'SORRY ELTON' on 12 December 1988, in which they apologised profusely, including for the initial

---

* Yes, I know judges don't really use gavels. Don't you fucking dare tweet me.

story alleging he had been seeing rent boys, saying 'we are delighted that the *Sun* and Elton have become friends again, and are sorry that we were lied to by a teenager living in a world of fantasy'.

Kelvin MacKenzie was later asked about the saga by *Press Gazette*.

'When I published those stories, they were not lies,' he told them. 'They were great stories that later turned out to be untrue – and that is different.'

Not exactly journalism though, is it, Kelvin? Journalism is the bit before you hit print where you fact check.

For a paper that seems to think smacking will solve bad behaviour, they didn't learn their lesson too quickly. They would go on to do one more bit of dog-based Elton John defamation in February 2016, when they claimed his dog had inflicted 'Freddy Krueger-like' injuries on a five-year-old girl, before not making any effort to check how the girl was. The injuries were not serious, and Elton and his husband David Furnish had in fact made several enquiries into the girl's health in what was a minor attack, establishing each time that she was fine.

MY SEX ROMPS WITH
MR ORVILLE

1 December 1988

YOU COULD TELL THAT PUPPET WAS A HORNY DEVIL JUST BY LOOKING AT HIM.

The *Sun* has run a whole load of sexposés over the years, and as I was scanning through them I became obsessed with knowing what their cut-off point is. Who was so low or just plain innocent on the celebrity ladder that if someone rang with a sex story they'd say 'The guy who voiced Alvin from *Alvin and the Chipmunks*? No thanks, I don't care if he has been snorting crack off Peppa Pig, we just don't class him as a celeb.'

I don't think we'll ever know the line, but I feel like I've got a rough idea of how low they'll go in terms of publishing the sex-life details of somebody who you just don't need to know sex-life details about, after stumbling across a front-page story from 1988 which read 'MY SEX ROMPS WITH MR ORVILLE'.

Keith Harris, for those of you too young to remember (like I am), was a ventriloquist who had a big green duck puppet called Orville. I'm informed (I'm not old) that this pair were huge [apologies, this is what happens when you spend months in a library reading puns about tits]. As well as all the Thatcher, homophobia and a distinct lack of Pokémon GO, people in the eighties had to endure prime-time TV involving a man pretending to have an argument with a puppet.

Which sounds just awful, but I realise it's not your fault if people working in television at the time couldn't be bothered to create *Breaking Bad*. Keith Harris is not an obvious target for a sexposé, though. In terms of levels (or style) of celeb, it would be like if nowadays we found out who and precisely how Tinky Winky's been fucking.

And yet, into detail the *Sun* went. First up, they thankfully clarified the headline. The woman on the other end of the romp was having it off with the recently divorced Keith Harris, not banging the duck puppet as the headline implied. Small mercies.

The *Sun* then painted in grim detail the 'bonking' sessions (such a sexy word) of someone you should never have to picture having sex. She even marked his performance, calling him 'average' but adding 'I suppose he performed quite well considering he was supposed to be broken-hearted'.

You're probably wondering why I've included this example. 1) Honestly, because these kinds of celebrity tittle-tattle stories happened in the *Sun* quite a bit and I felt like this book should reflect that in some way rather than gloss over them entirely. 2) This is a particularly weird example of a target for a tell-all story; he's just some childhood hero who rams his hand up a puppet, not Tom Cruise. 3) Because I can't erase this next quote from my mind:

The cheeky comic even quipped to her: 'It's a shame you're not Orville, then I could stick my hand up your bottom.'

Which (although he almost certainly didn't say it) has made me see all forms of puppetry as some sort of sexual act, and now you will too. You're welcome.

THE TRUTH

19 April 1989

On 15 April 1989, a disaster unfolded during a football match at Hillsborough Stadium in Sheffield that would claim the lives of ninety-six people, and injure 766. A build-up of fans in the standing pens, followed by a decision to throw open a second gate, which also funnelled through into the same overcrowded stands, led to a crush of people that resulted in the deaths of many fans, including young children.

An inquiry in 2016 found that they were unlawfully killed due to a failure of police and ambulance services, whose gross negligence was ultimately responsible for their deaths. Back in 1989, the police tried to shift blame for the disaster onto the fans, claiming that they had gained unauthorised entry through the exit gate, when really this had been opened on police orders, due to concerns of a crush around the turnstiles.

Four days later, the *Sun* would print a list of offensive lies about the behaviour of fans during the disaster, directly under the headline 'THE TRUTH':

'Some fans picked pockets of victims'

'Some fans urinated on the brave cops'

'Some fans beat up PCs giving the kiss of life'

The story claimed that 'drunken' 'hooligans' had attacked rescue workers including police officers, firemen and ambulance crew, as well as urinating on them and the dead.

'Some thugs rifled the pockets of injured fans as they were stretched out unconscious on the pitch.

'Sheffield MP Irvine Patnick revealed that in one shameful episode a gang of Liverpool fans noticed that the blouse of a girl trampled to death had risen above her breasts. As a policeman struggled in vain to revive her, the mob jeered: "Throw her up here and we will **** her."'

Footage would confirm that fans who had escaped the crush and onto the pitch helped lift more fans to safety. Others assisted the emergency services, turning advertising boards into makeshift stretchers to carry out the injured, and treating victims themselves on the pitch. Claims of pickpocketing were also false.

The article, by way of adding extra weight to the claims, said that they were 'backed by Sheffield MP Irvine Patnick', who had not been at the game but had merely 'spoke[n] to officers on duty in the mortuary hours after the tragedy'.

During the Falklands War, the *Sun* had had a go at other papers and news programmes for questioning the version of events of those in power (see page 210). True to their word, they were now publishing the words of the police and an MP – who had heard information second hand – as if it were the objective truth. If I had to guess what happened here, and why they made such an awful misjudgement, it's that this is what happens when your newspaper has picked a team to root for instead of trying to establish the truth. The *Sun* had written pieces about football hooliganism before, and weren't big fans of it. They saw themselves as on the side of law and order. The police over louts. Thatcher over the miners. So when they heard the appalling claims about the behaviour of fans, they didn't think, these are awful claims that need investigation, but *gotcha*. Fans apparently behaving the way the *Sun* thought they would behave was one over on the other side, a bizarre victory of sorts, and it was enough to turn off their scepticism.

Kelvin MacKenzie had apparently spent quite some time trying to decide between two titles for the piece. He eventually chose the headline 'THE TRUTH', discarding his second option, 'YOU SCUM'.

It's a testament to how terrible both options are that I can't tell which is more offensive: calling the victims and witnesses of a tragedy 'scum', or printing horrific and untrue allegations about the same victims and distressed witnesses under a headline that implies they're just facts.

Either way, the headline would have consequences for the paper for years. The *Sun* did not deal well with the fallout from their terrible coverage of Hillsborough, unless being boycotted by the whole of Merseyside for all time is part of some kind of unfathomable master strategy that us non-editors are too blind to see. Sales in Merseyside dropped from 524,000 to 320,000 overnight, and the paper was burned in the streets for good measure.

The *Sun* hadn't been the only paper to carry the unverified reports of the police officers. The *Mirror* had gone with 'FURY AS POLICE CLAIM VICTIMS WERE ROBBED' and the *Star* went further, with 'DEAD FANS ROBBED BY DRUNK THUGS'. But both papers, while still giving too much prominence to claims, put in caveats that these were allegations by the police, whereas the *Sun* had gone with THE TRUTH. The *Star*, for its part, apologised the next day for its own terrible front page.

Offensive though it was, it's possible that the *Sun* could have avoided what was to come if they had done the right thing and apologised immediately. But instead they doubled down.

'On Page One yesterday, we reported the unpalatable facts about the behaviour of SOME of the Liverpool fans at Hillsborough,' they wrote in a front-page opinion piece the following day, under the title 'The truth hurts'. Then they repeated the urination and looting claims and said their reporting of such was to prevent the same from happening again.

On top of this, they published a selection of comments on page 4. One man accused the police of trying to 'squirm out of it'. For this he was described as 'sobbing scouser Joseph Murray'.

MacKenzie did end up apologising, on Radio 4 on 30 July 1989, saying: 'It was my decision and my decision alone to do that front page in that way and I made a rather serious error.' He then rolled it back a bit in 1993, telling the House of Commons National Heritage Select Committee, 'I regret Hillsborough. It was a fundamental mistake. The mistake was I believed what an MP said. It was a Tory MP. If he had not said it and the chief superintendent (David Duckenfield) had not agreed with it, we would not have gone with it.' By 1996 he had absolved himself of even more responsibility, telling Radio 4 'The *Sun* did not accuse anybody of anything. We were the vehicle for others.'

The *Sun*, under new editors, have attempted in later years to make up for their coverage. When the findings of the Hillsborough Independent Panel were published in 2012, they published the headline 'THE REAL TRUTH' in which they stated 'cops smeared Liverpool fans to deflect blame' and 'we are profoundly sorry for false reports' (12 September 2012).

For many, and especially in Merseyside, it was too little, too late. A boycott of the *Sun* in Liverpool has been going strong for thirty years now. Major supermarkets in the city have stopped selling it, because there's no demand. People – not just in Liverpool, of course – refer to it as the Scum or the S*n, as if it's a swear. Even people I know who'll happily use the c-word around their nan like it's punctuation.

Perhaps believing they were best to just ignore it, or perhaps because they thought that David Cameron's aides using WhatsApp to coordinate referendum tactics was a bigger story, in 2016 the *Sun* decided not to put the eventual Hillsborough inquest jury ruling on the front page. The story that the ninety-six victims were found to have been unlawfully killed was pushed back to pages 8 and 9 instead.

I guess the truth hurts.

IT'S WALL OVER

10 November 1989

On the day the Berlin Wall fell, the *Sun* dedicated half their front page to pictures of children's TV presenter Michaela Strachan in her underwear because she'd said she didn't like to be seen as a sex object.

While the other national newspapers recognised that the Berlin Wall being torn down was one of the most important events in modern history – and wrote of the end of an era over a full front page – the *Sun* looked at it and thought, hmmm, needs more tits. Before deciding in the spirit of the triumph of capitalism over communism that they shouldn't be volunteered.

'Here is kids TV presenter Michaela Strachan as you have never seen her before – and how she prayed you would NEVER see her!' the exclusive started, letting you know immediately this was not a consensual arrangement.

'The *Sun* today reveals how pretty Michaela – who hates being seen as a sex object – once worked as a £15-a-night **STRIPPOGRAM** girl.'

The focus of the piece, which continued over a further two pages, was twofold: saying that Strachan, twenty-three, didn't like to be seen as a sex object, and printing pictures of her she didn't want people to see, as a seventeen-year-old in her underwear, while calling her 'shapely' and 'saucy'.

The article described how earlier that month men in a nightclub had chanted 'get your t**s out' at Michaela, genuinely censoring the word in an article humiliating a woman by displaying said tits. They then went on to describe her suffering sexual harassment, writing 'mini-skirted Michaela seethed: "I'm a TV presenter, not a bimbo". But just a few years ago, Michaela had no qualms about revealing her body,' as if that made her a hypocrite for not displaying her breasts now because a gaggle of perverts demanded it in song.

Strachan told the paper that she was 'extremely naive' when she worked as a strippogram at seventeen, adding 'I'm just upset that all my fans are going to see me like this'.

As well as being a complete non-story (ha-ha, this person doesn't like to be seen as an object but we've got photos of her in underwear!), the thing that gets me is how urgent they found it. The Berlin Wall had just fallen and they thought, this can't wait another day, as if the employment history of a children's TV presenter was suddenly going to change if they held it back till Saturday. The paper clearly calculated that though their readers had some interest in the collapse of communism and the world changing probably for ever, they were far more interested in seeing tits.

As I've been writing this book, I've often thought, what would some-one think if they only got their news from the *Sun*? If you'd just arrived from space and found a copy on 10 November 1989, you'd have to assume that the symbolic fall of communism was roughly on par, in terms of importance to humans, as a woman ever so nearly getting her bum out five years prior.

FERGIE IS FINISHED

22 August 1992

Shortly before Dianagate (it's coming, folks, brace yourselves – the book's about to turn into the *Daily Express*), the *Sun* published extensive creepshots of the Duchess of York in (and out of) a bikini. The pictures were part of a legal battle in France, so at first, on 19 August 1992, the *Sun* merely printed that the pictures were in existence, under the front-page headline 'QUEEN IN RAGE AT TOPLESS FERGIE' and trailing 'snaps may be seen by world' and assuring readers that 'deals are being negotiated' for the pictures.

In the meantime, they decided to publish a story about the pictures and ask their readers what they reckoned Fergie's tits looked like. They asked, 'Come on folks, as the snaps may never be seen, what do you think Fergie would look like without her bikini top?' before encouraging readers to send in their 'tasteful' drawings.

The Duchess of York, better known as Fergie, had split from Prince Andrew (now an infamous diner at a Pizza Express in Woking) and she was seeing a new man, John Bryan, with whom she'd gone on holiday. The aforementioned photos were taken by a man with a camera during a hangout at the pool, and included a shot of Bryan 'sucking' Fergie's toe (he would later claim it was just a toe kiss) and a topless picture of Fergie. I know you think this telephoto lens-wielding photographer (who could have been in the next county, so grainy are the photos) sounds like some creep who should be immediately arrested, but he sold on the pictures to the press for money, which made him a professional photographer rather than just some very arrestable fucking pervert.

Soon good news came for invasion of privacy fans. The *Sun* wouldn't have to print the drawings after all, as Bryan's court battle was lost and the *Sun* (and other tabloids – the *Sun* weren't alone in this) could publish the photos.

The photographer had only managed to get a picture of the one breast. Making the best of a bad job, on 22 August 1992 the *Sun* published it under the title 'FERGIE'S FINAL BOOB'. They hyped up the photo as '**THIS is the most sensational picture of a royal ever taken**'. Keeping focused on what this meant for the royal family and not just printing sleaze, they trailed 'more amazing pictures pages 4, 5, 14, 15, 21, 22, 23, 24'.

On Page 3 they had the headline 'A YORKIE BARE', which is a classic example of a good pun being ruined by the writer being on the side of Satan. Almost by way of apology for only having the one breast, they stuck Fergie's head on to a Page 3 model and urged readers to 'GIVE stunning Sarah Windsor a right royal welcome to Page Three folks – thanks to the *Sun*'s own picture wizards.' I cannot stress how shit this fake was: it looked like a child had mashed her face on there with a Pritt stick before taking a photo of it with a damaged digital camera and then heavily compressing the file. They then promised 'NOW SEE THE REAL THING – PAGES 4, 5, 14, 16 and 17'.

A palace statement said, 'We strongly disapprove of photographs taken in such circumstances,' to which Sun Says replied: '**[The Queen] must stop**

blaming the messenger when it is the message that is rotten.' Which roughly translates as 'stop blaming us for printing creepshots of tits; she shouldn't be waggling them around in private'.

The *Sun*'s 'angle' on the 'story' seemed to be that they thought it a scandal that Fergie should still be a royal, printing calls from MPs to 'STRIP HER OF HER TITLE'. But it's hard to hold the moral high ground when you're also publishing a Fergie creepshot extravaganza pull-out (which they called *The Fergie Collection* and included a 'souvenir poster' of her with her boob out for readers to put up on their walls).

DI WORRY OVER SMASH

28 August 1992

IT'S ALMOST AS IF HE DOESN'T *WANT* ME TO TAKE HIS PHOTOGRAPH.

The *Sun* were pioneers both in pursuing celebrity stories as entertainment (or 'tat', as I've been filing these stories under on my desktop) and in treating the royal family as celebs pretty much like any other. They started that with Charles and Diana, giving them even more attention than Prince Andrew gives a convicted sex offender with whom he wants to have no more contact. They followed the romance, the fairy-tale wedding, and then their eventual split in 1992. Far from being the end of the coverage, this just gave them twice the number of potential new royal romances to cover.

And so, in 1992, the *Sun* obtained tapes of Diana talking on the phone to a mystery person, a man who called her 'squidgy' and 'darling', and who blew kisses down the line to her. They published long transcripts of the private phone calls, which covered topics from Diana being unhappy in her marriage – '[Charles] makes my life real torture' – and the weird looks she was getting from the Queen Mum – '[She] looks at me strangely. It's not hatred, it's pity and interest mixed in one' – to fears that she might be pregnant.

The call – which took place in 1989 – also touched on how Jimmy Savile had rung her the previous day, which is weird and something I'd like to go into but feel we'll lose some of the momentum we've built here if I have to explain that yes, she was phone buddies with Britain's now most-famous paedophile.

They milked the tapes for all they were worth. 'I TAPED DI', the front page read the following day, revealing that an ex-banker had 'heard her by chance' as he 'innocently' searched the airwaves with his radio scanner in order to listen in on the conversations of strangers without their consent.* They had columnists speculate whether the tape was genuine and took polls of whether 'Dianagate' (aka Squidgygate) was more or less damaging to the royal family than when Fergie had been pictured with her top off (photos which they, of course, had printed).

Column inches were filled with justifications of 'WHY YOU HAD A RIGHT TO KNOW WHAT IS ON THE TAPE' from writers on the royals, as well as from the *Sun* itself. If you're interested, they say it's because they'd had the tapes for years and excerpts had been published in America, and the *Daily Express* had printed an extract too:

'We decided to publish yesterday because we wanted to spike damaging rumours about Diana which were circulating,' they wrote, the absolute heroes, adding:

'The *Sun* and all its readers want Charles and Di to smile again. We want the Queen to reign over us, happy and glorious. **For many, many years.**'

Which is a nice sentiment, but for one minor twist in the tale. Whilst pursuing the story, their photographer and the person they believed was Diana's mystery caller – James Gilbey – smashed into each other in their

---

* It's not clear-cut that this is what happened. Analysis from surveillance firm Audiotel International and others suggested that it came from a local tap, but again we're straying from the point.

cars. The photographer then chased Gilbey down the road, snapping photographs to be published, when what they both really needed was hospital treatment.

So that's a car crash, one of Diana's (possible) boyfriends and a paparazzi chase. This scene is going to be torn to shreds by the critics for the 'heavy-handed foreshadowing' in series 34 of *The Crown*.

DI SPY VIDEO SCANDAL

8 October 1996

'A MYSTERY snooper filmed Princess Diana frolicking with James Hewitt during their affair, the *Sun* can sensationally reveal today,' the *Sun* wrote on 8 October 1996, proudly proclaiming it a 'SUN ROYAL WORLD EXCLUSIVE'.

As you are probably aware, there's famously zero videos of Diana frolicking with anybody, so the word 'reveal' on their front page was doing quite a lot of heavy lifting. Nevertheless, they printed many stills from a video reportedly showing Diana stripping off with Hewitt, dancing for and making out with him in astonishingly grainy footage, even for a creepshot taken in the nineties.

In a Sun Says column, they first judged the filmmaker in the harshest possible terms for the footage they would publish to an audience of millions.

'The 80 seconds of tape handed to the *Sun* prove that there was no depth to which the spies would not sink,' they wrote with all the self-awareness of a potato. 'It was a calculated invasion of Diana's privacy at a time when she was most vulnerable,' they continued, really taking the piss now. While they judged whoever had given them the video, this didn't stop them from using subheadings like 'tantalising' and captions like 'revealed . . . Di in her bra as he watches' when talking about the contents.

They went on to explain that they were publishing pictures from the video for Diana's sake, of course, to let her know that she wasn't imagining things and she really was being watched.

'We believe that any embarrassment our action may cause to Diana is tiny compared to the satisfaction she will feel in knowing that she was right all along about the dirty tricks.'

Satisfaction that clearly could never be gained from having a quiet word and giving her the tapes to hand over to whatever authorities she felt fit. Their only option was to splash the story over several pages and draw attention to the frames where you can almost see her boobies. You see their predicament.

The bizarre video shows 'Diana' stripping down to her underwear and riding around on top of 'Hewitt' like a horsey. If that and my use of inverted commas hasn't made you ask a few stern questions, congratulations: you are exactly as rigorous as a *Sun* editor. The tapes were a fraud. It was just some woman who looked a bit like Diana riding around on some bloke.

After splashing the story and getting experts to speculate wildly on who might have made the film, the *Sun* were forced to admit the following day that they'd been conned.

They admitted they'd been taken in by two men who had 'acted as intermediaries' – they had presumably been the conmen. The editor said the *Sun* had been 'the victims of a highly sophisticated hoax'. Even though in terms of sophistication it was on par with writing 'delicious pie, please eat me' on a box of laxatives in the boss's fridge and telling them 'That pie in there looks nice' around lunchtime. The footage was blurry, the figures indistinguishable, and I really must stress the Diana actor was riding the Hewitt actor around like a horse, man.

Showing off one last bit of the investigative journalism prowess of the best-selling paper in the country, the *Sun* appealed to readers to phone in if they had any information on 'the sting', like a victim in an episode of *Crimewatch*.

Meanwhile the Diana lookalike – who had been unaware how the footage would be used when she filmed it – came forward after suddenly finding herself on the front page of a national newspaper.

QUEEN OF ALL OUR HEARTS

1 September 1997

In the weeks leading up to Diana's death, the *Sun* printed a series of articles about Diana's new love interest, Dodi Fayed, being shit in bed.

They got their exclusives from Dodi's ex-fiancée, Kelly Fisher. Printing 'DODI IS A DUD IN BED' (18 August 1997 – thirteen days before Diana and Dodi's deaths) and 'DODI'S NO GREAT LOVER, HE DOESN'T KNOW HOW TO PLEASURE A WOMAN'. Dodi and Diana were trying to dodge the press, who were trying to snap their every move. It wasn't just the *Sun*. When she kissed Dodi on a yacht, the tiny pap shots received bids of £500,000.

The *Sun* also featured snaps of Diana buying gifts for Dodi (20 August 1997 – eleven days before they died). Two days before her death, they printed pictures taken from a distance of Diana trying to get onto the back of a jet-ski behind Dodi on their front page under the headline 'DI'S LEGOVER', with more shots on pages 2 and 3.

Then, as I'm sure you're aware, unless you found this book at some far-off date in the future, or are ten, she was killed while being pursued by paparazzi through a tunnel.

'This is not a time for recriminations, but for sadness. However, I would say that I always believed the press would kill her in the end,' Diana's brother, Earl Spencer, said in a statement the day after Diana's death, when details of the accident were still sketchy.

'But not even I could imagine that they would take such a direct hand in her death as seems to be the case. It would appear that every proprietor and editor of every publication that has paid for intrusive and exploitative photographs of her, encouraging greedy and ruthless individuals to risk everything in pursuit of Diana's image, has blood on their hands today.'

Though the paparazzi would later be cleared of causing her death, you'd think under these circumstances the *Sun* and any other papers who used paparazzi shots would lay low, but the *Sun* laid on a mourning extravaganza like a murderer at a funeral trying to throw off suspicion by crying the loudest. They'd spent years loving but also sometimes hating on Diana (Richard Littlejohn said 'Di is so dim she thinks opera is a chat-show host' in one column that particularly stood out, from 6 March 1993) before bursting into a chorus of 'GUBAAH ENGLAND'S ROSE' the second she died.

Having harassed Diana for sales and printed sleazy stories about her boyfriend for sales, the *Sun* switched to mourning her loss for sales, like someone who's bullied you for all your life showing up to your funeral with a coin bucket.

Many editions ran with Diana on the front page, with headlines through the papers like 'GOODNIGHT, SWEET PRINCESS' and '*SHE WAS SPECIAL* ... BECAUSE SHE WAS ONE OF US' and a tribute titled 'She was so Special'. Years later, they'd even get Andy McNab to speculate whether she'd been murdered by secret agents. Just because she's dead doesn't mean she can't be milked for money.

But buried in amongst the tributes on 1 September was something of a telling excuse, as they tried to wash their hands of their part in things: a small Sun Says titled 'DON'T BLAME THE PRESS'. In the short piece they said they understood Diana's brother was 'entitled to be bitter about her death' but the 'press' should not be blamed, and no 'draconian privacy laws' brought in.

'Diana died in France, a country with [. . .] the wildest of the paparazzi. They sell their pictures to a world market [. . .] even the harshest of privacy laws in the UK would not have stopped the terrible, terrible events of yesterday morning.'

'No British law could prevent editors in [other countries] from reaching for their cheque books. Nor could it stop the activities of foreign cameramen in foreign countries.'

The day after Diana's death, their argument – before the facts were known – was essentially that the UK should be able to carry on buying pap pictures at the potential cost of a human life because other places were doing it too. Before printing a 24-page Diana tribute pull-out, after dedicating their paper entirely to Diana (there were basically zero other stories in the edition), for all your mourning needs.

VOTE OUT THE PIG

3 July 2002

During the seventies, eighties and nineties, the *Sun* had sold millions and millions of papers through covering the lives of celebrities. It started with the royals before moving on to the cast of *EastEnders*, then before you knew it they'd talk about anyone famous at all. If you had appeared on telly and at some point had a 'romp', they were basically interested. Then, in the noughties, something incredible happened: a whole new type of celebrity to tap up emerged. Regular people famous for ... being regular people. All their wanks had come true. Suddenly, instead of having to invent tenuous reasons why reporting on the sex lives of, e.g., Showaddywaddy was in the public interest, there was an army of people who were willing to be famous and deal with the consequent invasion of their privacy. Even better, they didn't have a fucking clue what they were letting themselves in for.

57

Because the *Sun* – and the right-wing press in general: let's try to keep in mind they're also shits – will turn on you in an instant if they sense it's what the public wants. One second you're up and doing nip slips, the next you're on your way out and pictured looking glum in a hoodie, carrying a can of Pepsi.

One of the most whiplashy of examples is how they went from turning reality TV star Jade Goody into a figure of hate, calling her a bully and comparing her on the regular to a pig, a baboon and a horse, to cashing in and doing a twelve-page tribute to her when she passed away after getting cancer. If you'd not been paying attention you'd probably think, hmmm, I get that it's sad that she's died, but why are they dedicating a third of the newspaper to a racist baboon horse bully?

Jade, a dental nurse from south London, was catapulted to fame when she appeared on the third series of *Big Brother* in 2002. If you're unfamiliar with the TV show, it was sort of like a zoo for humans, except all the visitors were behind TV screens and were extremely judgemental of all the animals. Like if you and all your friends went round Sea World calling the sharks 'little swimmy arseholes' or 'sub-par dolphin cunts'.

During Jade's time on *Big Brother*, she became a hate figure for the *Sun*. She'd been a bit loud and brash, and let's just say not the most knowledgeable of contestants. For this, their showbiz columnist urged readers to 'VOTE OUT THE PIG', based on his perception that she looked a bit like a pig. This was real Oscar Wilde stuff.

'The pig with the biggest mouth on TV has finally been nominated for eviction and now YOU have the power to roast her,' he wrote, adding, 'she doesn't deserve to win the £70,000 prize and you can help stop her getting her trotters on it.'

But then it became apparent from the show's evictions that the public were actually quite keen on Jade, so before you could say 'ow my neck' the paper switched to liking her too, and she ended up coming fourth. Years went by and barely a bad word was said about her, bar a column from Jeremy Clarkson on 1 March 2003, titled 'Jade Goody should never get her hooves on a driving licence', next to an unflattering picture of her juxtaposed with a photo of Red Rum. This was after she took part in driving lessons on TV for Comic Relief. Don't do charity if you don't want to be compared to a horse, that's my advice.

Then, in 2007, she was deemed a big enough celebrity from her appearance on *Big Brother* for her to enter *Celebrity Big Brother*, a sort of human centipede of fame. She had slimmed down somewhat in the intervening five years, taking away the *Sun*'s opportunity to call her a pig or similar. No matter. They discovered that she hadn't lost weight through a fitness routine so – on the front page on 10 January 2007 – they wrote that 'Jade Goody is exposed by the *Sun* today as a big fat liar who created her sexy new shape through LIPOSUCTION' and complained that 'Jade's body is bought.. not earned' in a piece in which they casually called her a 'gobby cheat'. So long as the public like you, the *Sun* likes you – until you do something truly EVIL, like trying to get thinner through surgery, and then all bets are off.

Once she was in the house, Jade and other contestants – including her boyfriend, her mum and fellow contestants Danielle Lloyd and Jo O'Meara – behaved in a bigoted, sometimes racist, way towards their fellow contestant, the Indian actress Shilpa Shetty. None of them covered themselves in glory (which is to say they acted like arseholes), with Jade's boyfriend Jack Tweed calling Shetty a 'cunt', Lloyd calling her a 'dog' and saying she didn't like Shetty touching her food because she didn't know 'where her hands have been' and that she should 'fuck off home'. Goody referred to Shetty as 'Shilpa poppadom' and said that she needed a 'day in the slums'.

The public were outraged and Ofcom eventually received more than 44,500 complaints, the second highest number of complaints ever received. The *Sun* joined in, centring their coverage around Jade, even though half the house had been quite racist towards Shetty, with Lloyd arguably using stronger language. They ran headlines like 'BEAUTY VS BIGOT', pitching Shilpa against Jade, 'evict face of hate', 'national disgrace' and, on 20 January 2007, 'GOODY RIDDANCE: Bully Jade booted out'.

The hatefest got to Goody, who seemed genuinely distraught at what she'd done, and said she felt suicidal following the events. Meanwhile, the *Sun* covered the fellow contestants caught up in the racism scandal like nothing had happened, under headlines like 'Danielle has Jack-uzzi', detailing the thrilling and newsworthy event of two people having a swim.

Jade attempted to make amends by appearing on the Indian version of *Big Brother*. As the saying goes, when you're a contestant on *Big Brother* every problem begins to look like an opportunity to appear on *Big Brother*. While on the show, she received a cancer diagnosis (live on air, just to clarify) and returned to the UK, and the *Sun* forgot the times they had vilified her and instead deified her during her last few weeks of life. Jade had decided to try to make money for her children by selling stories to the tabloids, resulting in her last days being covered in distressing detail, with headlines like 'JADE'S GOING BLIND' (10 March 2009), 'Jade tells youngest son: The angels are calling Mummy' (16 March 2009), and 'JADE: KILL ME NOW' (25 February 2009).

When she died on 22 March 2009, their front page read 'AT PEACE ON MOTHER'S DAY', with a mournathon of stories on her demise running all the way to page 10, but forgetting to mention how, at times, they'd pointedly chosen to turn her into a baddy and had kept on calling her a pig.

HARRY GIRL'S ON PORNHUB

4 November 2016

In June 2016, Prince Harry met Meghan Markle and the two began dating. For this heinous crime they were hounded by the media from that point forward.

The *Sun* were quick off the mark in deciding that Meghan was terrible, printing headlines like 'Don't fall for my little sis, Harry, she'd be the next ... PRINCESS PUSHY' (2 November 2016) based on an exclusive interview with Meghan's estranged-for-nearly-a-decade maternal half-sister, Samantha. They called her 'her sister' for short.

Soon they moved on to implying she was a porn star, under the grammatically quite frightening front-page headline 'HARRY GIRL'S ON PORNHUB'.

'Prince Harry's new love Meghan Markle features on adult site Pornhub.

She can be seen stripping off and groaning in,' the teaser read, before enticing readers to turn to page 5 to read the rest. From the text you'd be forgiven for thinking she'd actually done something pornographic, when in actual fact some perv had just uploaded to Pornhub some of Meghan's scenes from the TV show *Suits*, which is rated suitable for twelve-year-olds.

They inevitably had to apologise, saying, 'We would like to make clear that Miss Markle has never been involved with [making] such [pornographic] content and had no idea that the video clip had been published illegally on this website.'

From that porny low point, the relationship between the press and the couple deteriorated, not just with the *Sun* but with other tabloids like the *Daily Mail* and the *Daily Express*. For instance, Meghan once served avocado on toast, a fairly innocuous act, at which, on 22 January 2019, the *Daily Mail* went with the headline 'AS THE DUCHESS SERVES AVOCADO ON TOAST FOR TEA … IS MEGHAN'S FAVOURITE SNACK FUELLING DROUGHT AND MURDER?' about the avocado trade. She can't even eat guac without it being linked to a war crime.

Let's not beat around the racist bush in your neighbourhood that keeps on shouting racial slurs, as Harry himself said in a statement in 2016:

'Meghan Markle has been subject to a wave of abuse and harassment. Some of this has been very public – the smear on the front page of a national newspaper; the racial undertones of comment pieces …'

No matter how much the *Sun* and other newspapers protest, there's a notable difference between how they treated the story of (white) Kate falling in love with Prince William and how they treated the story of (mixed-race) Meghan falling in love with Prince Harry. Take, for example, the tales of how the women touch their bumps during pregnancy (like just about every pregnant woman is known to do from time to time).

'There she glows: Pregnant Kate cradles her burgeoning baby bump as she waves to crowds at mental health forum,' the *Sun* wrote about Kate in 8 November 2017, which is reasonably normal if you ignore the inherent weirdness of royalty being a thing in the first place.

See if you can spot any subtle differences in this headline about Meghan from 28 January 2019:

'Gone gaga: Meghan Markle's constant bump-holding is "just for a photo op and she should take her 'Baby Bump Barbie' act down a notch" critic slams.'

The *Sun* and others have kept up their dislike for the couple, bar a few moments such as their wedding and the birth of their child, when it might go against the public mood somewhat to call her a pushy avocado-eating doolally bitch.

They noticeably changed their tone when, on 27 September 2019, Harry began legal action against the owners of the *Sun* and the *Mirror* over the alleged interception of voicemails – likely, in the *Sun*'s case, to be related to matters at the *News of the World*. By 4 October the *Sun*'s Twitter captions for articles about the couple went from things like 'While Meghan Markle whinges about Wimbledon photos the Queen gives a masterclass on how to behave' (9 July 2019) to the absurdly over the top 'Busy mum Meghan Markle scheduled the royal tour around Baby Archie's feeding times – she's such a good mother' followed by a heart emoji (2 October 2019). They might as well have tweeted out 'please stop your legal action'.

But it didn't last – negative and often inaccurate coverage painting Harry and Meghan as some kind of evil duo, a real-life Michael Gove and Sarah Vine if you will, continued.

Coverage of royalty is obviously one of the areas where the media has most influence over reader opinion. It's not like you can get hold of information about their lives without it, unless you happen to be the 'plays polo' level of posh. They aren't like other celebs desperately chasing the spotlight, they don't do anything particularly newsworthy (I've never seen any extensive coverage of a non-royal doing a bit of a wave) so everything you learn comes through the lens of the media first.

There's a stark divide in how favourably the people of the UK view the royals. YouGov polling using data from May 2019 to May 2020 showed 40 per cent positive opinion about Meghan vs 32 per cent negative. Meanwhile,

Kate had a whopping 64 per cent positive opinion vs 10 per cent negative. Call me an optimist, but I refuse to believe that the stark difference is purely to do with the public being racist (though I'm certain prejudice plays some part). It's more likely that the relentless press coverage of Meghan – itself probably rooted in prejudice – has shifted public opinion against her.

When – brace yourself – Megxit (ugh I've just been sick in my mouth) happened, the *Sun* published letters (15 January 2020) from a selection of readers who were mad about somebody they'll never meet in a million years moving somewhere else. The letters mimicked some of the language used by the media, with one reader calling Meghan 'controlling' and another insisting that '"woke" lefty liberal' claims that 'the Sussexes are being driven out by racism' were 'nonsense and a disgraceful slur on this country', two days after a story titled 'Meghan Markle is not a victim of media racism, insists Priti Patel', which argued much the same.

So why does the media go after her and not Kate? I'd guess a lot of it is to do with Harry and Meghan not playing ball.

Harry has never come across as being as comfortable as his older brother with having been born into an institution as thirteenth-century as the royal family, and it probably doesn't really suit him as a person. To bring up the obvious example, there was that time the *Sun* splashed an image of him across the front page showing him at a fancy-dress party wearing a swastika armband, under the headline 'HARRY THE NAZI' (13 January 2005). William, meanwhile, had gone in a 'homemade lion or leopard costume', according to the *Guardian*, which is a damning indictment of his needlework. He's either blind to the scrutiny, or is unaware of how it works that he didn't even consider that rocking up as a party Nazi would invite a fair bit of it.

William has played ball with the press, but Harry not so much. As well as the Nazi incident and reports of him smoking weed, the *News of the World* obtained a video of him using racist language about a fellow army cadet, including the P-word, as a teenager (10 January 2009).

Then there was that time, on 23 August 2012, that the *Sun* published photos of Prince Harry naked with an unknown woman in a Las Vegas hotel, playing some sort of game of strip billiards. Just because you're nude, it doesn't mean you can't be posh. In that edition, they explained in an editorial headed 'WE FIGHT FOR PRESS FREEDOM' – which is rather a grand title for a piece in which you were explaining why you were posting pictures of someone cupping their balls – that they were 'publishing the photos because we think *Sun* readers have the right to see them' in spite of 'warnings from the Royal Family's lawyers'. They felt the photos 'generated a legitimate public debate about the behaviour of the man who [was] increasingly taking on official duties, as he did most recently at the Olympics' closing ceremony'. Ah yes, famously, if you're going to do something like attend the Olympics, you are required to have never got your bum out in private near a woman.

Meanwhile, the most interesting thing William did was go bald. Which the *Sun* did get a surprising number of articles out of, including one where they photoshopped different hairstyles onto him if he wasn't bald (20 January 2018). Now he's even had that taken away, since they've gone on bald watch for Harry, resulting in the article 'Prince Harry's bald patch has doubled in size since marrying Meghan Markle and becoming a dad, claims hair transplant surgeon', which made it sound like Meghan is partly to blame for his genetic baldness.

So Harry was more interesting to the tabloids, and clearly hates them with a passion. Since he and Meghan have been together, it seems their willingness both to pull away from royal life and to take on the newspapers has escalated the situation (that situation being that the tabloids are bloodsucking parasites who want to drink them dry).

Even as they've tried to pull away from public life, the *Sun* continue to pursue them and write story after story, maybe as a warning or in hope they'll back down, or just because they think it's what their audience want and they aren't going to let a pesky thing like Harry not wanting to be in the spotlight any more stop them.

To cap it all off, Harry and Meghan have been portrayed as attention seeking for ages, even though attention is the one thing they've repeatedly made clear they don't want at all. As 'leave me alone' signals go, they don't get much clearer than physically moving yourself to a different continent. On 21 April 2020, the *Sun* reported that 'The Duke and Duchess of Sussex have announced that they will no longer be speaking to a hefty slice of the British media – including the *Sun*. Begging the question: Will any of us actually notice?'

If you search 'Princess Meghan and Prince Harry' on Google and limit it to results from the *Sun* website, there are 6280 results.[*]

---

[*] Correct at time of writing (25 May 2020).

'ROSS BARKLEY: SUN APOLOGY'

22 April 2017

In April 2017, Kelvin MacKenzie got suspended from his job as a columnist on the paper he used to run, after he compared footballer Ross Barkley – who has a Nigerian grandfather – to a gorilla.

'Perhaps unfairly, I have always judged Ross Barkley as one of our dimmest footballers. There is something about the lack of reflection in his eyes which makes me certain not only are the lights not on, there is definitely nobody at home,' he wrote. 'I get a similar feeling when seeing a gorilla at the zoo. The physique is magnificent but it's the eyes that tell the story.'

Accompanying the article was a picture of Barkley next to a gorilla, with the caption 'Could Everton's Ross Barkley represent the missing link between man and beast?' in case the racism was too subtle.

The paper apologised a week later, on 22 April 2017, after criticism and complaints of racism, including 219 complaints to the Independent Press Standards Organisation (IPSO) and Liverpool's mayor reporting it to the police as a 'racial slur'.

They claimed that, at the time of publication, they weren't aware of Barkley's background, and as soon as they became aware they took the article down and made an apology.

The paper didn't apologise for other parts of the piece, which had suggested that the only other people to earn footballers' wages in Liverpool were drug dealers. When you've already reported that Liverpool fans urinated on the dead at Hillsborough under the headline 'THE TRUTH', I guess it's just open season: it's not like Liverpool can be more mad at you.

It also wasn't MacKenzie's first racist rodeo. During his time as a columnist at the *Sun* he drew a lot of complaints, such as when he wrote on 18 July 2016 that 'I could hardly believe my eyes' when a Channel 4 News presenter presented the news whilst being Muslim, and wearing a hijab.

'Was it appropriate for her to be on camera when there had been yet another shocking slaughter by a Muslim?' He also claimed that 'all the major terrorist outrages in the world [are] currently being carried out by Muslims', even though they quite obviously aren't.

After the Barkley incident, the *Sun* and MacKenzie finally parted ways, clearly deciding that it's three strikes and you're out (and, personally, I'd count his time as editor as a very fucking big strike one).

STABBED TEENS DIE ON STREETS

29 May 2018

> RAHEEM STIRLING AGAIN IS IT?
> WHAT'S HE DONE THIS TIME?

> HE BOUGHT A NEW SINK FOR HIS
> MUM THE ABSOLUTE D**KHEAD

Raheem Stirling – one of the few football players whose name I actually know, because he sometimes occupies the position of striker, aka 'where I'd expected Alan Shearer to be when I last watched a World Cup' – has had more than his fair share of media attention. His every action on and off the pitch has been scrutinised to a degree that other (let's be frank: white) players just aren't.

The *Daily Mail*, for instance, spent one match report banging on about how shit he was in a game where he scored two out of the three goals in a 3–2 victory (15 October 2018), berated him for enjoying an ice-cream with his fiancée 'after England's World Cup devastation' like his performance meant he didn't deserve pudding any more (27 July 2018), and implied he was cheap for taking an easyJet flight home from his holidays (24 October 2016) instead of e.g. renting out some piggyback space on a Sherpa.

As well as having to worry about being cheap, he also has to worry about spending too much, in a way that fellow obscenely rich footballers just don't. The *Sun* once sat down and costed up the price of every car he's ever driven, something they've never done for Alan Shearer. Other examples include:

- A front page on 30 June 2016, declaring 'England failure steps off plane and insults fans by showing off blinging house OBSCENE RAHEEM' after he posted a video of a nice sink he'd bought on social media. They somehow failed to mention that he'd bought the sink for his mum.
- A front page from 4 June 2017 ran 'PREM RAT OF THE CARIBBEAN', implying he was cheating on his girlfriend because of a picture showing him on holiday next to a friend.
- Yet another front page, from 22 October 2014, talked about Raheem going to a nightclub a day after being too tired to play a match, as if going for a dance with your friends is on par with the kind of fitness levels you need to perform at an international standard in football. If you can eat a kebab at 3 a.m. you can play against Spurs, that's just how it is.
- A needlessly insulting tweet from the *Sun* account that simply read 'From troubled youth to £100k a week – The life of footie idiot Raheem Sterling' (30 June 2016).

In a particularly grim example, Sterling famously got a tattoo of a gun on his leg, as a reminder of the tragic death of his father.

'When I was two my father died from being gunned down to death,' he wrote on his Instagram page, explaining the tattoo. 'I made a promise to myself I would never touch a gun in my lifetime. I shoot with my right foot so it has a deeper meaning.'

The *Sun* ignored this and went full throttle at him, printing several front pages as if he was endorsing guns, which he wasn't. One, from 30 May 2018, quoted murdered Damilola Taylor's dad calling for him to 'Say sorry for gun tattoo, Raheem.'

But the weirdest part of the whole debacle came when two teenagers were stabbed in Sheffield and the *Sun* decided to crowbar Sterling into line one of the story.

'TWO more teenagers were killed over the weekend as Sterling revealed his controversial gun tattoo.'

But I suppose if he didn't want this kind of coverage, he should personally prevent all people in the country from getting stabbed, shouldn't he?

PERVERTS WHO TAKE PICTURES UP WOMEN'S DRESSES FACE TWO YEARS IN PRISON AS UPSKIRTING FINALLY MADE A CRIMINAL OFFENCE

15 January 2019

In 2019, the 'upskirting' law came into effect, making it illegal to take photographs up people's skirts without their consent.

The *Sun* came down strongly in favour of the law, branding people who take upskirt shots 'perverts'. Not the kind of reaction you'd expect from a newspaper that has an entire tag on their website devoted to celebrity wardrobe malfunctions.

Indeed. The *Sun* has an entire archive of shots of the more intimate parts of celebrities' bodies that they've taken without their permission, or purchased from photographers who've trailed celebs at beaches, hoping one of the sexier body parts might pop out. Point of order: it's not really a 'wardrobe malfunction' if the skirt only malfunctioned from your specific angle of waiting patiently on the floor. If the law had come in earlier they could have just retitled the celebrity wardrobe malfunctions topic on their website 'evidence on behalf of the prosecution' and saved the CPS a shitload of time.

They've even got stories from times when creepshot photographers have narrowly failed to fulfil their brief, with '*Stacey Solomon narrowly avoids embarrassing wardrobe malfunction as she adjusts her bikini on the beach*' from 22 August 2016 and another from 12 October 2017 titled '*Amanda Holden's boobs almost pop out of her dress as she struggles to avoid flashing her knickers*'.

Imagine getting into journalism, maybe inspired by journalists unearthing big political scandals and hoping to speak truth to power, only to find yourself writing a 300-word story about how some photographer nearly saw a tit.

If you think the *Sun* are above publishing paused TV in order to give their readers a view of a BBC presenter's pants, you have severely underestimated their determination to see vaginas without consent. They ran a piece on their website titled 'MORNING FLASH Steph McGovern accidentally exposes underwear during BBC Breakfast'.

If you're pervy enough to click the link, you'll be greeted with McGovern accidentally showing her knickers while holding up a newspaper showing the carnage from the 2017 Tube bombing and will have to decide whether or not to continue to have the horn. This choice is known in philosophical ethics circles as the *Sun* Reader's Dilemma.

Then in one issue from 3 November 1998 I stumbled across a story where they condemned a pervert who had placed a spy camera in a toilet on a plane.

Two pages later, they printed sneak shots of Pamela Anderson's arse under the headline 'That's rearly tricky Pammi'. Finding and condemning upskirt creeps is a good thing, but when they do stuff like this you get the sense that the *Sun* do it with the demeanour of a drug cartel dobbing in the rival gang to give themselves a monopoly on crack cocaine.

The *Sun* have now – as with publishing pictures of topless sixteen-year-old girls – stopped the practice after a change in the law. From now on nip slips and wardrobe malfunctions are only fine if you got them by genuine accident rather than massive patience and a telephoto lens. Yet again, they stopped doing something incredibly creepy not because they realised how damaging it is to women and society to treat women like objects who are there to be gawped at by horny old men with or without consent, but because it would get them thrown in with the nonces.

STOKES' SECRET TRAGEDY

17 September 2019

Occasionally the *Sun* seems to confuse 'public interest' with 'things nosy shits are interested in', and 'news' with 'dredging up deeply personal family tragedies from thirty years in the past for money'.

Like just about everyone in the *Sun* spotlight, England cricketer Ben Stokes has seen mixed coverage over the years. He was on the front page when he was prosecuted following a fight outside a nightclub involving him and several others. The *Sun* went for the headline 'Out of control' on 7 August 2018, accompanied by a photo of the incident and the bullet points 'Stokes' "gay taunts"', and 'KO'd two other men'.

There was a media furore, but when it came to court Stokes was acquitted. During the trial he told the court that he had been defending a gay couple from homophobic abuse. The couple thanked him for his help.

The following year, when he was good at cricket – hitting and/or catching those cricket balls in a way the *Sun* found to be quite pleasing – they forgot about the time they'd gone with the 'guilty until proven innocent' angle and led with 'GO URN MY SON', with a photo of him striking a heroic pose (26 August 2019).

But then [steeples fingers together like Mr Burns] it was time to fuck him over again. The following month, Stokes said the *Sun* sent a reporter to his parents' home in New Zealand in order to ask them questions about a family tragedy from three decades earlier, which had been covered in the newspapers at the time but had since been mostly forgotten. The result was an online article in September 2019 titled 'STOKES' SECRET TRAGEDY' and a front-page 'Hero Ben's brother and sister were shot dead'. The article described how his mother's ex-husband had killed their two children before dying by suicide.

Here they were, digging around in his past and waving some tragic memories in his face at possibly the peak of his career, when they thought he was – in their own words – a hero. It's like seeing your own personal hero, be it the guy who shoves his hand up Orville, or Tom Cruise, and getting their attention by shouting 'I HEAR YOUR NAN DIED OF GONORRHOEA, LET'S BE FRIENDS'.

Stokes described the story as 'the lowest form of journalism, focused only on chasing sales', especially the intrusion on his family. 'To use my name as an excuse to shatter the privacy and private lives of – in particular – my parents is utterly disgusting.'

'The article also contains serious inaccuracies which has compounded the damage caused. We need to take a serious look at how we allow our press to behave.'

A spokesperson for the *Sun* said that 'it is only right to point out the story was told with the cooperation of a family member who supplied details [. . .] The tragedy is also a matter of public record and was the subject of extensive front-page publicity in New Zealand at the time.'

Which is like saying, 'Look, I know I keep shouting it around the office that your mum's dead, Jeff, but in my defence people in your village eleven thousand miles away did talk about it a fair bit at the time, didn't they?'

And so, because the *Sun* determined there was interest in the backstory of a man who's good at hitting stuff, he and his family had to have tragic events from their past thrown up in front of millions of people. He hadn't done anything wrong. He hadn't hurt anyone. He just had a tragic (and saleable) backstory and was very good at hitting balls.

CRIME

THE ANTI-HANGMAN

17 December 1969

Whilst reading through the archives, I couldn't help but get the impression that the *Sun* isn't a soapbox for some mad right-wing autocrat, as a lot of people would have you believe. Rupert Murdoch is right wing, yes, but I don't think that's the driving force of the paper; I reckon he'll let the paper take whatever stance they think their readers want. I'm not sure whether this makes the paper more or less harmful to society, but I believe his editorial line is dictated more by how many sales he can make in comparison to other papers than anything as trivial as ideology or basic human decency and principles. Oh wait, no, maybe I am sure.

When Murdoch acquired the *Sun*, it was a Labour-supporting paper for left(ish)-leaning people. Readers the paper had to retain and build upon, whether or not they were Remoaner snowflake millennials. It would therefore take left-leaning stances on a number of issues, including the abolition of the death penalty, which took place the month after the *Sun* relaunched.

The *Sun*'s coverage of the abolition was broadly in favour of it, and actually quite good. As well as fairly well-balanced reporting of arguments in the Commons, the *Sun* (as is their style) also printed more sensationalist pieces, including a portrait of a hangman who had executed 450 people and now supported abolition of the death penalty. They dubbed him the 'anti-hangman'.

But as time went on, the *Sun* moved away from this stance and much more towards that of an angry, braying Stuart attending the execution of Guy Fawkes. This reflected the outcomes of various polls the *Sun* ran (see page 83), and it was clearly a mood that was growing in parts of the country: in 1983 and 1987 there were debates in the Commons to reintroduce capital punishment, which lost both times but still got a good chunk of votes in favour. Ah the eighties: a magical decade of shoulder pads, technological advancement and that good old-fashioned 'burn 'em' mentality.

Consequently, *Sun* readers weren't just treated to articles about murderers, they were also given quotes from people calling for the murderers' execution, often with these requests making the full headline. 'STRING HIM UP' one read on 29 October 1987, accompanied by comments from the victim's family that the authorities should 'let the bastard swing'.

Another example, from 9 September 1988 and filled with weird reporting, told of a 'SPIKY-HAIRED punk accused of two murders' who 'snarled' in defiance at a 'mob baying for his blood'.

The article told how the 'jobless 21-year-old' (which, when you're accused of murder, isn't really the main thing about you, is it? If someone you don't like is accused of murder you can drop the 'also, he's shit at chess' details from your attacks, no matter how much you want to denigrate chess players as a group) had been heckled as he was charged for a second murder. The headline they'd chosen for this story was 'HANG HIM NOW!', based on the chants of crowds at the trial. It's never great when you're getting your headline ideas directly from people you call a 'baying' 'mob' in the first sentence of your article, without even using inverted commas.

99 PERCENT OF YOU WANT THIS

9 September 1988

As discussed on the previous page, it's fair to say the *Sun*'s readers had developed their appetite for execution by the eighties. We can deduce this because occasionally the paper would ask their readers if they liked hanging in general, or if they'd like to 'string up' somebody in particular, and get them to phone in to vote for their favourite option, like an insane early prototype of *The X-Factor*.

In one poll they asked readers if they'd like IRA members involved in the 1987 Remembrance Day bombing to be hanged, as if the judge was going to say 'Sure, hanging's been illegal in Northern Ireland since 1973, but look at those numbers – fetch the rope.' The poll, conducted a few weeks after the bombings in November 1987, received 35,246 votes in favour of hanging. Only 1652 dialled in to say that they didn't fancy a bit of execution.

Rather than thinking, OK, 35,246 of our readers were prepared to ring a hotline – with no sway over anything – to register that they'd like someone to be hung by the neck until they're dead, that's fucking terrifying, and taking a long hard look at what they'd done, they continued with their usual murder content and its decidedly pro HANG THEM ALL slant, satisfied they'd judged their quite Manson-y audience correctly.

By 2008 they'd shed even more of those woolly liberal types who don't even want the state to murder people to death on their behalf. A poll they conducted in 1988, in the wake of the convictions of brutal murderers Mark Dixie and Steve Wright, concluded that '99 PERCENT OF YOU WANT THIS', 'this' being execution. That was the headline they ran on the front page over a picture of a judge with the quote 'You will be taken hence to a place of lawful execution and there be hanged by the neck until you are dead.'

The story was accompanied by lovely quotes from the public like 'beasts like them don't deserve to breathe the same air as decent people – they should hang' and 'Men like Dixie are like a dog. Once they draw blood they should be put down. I wish this was America and we had the lethal injection.'

My guess would be that two things had happened to push readers to a much more killy stance. By this point the *Sun* had encouraged their audience towards a more right-wing view on crime and criminals through years of covering sensationalist crime stories in which perpetrators were labelled as 'monsters' and 'evil' (rather than perhaps trying to understand what led them to be that way), and as they lost their more liberal and lefty readers they were replaced by people who happen to like the idea of hanging, these people having seen copies of the *Sun* also yelling 'STRING HIM UP' and thought, aye, that's the paper for me.

NO GIRL IS SAFE

18 August 1993

On 15 July 1992, twenty-three-year-old model Rachel Nickell was stabbed to death on Wimbledon Common in front of her two-year-old son.

A media frenzy ensued. It had all the usual factors the *Sun* liked in a murder mystery: an attractive (or, in the case of child murders, 'adorable') victim, and a murderer presumed to be a stranger still on the loose. The *Sun* called the case 'beauty slain by the beast'.

The police were under pressure to find the killer, although this does not excuse what happened next. They arrested a lot of suspects. Not just a few, but a number that makes you think they were employing the 'murderer says what?' method of building a case to round up some more suspects, or even 'he who smelt it gets twenty-five to life'.

On the twenty-seventh arrest (not the last), the police finally thought they had their man. They do say twenty-seventh time's the charm (I imagine, probably after they've fucked up the first twenty-six). This was Colin Stagg, an unemployed man from nearby Roehampton who regularly walked his dog on the Common.

The police had launched a (highly unethical) sting operation, getting an undercover cop to pose as someone romantically interested in Stagg and also in satanism over the course of five months, in an attempt to get him to confess to a murder he didn't actually do by saying subtle stuff like 'If only you had done the Wimbledon Common murder, if only you had killed her, it would be all right.' He didn't confess, because when you're not into satanism or murdering you tend not to, even when asked by a date, but spent a year in custody before the judge threw out the case, calling the sting operation 'deceptive conduct of the grossest kind'.

The *Sun* covered this under the headline 'NO GIRL IS SAFE Rachel murderer will strike again'.

(By the by, it strikes me as quite weird to say 'girl' when you mean an adult woman. I can't imagine how it must have felt to read that headline and feel both overwhelming existential dread and also quite patronised. Like someone saying, 'There, there, you're going to die, little lady.' But as this kind of language was pretty standard for the *Sun*, let's get back to Stagg.)

Along with the headline they had prominent pictures of Stagg looking like, well, a bit of a murderer (sorry, Colin). The piece asked '*PRIME SUSPECT CLEARED – SO WHO IS THE KILLER?*', but still the media trial went on. The *News of the World* had Stagg take a lie-detector test, which he passed (lie detectors are dodgier than an undercover police officer posing as a satanist, but let's ignore that for now).

The papers continued to vilify him. Stagg 'slowly settled into the life of a recluse', as he wrote years later in his book about his experiences, *Pariah*. The real killer, Robert Napper, would later confess to manslaughter on the grounds of diminished responsibility – while already serving a sentence for two other murders – clearing Stagg entirely.

Stagg was awarded £706,000 compensation from the police, which the

Sun took exception to. 'STAGGERING', they wrote on the front page, 'fury at £706,000 for suspect cleared of Rachel's murder' (14 August 2008).

I'll be honest, it seems a tad unfair to be so angry at a person your own headline explains was cleared of murder. He was innocent, but I'd argue the headline made it look at first glance like there was some doubt there. Imagine being branded 'not a murderer Colin' for the rest of your life, while all the other Colins are just called 'Colin'. It's like calling someone you don't like from accounts 'not a sex pest Jan' or 'definitely not into a bit of GBH Pete'.

They still weren't done with him, and later published a piece on how 'Colin Stagg has spent ALL of the £750k payout he got for being wrongly accused of murdering Rachel Nickell – after blowing the cash on luxury cars and holidays' (10 July 2017). A real 'innocent man used his own money how he wanted to use it' shocker. The piece – as well as awarding him an extra £44,000 payout he wasn't given – made it clear the real killer had been arrested, at the same time as using needlessly ambiguous phrases like 'Stagg (pictured in 1994 leaving the Old Bailey) became the most hated man in Britain when he was jailed for the stabbing – but was later freed'.

Suspicion around Stagg continued long after he was found to be innocent, and pieces about his intimate life – which he says were untrue – published in the *News of the World* alleged that the 'weirdo' had asked for 'bizarre sex' with his 'terrified' girlfriend close to where Nickell was murdered.

In a rare happy(ish) ending, Stagg ended up getting some more money, and from News International – the parent company of *The Times*, the *Sunday Times*, the *Sun* and the *News of the World*, now known as News UK – itself. In 2011, he was informed by the Metropolitan Police that he had been hacked by the *News of the World*, *six years* after he was acquitted of the murder.

He ended up accepting substantial damages from the paper in an out-of-court settlement. He saw this specifically as 'sweet revenge' on the *News of the World* itself, which had also blagged their way into getting his medical records.

'They published two pages of complete lies about my so-called deviant sex life,' he told the *Evening Standard* at the time of the settlement in 2012.

'It was total make-believe, but at that time I had neither the money nor the reputation to fight back. All that changed when the Met contacted me 18 months ago to reveal I had been a hacking victim in the early 2000s.'

'Justice has been done and I'm very pleased. I look on this money as part payment for all the years of vilification I suffered at the hands of the press in general.'

THE *SUN* GOES INSIDE ALCATRAZ

27 January 2001

The *Sun* are more obsessed with life in prison than a nine-year-old who's accidentally stolen some sweets from a shop and thinks that at any second they're going to be thrown in solitary for three to five. The focus of their coverage has been on high-profile killers, who they follow around like they're especially difficult to follow celebs, but without the chance of a nip slip because of the jumpsuits. (Before you get mad at me for saying they wear jumpsuits when they don't, I should add that all robbers go around in little black and white costumes and carry a big bag marked 'swag'.)

They've run stories on everything from minor inside punch-ups involving the Kray twins and prison moves of the Yorkshire Ripper (sort of like a 'where are they now' but the answer is always 'in solitary') to celebrating when Harold Shipman killed himself ('SHIP SHIP HOORAY') and 'HAPPY NOOSE YEAR' when Fred West did the same over the holidays. A pun so bad that if he'd done it slightly earlier they would have presumably gone with Merry Noosemas.

They've gone to great lengths to get stories about jailed high-profile prisoners too. One prison officer was jailed in 2013 after it emerged that he'd sold information to the *Sun* about murderer Jon Venables. In 2014, during the phone-hacking trial, Rebekah Brooks admitted that sometimes the *Sun* would get someone to write to prisoners in order to gain information: 'to pose as a pen-pal to gather evidence'. They spoke to the most notorious killers in the UK and still somehow ended up looking like the baddies.

I bet you can probably guess exactly what their opinions on prisons are without looking. If you said: they think prisons are too soft on criminals and criminals should rot there for ever in what they just claimed are luxury conditions at the expense of the taxpayer – congratulations! Just from skimming comments online and letters to the editor, a lot of their readers are with them all the way to the torture wing at Guantanamo Bay. To give you a random selection from the last few years on their Twitter feed:

'I would hang him for this 🤮 What about his daughter and girlfriend who he brutally stolen (where is their rights) ⚖️ 🤬' in reply to a story about a cannibal killer (31 January 2020), which I include because I've never seen so many emojis in an appeal for hanging. And 'People today, run around riot and have no respect for themselves, others or country. Time to bring back the stocks, with sign of what a scumbag he is. Flogging and burning at the stake', which I include because it was in reaction to somebody pouring a milkshake over some Burger King customers (3 October 2018). While the Yazooed victims were a mother and child, it seems a tad disproportionate to hang people for getting other people milky.

But back to the *Sun* and their obsession with prisons being too cushty. They complained of 'LUXURY LIFE OF BULGER KILLERS' on 9 January 2001 after finding out the murderers were given an education whilst in prison, including one-to-one tuition which helped them pass their GCSEs, plus trips to theatres and '£10 on their birthdays' in order to prepare them for life on the outside. Presumably the *Sun* would prefer prisons to send child killers to solitary before saying, 'Right, your sentences are up, off you fuck and be good now,' and just vaguely wondering what they'll do next. Hard-working accountant, proctologist or serial killer – that's for the streets to decide.

They've published outrage stories of prisoners having an easy life on a regular basis, from Peter Sutcliffe mixing with female patients when he was moved to a psychiatric hospital, to terrorists being given comedy classes, revealed later in the article to be part of a course run by a non-profit that 'uses the arts as an education and rehabilitative tool'. Reading the *Sun*'s prison output, most of the time you'd assume it was like uni but without any of the sociology wankers.*

So it was nice to see an article where they actually visited a prison to see for themselves. The *Sun* visited Woodhill prison, nicknamed 'Alcatraz', in 2001.

'As we near A-wing we get a taste of the abuse staff get every day. One gruff voice barks out from behind a tiny slit in a cell door: Why don't you stick your ******* **** up you ******* ****' (27 January 2001). It's like a game of blankety-blank where one of the words almost certainly means cunt.

They then relayed anecdotes of how, two days before their visit, a prisoner 'bit an officer's hand down to the bone' and a separate prisoner had warned a guard he was going to 'stab you so many times that you'll end up like a teabag'.

The experience didn't change them, and they were soon back to telling their readers that prisons were like Butlin's, but free. Which, to be fair, does sound like a fate worse than death.

---

* I studied sociology, before you tweet me your complaints.

MILLY 'HOAX' RIDDLE

14 April 2002

During *News of the World* editor Andy Coulson's trial, which ended with him being sentenced to two years for conspiring to hack phones, his lawyer said in mitigation that Coulson, the *News of the World* and newspapers generally were not aware that hacking was illegal when they were doing it.

You can sort of buy this, considering they straight-up reported that they'd done it under the headline 'Milly "Hoax" Riddle':

'The hunt for missing Milly Dowler took a new twist last night when it emerged that messages had been sent to her mobile phone after she vanished,' the first edition of 14 April 2002's *News of the World* read. 'One of them appeared to be offering her a job in the Midlands.'

'Hello Mandy' – her real name was Amanda, but she went by Milly – 'We are ringing because we have some interviews starting,' the message said. 'Can you call me back? Thank you. Bye Bye.'

Revealing in print that you know the contents of a voicemail message of a missing person in an extremely high-profile case is like going to a Neighbourhood Watch meeting and loudly protesting 'I certainly didn't break into Mr Aggett's house by getting that key he hides under the third rock from the left and disabling his alarm using the code 301393659' before anyone had realised he'd been robbed.

They went further than this, contacting Surrey police directly on 13 April to let them know about the potential lead, like a loveable town scamp who you try to hate but always makes amends by confessing to his worst crimes. 'Fair play, Arson Joe burnt down another church but he did dob himself in, credit where credit's due.' The police did not investigate further.

The public wouldn't know about this until 2011, when the *Guardian* published an article revealing Dowler's phone had been hacked, leading to massive public outcry. While the public didn't get too wound up about celebrity hacks, they were a bit more pissed when a paper did it to the phone of a missing girl who it was eventually discovered had been murdered. Under public pressure, politicians – normally nervous about pissing off News International – even began to condemn the actions, with Prime Minister David Cameron calling it shocking and 'a truly dreadful act and a truly dreadful situation'.

Adding to the outrage, the *Guardian* also reported that the *News of the World* had deleted messages from Milly Dowler's voicemail, giving her family false hope that she might still be alive and deleting them herself. This wasn't actually true, but it was one of the many final straws that led to the paper's closure on 10 July that year, before that came to light. Before you cry them a river, they did something that was arguably much worse.

The *Wall Street Journal* discovered that *News of the World* journalists had been sent to an Epson ink-cartridge factory for three days on a lead that said Dowler was working there, information they'd got through hacking her phone. During the trial of Andy Coulson, the judge said *News of the World* journalists had put off telling police about the contents of the missing girl's voicemail until they realised they weren't going to find her all by themselves, adding:

'That was unforgivable ... The fact that they delayed telling the police of the contents of the voicemail demonstrates that their true motivation was not to act in the best interests of the child but to get credit for finding her and thereby sell the maximum number of newspapers.'

I can't help but wonder how aggressive the *News of the World* headline would have been on the 'SICK BASTARD HACKS DEAD GIRL'S PHONE' scale if they had found some random TV actor doing the exact same thing they'd done.

WHO'S NEXT?

26 February 2003

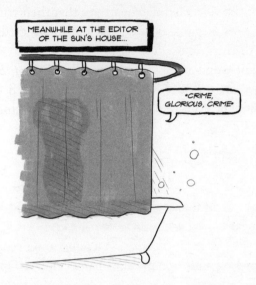

In the early days of the *Sun* as a tabloid, the headlines were quite quaint, with titles like 'MURDER AT THE GOLDEN EGG' from 16 August 1973. So far, so charming countryside murder mansion soirée that can only be solved by Poirot.

By the time Kelvin MacKenzie was in charge, there were full-on voyeuristic horror shows. One report from 28 October 1987 gave readers a 'picture special' showing the dinner table of the murdered, with 'half-eaten meals and unfinished glasses of wine' on the table under the headline 'THE LAST SUPPER'. If I hadn't already spun around and locked the door, the subheading 'then rapists stormed in at horror house' would have done the trick.

I can't help but feel the headline output did at times have the obvious subtext 'you should be shitting yourself right now; buy the next issue to find out about where the danger is lurking'. Below, to give you a sense of the coverage, are a few of the headlines that made me slightly worry about leaving the house, going to a church, staying in the house, and just generally existing near humans and/or cutlery.

HORROR OF DEVIL PRIEST

(27 March 1985)
Sound like a vague headline? The subheading explained 'he castrated the dead', making me wish I'd learned to live with the ambiguity.

MUM KILLS EASTER EGG KIDS

(4 April 1988)
This one went into lurid detail about how a mother had killed one of her children with a pyjama cord and another with a knife before she 'tried to cut her own throat before throwing herself in a pond and drowning'. They were dubbed the Easter Egg Kids because they had been unwrapping Easter eggs at the time.

WOMAN No. 2 SLASHED BY RAIL RIPPER

(4 June 1988)
'Jack the' will be spinning in his grave to learn that the number of murders you need to commit to gain the horrifying title 'Ripper' is now one. 'It was tougher back in my day,' I'm sure old Jack would tell you.

HAMMER MANIAC SMASHES BRAVE PC

(5 February 1988)
Pretty self-explanatory this one: a hammer maniac (that's someone with

a hammer who is a maniac, not someone who just really likes hammers) smashed a brave police officer.

NUKE BOFFIN IS MURDERED

(12 February 1988)
Imagine getting murdered, then being called a fucking dork in the headline about it.

SHOT DEAD FOR 26p 'Gunman's eyes were crazy. He was hungry for blood'

(24 February 1993)
The kind of headline that makes you need to calm down, and maybe take a nice relaxing bath.

They all thought he was a saint . . . but he was a devil plotting perfect murder of wife in electric bath

(16 November 1993)
Oh no. Maybe a stroll in the park?

BOY, 2, SEES GRAN RAPED IN THE PARK

(18 February 1993)
Maybe a nice lie down.

COUPLE IN BED MURDERED BY KNIFE MANIAC

(18 May 1979)
Oh.

NUDE ROMP LOVERS ARE MURDERED

(6 February 1984)
On this one you could turn to read more about how nude they were on page 2, under 'NUDE COUPLE ARE KILLED'.

DAD 'BUTCHERED SONS WITH A SCREWDRIVER' and SCREWDRIVER KILLER MADE HIS KIDS EAT HIS WIFE'S ASHES

(11 March 2003 and 26 March 2003)
Just when you think a screwdriver killer couldn't possibly get any worse.

WHO'S NEXT?

(26 February 2003)
Perhaps the most overt of the 'you should be scared' stories, the *Sun* reported on a woman murdered with a hammer with the headline 'WHO'S NEXT?' next to a massive picture of a hammer.

Feel safe? You sure? What was that noise?

WE'RE WITNESSING THE DOWNWARD SPIRAL OF BRITAIN.

21 September 2008

Most people don't have crimes committed against them personally or witness them year in year out, meaning that pretty much all the information we get about them is from secondary sources, whether that's from the TV, print media or your knife maniac/dealer friend just telling you about their day.

What you think is going on in terms of national crime trends is very much influenced by where you're getting your information. The National Crime Survey regularly shows that more non-victims (6 in 10, to pick 2015/16 at random, though the trend is consistent over time, both here and in the US) think that crime has risen nationally over the last year than non-victims who think that crime has risen in their area (3 in 10). When asked about the level of crime in their local area versus the level nationally, only 9 per cent thought crime in their local area was above average and 55 per cent felt it was below average. Their view of what's going on nationally is at odds with what they're seeing in their own locality.

People get their views on national crime from a range of sources, but there's a not insignificant difference between tabloid readers – 70 per cent of whom thought that crime had gone up – and broadsheet readers (43 per cent). *Sun* readers were bang on average, at 70 per cent.

Essentially, imagine you're shut in a house, witnessing nothing outside, and have to rely on someone who comes to your house to tell you what's going down. The broadsheets are like a person calmly telling you there's been a slight increase in bad things out there (or decrease, as it may be) but generally everything remains calm, while the tabloids are like a guy panting his way into your lounge covered in blood, saying 'Holy shit, it's a bloodbath out there – I saw a nun kill a dog with a whisk,' before enacting the scene for your kids. Without mentioning that outside is largely dog-murdering-nun-free, bar the occasional dog-murdering-nun spree, which has actually even decreased over the past few years. They both saw the same crime, but their different slants on it kind of skew your perspective of what it's like outside.

Look, there are merits to both methods – for instance, if the nun is just outside my door I want to know about it in more detail than just 'there's been an uptick in religious dogicide in the UK but rates remain low nationally'. But when you aren't in any immediate danger, you have to wonder about the motive of the strangers coming around to your house to tell you about the crime. One of them seems to want to tell you about the stats and give you the context while the other seems to want to keep you afraid.

To pluck one headline at random, the *Sun* dedicated the front page on 21 September 2008 to a reader letter, headlined 'We're witnessing the down-ward spiral of Britain. Decent members of the public are being murdered by feral youths on our streets. MPs just give us sad eyes and soundbites. This is the 2008 equivalent of Nero fiddling whilst Rome burns'. Surrounding the letter, which warned 'if we don't act now, the problems of London and other cities will be in the suburbs and the rest of Britain tomorrow', were pictures of people who had been killed violently.

All these murders had taken place, and crime is a real concern. And I'm sure the reader was genuinely afraid of crime. But this was a time when violent crime – as measured by the police and the (more reliable) British Crime Survey – was actually falling. The headline may as well have read 'Man the media has scared shitless through relentless reporting on crime now fucking terrified of crime'.

If you're asking yourself why? Why would the *Sun*, Britain's best-selling newspaper, owned by a media-mogul billionaire, run a headline that directly contradicts the figures? I would venture that the clue is once again in 'best-selling newspaper' and 'media-mogul billionaire'. A year before the article in question, on 4 September 2007, the *Guardian* ran a piece called 'The good news about bad news – it sells'. It summarised substantial surveys (done in America, but hey, aren't we all ruled by the same bots?) that showed people who said they followed the news very closely dipped in the nineties to 23 per cent, compared with 30 per cent in the eighties and noughties. This was despite people's main motivations for following the news staying the same – namely war, weather, disaster, money and, you guessed it, crime. The conclusion was that people are more engaged with news when there is 'a perceived threat to their way of life'. Broadsheets – aimed at readers who are (stereotypically) engaged in the news no matter what's going on – maybe don't need as much coverage of a perceived threat to their way of life to keep them coming back. But for everyone else, if fear and danger sell papers, then like a crack dealer trying to unload his product after a shipping error landed him with way more crack than he needs, the *Sun* is going to give it to you.

PREJUDICE

I'D SHOOT MY SON IF HE HAD AIDS, SAYS VICAR!

14 October 1985

On 5 June 1981 a medical case report first documented a cluster of pneumonia cases amongst gay men, the cause of which was unknown. Before we knew much about the syndrome and realised our mistake, it was largely believed to only affect gay men and drug users, and was even termed 'Gay Related Immune Deficiency', before switching to Acquired Immune Deficiency Syndrome (AIDS) in 1982. The syndrome – caused by HIV – spread around the UK, with resulting deaths peaking in the nineties. As well as the tragedy of thousands of people dying of the disease, the stigma surrounding it was immense. Nowhere was that more evident than in the pages of the right-wing press like the *Daily Mail*, the *Daily Express*, and, of course, the *Sun*.

There are sensitive ways to cover a disease that's killing people, there are insensitive ways to cover a disease that's killing people, and then there's finding an insane clergyman who's willing to say he'd shoot his own son if he ever caught it, and then publishing his rantings about gay people. The *Sun*'s coverage of AIDS during the eighties strayed into the latter end of the spectrum.

In a particularly unhinged story – if you can call the garbled ramblings of an unhinged reverend a story – on 14 October 1985, they wrote of a vicar who 'vowed' he would take his teenage son up a mountain to shoot him if he ever contracted AIDS.

'Chris would not get closer to me than six yards,' the Reverend Robert Simpson told the paper, a perfectly normal thing to say about your loved ones. 'He would be a dead man.'

He added that he'd pull the trigger on the rest of his family too, which at least where the children are concerned is pretty great parenting – there'll be no playing favourites in this household.

To show everyone he was deadly serious, the *Sun* took him up a mountain for a photoshoot, where Simpson was pictured pointing a shotgun right at his son's chest. Imagine being the son being led up the mountain, thinking, on the one hand, it's bad that all my friends are going to see this, but on the other, at least he's probably not going to actually pull the trigger in front of invited witnesses.

'I don't think I would like Dad to shoot me, but I know there's no chance with AIDS,' Chris told the *Sun*, genuinely adding, 'Sometimes I think he would like to shoot me whether I had AIDS or not.'

It's unclear whether this quote was obtained while his father was pointing the shotgun at his heart.

The rest of the column was full of exactly the kind of garbage you'd expect from a man who'd let himself be photographed for a national newspaper while pointing a shotgun at his son's tits. He told the paper – which they then published without contradiction or context – that 'if [AIDS] continues it will be like the Black Plague. It could wipe out Britain. Family will be against family. Nobody will trust anybody else and gun law will prevail', before calling on the government to repeal the laws which legalised homosexuality.

The piece is spectacularly bad. It runs wild with the idea that people with AIDS should be feared. It doesn't contextualise any of his comments, e.g. by mentioning they're fucking insane. Next to the headline, the *Sun* wrote in large letters 'another red hot *Sun* exclusive', as if all the other papers were desperate to get the rights to a homophobic shotgun-owning vicar desperately in need of help chatting casually about how he'd murder the fuck out of his own family. It even ends by throwing in a second, unrelated single-line scare story saying a toddler with AIDS had been banned from kindergarten in Australia after biting his friend.

If you're a responsible newspaper and a vicar says 'I want to kill my family', maybe the first number you should think of isn't the circulation figures, but 999.

WOULD YOU LET THIS MAN NEAR YOUR DAUGHTER

27 April 1987

On 27 April 1987, the *Sun* printed a Sun Says column about the poet and writer Benjamin Zephaniah which, as Zephaniah puts it in his autobiography, made him sound 'like I was some kind of rapist'.

The piece came about after Zephaniah went for meetings to discuss taking up a post of Fellow at Trinity College, Cambridge.

'Just what are his qualities which have appealed to Trinity College?' the *Sun* wrote. 'He is black. He is a Rastafarian. He has tasted approved schools and Borstals. And, oh yes,' they added, like an afterthought rather than the reason he was invited to the post, 'he is a poet.'

In case you thought they were focusing a bit too much on him being

Rastafarian and black, they printed one of his poems. One so horrible that you couldn't help but grab your daughter in fear and rip up her offer of a place at Cambridge lest this vile man be within fifty feet of her, by which I mean a fairly tame poem about how he met Lady Di but had a bit of a stomach ache because he didn't want to fart near a member of the royal family. For some reason, the *Sun* censored out the word fart, writing it as 'f*rt'.

Yes, that's right: of his body of respected (and enjoyable) work, they chose a poem about that time he needed to fart while meeting the royal family. Look, I'm not saying it's his best poem, but he's a hard worker. Some of his poems will be about Palestine, some will be about societal issues and some, as is inevitable when you work as prolifically as Benjamin Zephaniah, will be about trying not to fart in front of Princess Diana. Them's the facts. Seemingly, the *Sun* did this because they thought it meant they could go from 'he's made a fart joke' to a column questioning whether this man should be allowed near teenage girls. It seems a tad tenuous to me too, especially when it comes three pages after a picture of a topless woman. You can't go printing sleaze and sex scandals constantly, then clutch your pearls and start censoring the word 'fart' the moment a poet writes a poem about not doing a fart.

Finishing up the column, to add to all the damning reasons why you might not want your daughter to be near a talented poet, they said '**from his picture, Mr Zephaniah himself could do with a good shampoo and set**', referring to a picture they had of him looking normal and with dread-locks, again sounding a tad 'dog whistle played through a megaphone' levels of racist.

The correct answer to the question posed by the headline is yes, unless you're some sort of massive honking great racist, but the *Sun* went with 'our guess is that they would prefer their offspring to work in a hairdressers', taking a gigantic shit on barbers while they were at it.

FLY AWAY GAYS
AND WE WILL PAY

6 May 1987

On 6 May 1987, the *Sun* ran a Sun Says titled 'FLY AWAY GAYS AND WE WILL PAY' in which they claimed they weren't hostile to gay people, then offered to buy one-way tickets for some of them to fuck off to Norway.

'**The *Sun* has never been hostile to the gay community**' the piece began. (Later that week they would run 'GAY LESSONS "WILL END HUMAN RACE"', putting forward the views of a government minister, Dr Rhodes Boyson, that 'teaching homosexuality in schools' could 'bring death in one generation', with no opposing views within the article. So either they were lying about never being hostile, or they decided, 'fuck it let's turn on them' in an editorial meeting on Tuesday.)

'Thousands of them read our paper,' they continued, confirming what the *Sun* really like about gay people is money. 'This is why we reject the claim by **SOME** gays yesterday that the *Sun* and the *Daily Mail* have run a hate campaign against them.'

Gay rights campaigners had marched through London to 'seek asylum' in the Norwegian embassy as a stunt that week, saying Norwegian society treated gay people more sympathetically. The real point, of course, was to draw attention to poor treatment by the media and government in the UK. As the *Sun* put it, 'they said TORY policy of supporting the family will lead to repressive laws on homosexuals'.

Laws such as the private member's bill supported by the 'GAYS WILL END THE HUMAN RACE' guy from three paragraphs ago, which would have banned schools from teaching kids about gay relationships. Laws like Section 28, which would be passed the following year, a deeply homophobic amendment which stated that local authorities should not promote the acceptance of homosexuality as a normal type of family relationship.

In a normal and proportionate reaction to valid criticism, this was when the *Sun* offered to pay for plane tickets to get gay people to leave the country and not return.

'If this bunch of politically motivated publicity seekers really want to go to Norway the *Sun* is happy to help,' they wrote in the infamous Sun Says column. 'BA Flight 644 for Oslo leaves from Terminal One at Heathrow at 2pm. We'll pick up the bill for **ONE-WAY** tickets.'

They ended their piece '**<u>And bon voyage</u>**', which somehow sounds more like 'fuck off' than 'fuck off' does.

I'd hazard a guess this did nothing to soothe worries of gay people about the paper. When you raise concerns and the first reaction is to offer to pay for you to leave the country, you sort of take the hint.

WEREWOLF SEIZED IN SOUTHEND

24 July 1987

I'll give this to the *Sun*: they know how to sell a newspaper. I see the headline 'WEREWOLF SEIZED IN SOUTHEND' and I'm coughing up 20p to find out what the fuck they're talking about. Either werewolves are real or somebody's haired up a man, and I need to know which.

'A CRAZED "werewolf",' the story started, already implying with quotation marks that this isn't the confirmation of werewolves ~~I was~~ readers were hoping for, 'with amazing strength was seized yesterday after fighting a four-hour battle with eight terrified police.'

By paragraph six the quotation marks were dropped and they were just calling him 'the wolfman'. Just, oh yeah, he's 'the wolfman', like that's an established thing. The story told how police officers 'were thrown across the yard by the power-packed wolfman' and the coppers quoted as saying 'the man was snarling, his lips were turned back and his hands turned into claws'.

This is one of those stories that, the more you hear about it, the more awful it turns out to be. Like when you see a viral video of a dolphin doing what looks strikingly like the Macarena and then a few days later a dolphin biologist explains to the media that that's just the twitches dolphins make during the final stages of dolphin cancer.

The man (spoilers, but this wasn't actually proof that *Twilight* or any of the other less shit werewolf films were real) had been driven to the police station by a woman who had been spending time with him, after he had started acting strangely. After the fight with the police, they had got him into a cell, which the *Sun* called a 'cage' to make it sound more wolfy.

In the cell, he managed to smash his head through a door hatch, after which he was sedated by a doctor. Firefighters showed up and 'covered him in washing-up liquid and managed to squeeze him out'.

The *Sun* helpfully explained that the man was not a wolf, and was possibly suffering from lycanthropy, which is the (incredibly rare) delusion that you can turn into a wolf. It's often associated with schizophrenia, psychotic depression and bipolar disorder. The *Sun* stated that victims 'can develop incredible strength because their mind overrules the limitations of their body', which is only slightly less accurate than when they were calling him the wolfman: it does not imbue the sufferer with the strength and fighting prowess of a wolf, instead imbuing them with the regular powers of a regular unwell person urgently in need of treatment.

The *Sun*, ever the mental-health campaigners and bastions of sensitive coverage, printed a fun 'IS YOUR NEIGHBOUR A WEREWOLF?' guide on page 9, before interviewing the man in hospital a week later. In the interview, from 31 August 1987, they refer to him as 'the Southend werewolf', picture him baring his teeth and get him to 'admit' that he looks a bit like a werewolf. Which I imagine is exactly the right thing to say to someone with delusions of being a wolf.

DEATH LEAP!

28 July 1987

Suicide is a tough topic to talk about in newspapers, especially if your main specialities are bingo, scary crime and saucy stories about people making whoopie.

It's a subject where – if you're a responsible paper – you don't want to over-sensationalise. Nobody is saying don't cover it (it's the leading cause of death in under-35s, it should be covered in some way), but if you do, it should be done in a sensitive manner. Failure to do so can have consequences, and you might end up accidentally encouraging others to take similar actions. For instance, you shouldn't print a picture of someone leaping off a cliff to their death under the headline 'DEATH LEAP' on the front page of your paper, which the *Sun* did in a particularly crass edition on 28 July 1987.

The story was scarce on details about the sixty-four-year-old, as well as taste, noting that 'holidaymakers saw her run to the edge and hurl herself to oblivion for no apparent reason', before recounting those final few moments, and noting that she was the 'SIXTH victim this year to plummet to her death' from that particular location.

How could the *Sun* have known that mentioning a spot where people go to commit suicide could encourage others to go there too, or that putting someone's final moments on the front page of a national newspaper where any of her family, friends or acquaintances could see it was bad? How too could they have known it was distasteful to publish 'MONROE DOUBLE IN NUDE SUICIDE' (14 June 1989) about a Marilyn Monroe impersonator's death, along with details of how she'd killed herself and several photos of her in the nude for, uh, journalism reasons?

Then, in 1994, the Samaritans published guidelines, written with journalists, for reporting on suicides, with extensive advice for writers who are concerned about not making matters worse. The guidelines include a section on how to report celebrity suicides, given that research has consistently shown strong links between certain media coverage and increased rates in suicide, especially in the case of the deaths of celebrities.

They include simple things such as avoiding placement of the story on the front page or with large headlines, to avoid sensationalising the story, and avoiding explicit details of the method of suicide or what materials were used. News outlets should also take care to 'avoid speculation of causes or simplistic explanations – bear in mind that suicide is complex and seldom the result of a single factor, it is likely to have several inter-related causes'. All incredibly simple, so simple you can follow them by simply not writing a story if you can't be arsed to look them up.

With the guidelines there for everybody to see, there's no real excuse for choosing sensationalism over responsibility, and to be fair to the *Sun* they've been pretty good since. Except in 2019, when the Prodigy singer Keith Flint died and the front page on 5 March screamed 'PRODIGY KEITH'S SECRET AGONY', with a smaller paragraph mentioning a devastating split with his wife. And when Robin Williams died and they went with 'ROBIN: HIS FINAL HOURS' (11 August 2014), and included the method of suicide, along with other details of materials found near his body. And when Mike Thalassitis, a former *Love Island* contestant, died and they reported the method in the headline of their Twitter post (17 March 2019). And following Caroline Flack's death, when the method of suicide was right there on the homepage of the website (15 February 2020). But apart from that.

PULPIT POOFS CAN STAY

13 November 1987

In 1987 the Church of England was rowing horribly about gay members of the clergy, ending in a vote in the General Synod on whether to kick them out altogether.

The *Sun* couldn't wait to find out which way they'd go, and invited representatives from both sides of the argument to say their piece in the paper. In the 'yes we should kick them out' corner they had clergyman Tony Highton, who argued that 'our bodies are not made for a homosexual relationship' and quoted passages from the Bible about men being punished by God for being gay.

In the 'no we shouldn't kick out gay vicars' corner they had a normal human being making non-bigoted arguments.

The *Sun* then asked their readers to vote on it, seeing nothing wrong with asking readers whether it's OK for gay people to lead normal lives. They're like a movie studio that tests early cuts of a film on an audience and changes it based on their opinions, except the audience keeps saying 'more homophobia' or 'more racism', and you end up with *Transformers 2*.

7078 readers didn't find anything weird about this directive, voting in favour of 'booting out' gay people from the clergy, compared to 1586 against. To vote, you had to call an 0898 number. Don't want to be a stickler, but calling a hotline to have a go at gay people for the cost of 38p per minute doesn't strike me as very Jesusy.

The *Sun* clearly took their readers' views to heart, or were just planning on being homophobic shits anyway, because when the Synod voted to allow gay clergy they ran with a homophobic slur: 'PULPIT POOFS CAN STAY'.

'THE Church of England voted NOT to ban gay priests yesterday,' the front-page article started, '... despite hearing shocking indictments of perverts in the pulpit.'

The piece included examples of this behaviour by gay clergymen, as outlined by Highton. They included a 'deranged priest who beat up a man trying to protect an unwilling victim of his gay lust', a priest who had sex in a toilet (gay man in 'has sex' shocker) and 'the child-molesting school rector' who was convicted of child abuse, casually confusing homosexuality with paedophilia.

On the plus side, the article does go on to include an anecdote from someone sane. A reverend told of a man who'd been in a same-sex relationship for twenty-seven years, whose funeral he'd recently conducted. He said, 'I thank God that such relationships are becoming more common', and said homosexual relationships were part of the 'splendid variety of God's creation'.

But the final word was given to an anti-child abuse campaigner who condemned the move not to discriminate on the basis of sexuality, saying 'more and more vicars are molesting children sent to them in trust by their parents', too bigoted to realise that what she really wanted was a paedophile ban. 'The time has come for the Church to act.'

It's not clear how much attention the editorial team paid to reader polls, but from the outside the *Sun* sure looks like a newspaper that's willing to poll their readers on how bigoted they'd like them to be, and then implement the results. Insert your own Brexit joke here, in your heads.

PROUDEST DAY OF MY LIFE ... WHEN MY SON SAID HE WAS GAY

8 March 1988

I'll be honest, looking through the eighties coverage of gay issues has not been a pleasant task, and I'm coming at it from being a straight man thirty to forty years in the future.

I know part of it was the media were reflecting the homophobic attitudes of the time, but the casual homophobia and use of the word 'poofs' grates on you. For gay people actually living through it, it must have been hell.

I'd been looking for some sort of turning point in their coverage, where the casual homophobia would disappear and be replaced by some sort of more liberal view, or at least some sort of progress, when I stumbled across the story of a member of Status Quo discovering that his son was gay. The piece caught me off guard.

'STATUS Quo rock star Francis Rossi yesterday told of his "proudest moment" when his son Simon pulled him aside and admitted: "Dad, I'm gay."'

The tone of the piece was that it was a novelty that Rossi had reacted like this. You don't make it to page 1 by doing what the *Sun* believe to be an ordinary thing, after all. There are other problems too, including this quote: 'I even call him a big f****t. It's not an insult. There is no problem with his sexuality.'

They left the slur uncensored. Just to remind you, reader, two years earlier they had censored the word 'fart' in a poem, deeming it too rude for human eyes, and later in this piece they would censor the word 'pissed'.

Nevertheless, there were some signs of progress. They gave space to quotes from Rossi about how proud he was of his son. 'I love Simon exactly the same way as my other sons. There is nothing wrong with gays. They shouldn't feel they have to cover up in any way' and 'It took immense courage to tell me and I admired him for it. Coming out of the closet suddenly made him more mature.' Accompanying the piece, they even had advice from a counsellor on how to tell your parents if you're gay too.

They gave more space to Rossi saying how he could tease his son, 'saying he wants to be a great actress or actor, and he can take it'. The *Sun*'s message was very much that he may be gay, but that doesn't mean he's not an Absolute Lad. They were basically acting like a sitcom eighties dad would if their son had come out: trying to be supportive, but occasionally getting it wrong and being a bit of an obnoxious shit, before everyone learns a lesson about inclusivity.

If you were gay and reading the *Sun* (and Christ knows why you would do that to yourself) it must have felt like – not a triumph and that everything was going to be OK from then on, but a sense of relief that things weren't quite as shitty as before.

Then, on page 6, they had a cartoon of a gay son who was being hanged from a lamppost by his father, with his mother watching on and telling him, 'I said your dad wouldn't take the news so well, Rodney!' The punch-line being that while the Status Quo guitarist took it well, your own father might hang you.

SCRAP EASTBENDERS

26 January 1989

EASTENDERS IS SO DRAMATIC RIGHT NOW. THESE TWO CHARACTERS WHO HAVE BEEN IN A RELATIONSHIP FOR THREE YEARS HAVE JUST KISSED - FOR THE VERY FIRST TIME!

IN THREE YEARS ON CORRIE THEY'D HAVE KISSED, SHAGGED, GOT MARRIED, CHEATED ON EACH OTHER WITH THE OTHER'S BEST FRIEND, GOT DIVORCED, GOT RE-MARRIED AND THEN ONE OF THEM WOULD HAVE BEEN MURDERED ON THE SECOND HONEYMOON FOR THE LIFE INSURANCE, ONLY TO BE RESURRECTED TEN YEARS LATER.

In 1986, *EastEnders* introduced their first gay character – Colin Russell. For the next three years, Colin would face issues that a lot of gay men went through at the time (and still do), including rampant homophobia from Dot Cotton types – in this case, from the actual Dot Cotton.

But he and his boyfriend Barry never got to do any of the fun, normal relationship stuff like all of the heterosexual characters on the show. They never kissed. They were never cut to in bed. They were never even shown heading to the bedroom while tasteful porno jazz played in the background, indicating they were about to go to Pound Town.*

EastEnders treated Colin and Barry like Bert and Ernie from *Sesame*

---

* Might be thinking of pornography rather than *EastEnders* here. My memory fades.

Street; everyone knew they were gay, but you never got any on-screen hints that they bang, unlike Kermit and Miss Piggy, who you could tell from the way they interacted on screen were porking the moment the *Muppet Show* cameras turned off.

Then, in 1989, the show finally took the much-needed and realistic step of having Colin – who had been in several relationships over several years on the show – actually kiss someone on screen. The showmakers explained they did it for realism. It's pretty weird to have two people who are three years into a relationship without going in for a peck.

Twenty million people tuned in to see the first kiss – much higher than their average of seventeen million – and it can't be overstated what a big moment this was for gay viewers. Imagine growing up and never seeing someone like you making a basic show of affection on screen. For the first time, a lot of people were being represented on TV, doing a normal everyday thing they do. It was both a small step and a huge moment.

When the episode aired, the *Sun* covered it in a piece that mainly gave column inches to rampant homophobes using slurs under the tasteful head-line 'SCRAP EASTBENDERS', and after a brief introduction using some slurs of their own.

The two-page spread – written by Piers Morgan – began as it meant to go on:

'Furious MPs last night demanded a ban on *EastEnders* after the BBC soap showed two gay men kissing full on the lips.'

'The homosexual love scene between yuppy poofs' – these were the *Sun*'s own words, not a quote from a homophobic viewer – 'Colin and Guido was screened in the early evening, when millions of children were watching.'

The article – not content with merely sticking to their 'WON'T SOMEBODY PLEASE THINK OF THE CHILDREN' editorial line – then crowbarred AIDS into the discussion, by getting a quote from a bigot.

'It is completely irresponsible to show this sort of thing' – which, again, was two characters without AIDS having a bit of a smooch – 'when people are spending a vast amount of money to combat AIDS,' Cynthia Giles of Flax Bourton told the paper. 'And it could be counter-productive, with some people tuning in just to see two queers kissing.'

A second homophobe – who the *Sun* were in no way obliged to publish the views of – called the kiss 'despicable' and said that 'children should be protected from this filth'.

The showmakers explained that homosexuality is normal, and it's weird and unrealistic to not have men kiss at any point. As the actor who played Colin – Michael Cashman, one of the founders of Stonewall in real life – said: 'We cannot wrap children in cotton wool. We have to educate them so they are capable of dealing with everything the world throws at them. We showed two people in a relationship who just kissed.'

'I think people are fed up with homosexuals flaunting themselves on television,' one of the 'furious MPs' from the subheading, Terry Dicks, told the paper about – and I really must stress this – the first and only gay kiss to have ever been screened on television. It's like someone moaning 'I'm sick of these fucking moonmen' the second Neil Armstrong set foot on the Moon.

The *Sun*, then – ever the weathervane of bigotry trying to point in the same direction as its readers – invited 'You the Jury' (like a quick kiss with your boyfriend is a crime) to dial in with your 'verdict'. The results showed that 20,223 bigots voted 'against the scenes', compared to 6313 normals who voted in favour. Sure, the *Sun* had done something damaging and were definitely on the wrong side of history, but they'd got it bang on with what their audience wanted at the time. So, I guess, kudos, Piers.

STRAIGHT SEX CANNOT GIVE YOU AIDS – OFFICIAL

17 November 1989

The coverage of AIDS by the *Sun* had always been pretty shoddy, but in November 1989 it crossed the line into 'Are these guys in league with the virus?' territory.

In 1989, Lord Kilbracken – a member of the All-Party Parliamentary Group on AIDS – claimed there was only one person in the official figures who had developed AIDS from HIV transmitted through heterosexual sex, citing that of 2372 cases of confirmed AIDS, only one was someone who wasn't in a 'high-risk group'.

He thought that the government were overemphasising the risk of getting AIDS if you were heterosexual and not a drug user, stating 'I don't understand why the government and medical profession are misrepresenting the situation.'

I'm sure you're all screaming at your book, perhaps even looking up some stats this very second to include in said screaming, that you *can* contract HIV which *can* develop into AIDS through heterosexual sex – because you very much definitely can, and to tell people otherwise is very irresponsible indeed. Fortunately, some people from the past were of the same opinion, though they don't have your stats and can't hear you, so please stop shouting.

Lord Kilbracken's critics rightly said that by looking at just the cases of fully developed AIDS (rather than HIV cases and estimates of probable HIV cases), you would not be getting a clear view of the situation, as this ignored all the people who would likely go on to develop AIDS, which can take months to many years. You were certainly not getting enough evidence to claim that 'the risk to people outside these groups is statistically invisible' (17 November 1989), which is what he went ahead and said anyway.

That mattered not to the *Sun* – or they weren't aware enough to know of these problems, in which case, look into it next time, before you say something really fucking reckless – who went with a headline 'STRAIGHT SEX CANNOT GIVE YOU AIDS – OFFICIAL' on 17 November 1989.

They then printed an editorial going much, much further than the inadequate data had implied.

'AIDS – THE FACTS NOT THE FICTION. At last the truth can be told', the editorial that day read. They really do love to say they're about to tell you the truth before telling you some bollocks, don't they?

'The killer disease AIDS can only be caught by homosexuals, bisexuals, junkies or anyone who has received a tainted blood transfusion.'

The column advised that people 'FORGET' – side note, but why do they always have to shout? Use your indoor voice – everything from the TV adverts to 'boring TV documentaries' and, most irresponsibly, to 'FORGET the idea that ordinary heterosexual people can contract AIDS', going on to call it 'impossible'. Anything else, they said with an air of Alex Jones, is 'homosexual propaganda'.

I know you think basically telling straight people to bang away and assume they're completely safe from AIDS is bad. And calling heterosexual people 'ordinary' is bad, and using phrases like 'homosexual propaganda' to describe attempting to stop the transmission of a virus is bad (and it really, really is) but the *Sun* weren't quite done with being awful reckless shits just yet . . .

AIDS DOCTOR BLASTS THE *SUN*

18 November 1989

The day after claiming that straight sex can't give you AIDS, the *Sun* of course faced a backlash from people who actually knew what the fuck they were talking about.

The head of the British Medical Association's AIDS division said that 'the editorial in the *Sun* was grossly irresponsible and is likely to increase the risk of people acquiring HIV and AIDS.

'There are hundreds of thousands of cases which have been acquired as you would say through ordinary heterosexual intercourse in other countries. There are 714 people in this country known to the authorities to have acquired the infection heterosexually and probably thousands more who have not been tested.'

The *Sun* responded, saying that 'we report the facts on AIDS as we do all issues. Our readers know that', before adding in some more confusing information that could easily mislead their readers.

They brought in the comment of another doctor (who wasn't, e.g., head of the AIDS division at the British Medical Association), who told the *Sun* that 'there is no evidence that AIDS is spreading into the heterosexual population'.

This was of course missing the point that the *Sun* had told their readers that catching AIDS if you are heterosexual is 'impossible' – an entirely different claim that would require them to show heterosexual people can't transmit HIV, which the BMA had just told them they could and had.

Crass, scaremongering coverage of AIDS was typical of the *Sun* at the time: they referred to it as 'GAY PLAGUE' (6 February 1985) and ran stories such as 'HOW TO BURY A PLAGUE VICTIM' (20 February 1985) and 'AIDS: You CAN catch it from kissing' (7 March 1988), which also claimed that you can catch AIDS from a toilet seat (you can't).

Fighting the BMA was a new, but unsurprising, low. Particularly as they had already run stories of women catching HIV from straight sex ('AIDS plague "putting wives in grave peril"' on 15 March 1985, for example). But then, who among us hasn't heard advice from a doctor like 'don't put your penis in a toaster' and agreed, before later dismissing it as bullshit and recommending it to a friend?

AIDS – THE HOAX OF THE CENTURY

18 November 1989

The *Sun*, having been corrected by the BMA for running false claims that you couldn't get AIDS from heterosexual sex, decided to double down in one of the most bizarre columns I've come across while reading this newspaper, or any other.

'The shadow of AIDS has taken the fun out of sex for too long,' the column by Vernon Coleman read, as though the real tragedy was that straight men were forced to wear condoms. 'The **TRUTH**' – there they go again – 'is simple. AIDS was never a major threat to heterosexuals.'

'AIDS was the hoax of the century, the crisis that never was.'

This line was underlined and in italics, really drawing attention to the part where he was wrong on the facts and basically saying, 'Now that we've established it's only killing the gays, I no longer deem it to be an issue. The straights are fine, so stop worrying.'

Now very much on the highway to Hot Take City, Vernon cranked it up a notch by claiming condom manufacturers – aided by prudes and 'religious maniacs' – were using AIDS to sell condoms to people having sex and to stop people having sex, respectively.

He claimed that clinics and international drugs companies were gaining from AIDS, adding 'needless to say condom manufacturers have got extremely rich out of the scare', as if telling people to protect themselves from sexually transmitted diseases was a scam by Durex to trick people into trying their new ribbed magnum sheath.

In the column – on the same day the paper was told they had fucked up a story so badly that they would increase the risk of their own readers getting AIDS – the *Sun* allowed their columnist to try to discredit the British Medical Association, the very institution that had corrected them.

'With all this profit to be made,' he added, while claiming that much of the 'hysteria' had come from the BMA, 'it's hardly surprising that many doctors have been enthusiastic supporters of the AIDS theory.'

And we still haven't hit the lowest point.

Closing the article, Coleman claimed that 'much of the misinformation' (which, in regular circles, is known as 'information') 'has come from gay campaigners worried that once it was widely known that AIDS was **not** a major threat to heterosexuals, then funds for AIDS research would fall'.

To recap: that's condom manufacturers, prudes, doctors and gays all teaming up to pretend that AIDS infects the straights in order to sell condoms, stop people having sex, bring in that sweet AIDS dollar and keep funding for finding a cure. Rather than admit that Lord Kilbracken might have been mistaken.

SWAN BAKE

4 July 2003

In a piece that seems like the *Sun* were hoping to do a pun so good that it justified the racism (or racism so good it justified the pun, depending on your opinions on racism and puns), the paper ran a story that asylum seekers were stealing swans and killing them for barbecues under the headline 'SWAN BAKE'.

It alleged that 'callous asylum seekers are barbecuing the Queen's swans' – just to imply a bit of treason in case you weren't already mad at people murdering some swans and then chowing down the evidence* – and

---

* A law change in 1998 means it's technically no longer treasonous to eat the Queen's swans, though it remains illegal to kill or consume them, but fuck you, reader, I'm leaving in the treason joke. The swans remain the property of the Queen, and by Christ that makes eating them treason in my eyes.

that 'East European poachers lure the protected Royal birds into baited traps, an official Metropolitan Police report says.'

The allegations – which get quite specific – were front-page news.

'Police swooped on a gang of East Europeans and caught them red-handed about to cook a pair of royal swans,' the story read. 'The asylum seekers were barbecuing a duck in a park in Beckton, East London. But two dead swans were also found concealed in bags and ready to be roasted. The discovery last weekend confirmed fears that immigrants are regularly scoffing the Queen's birds.'

It all sounds a bit suspect, doesn't it? Swans will notoriously follow you down the road against your will if you look a tad nervous, so why would anyone feel the need to set up an elaborate swan trap? And why would Eastern Europeans be doing this, when in Eastern Europe their favourite cuisines are – famously – *NOT SWAN*?

There must be some evidence to it, right? Because – and I'm being extremely fair here – claiming that a specific group of immigrants are luring swans to their death (like a pied piper whose pipe makes pleasing swan honks) and then whacking them on a barbecue *without any solid evidence of investigations or arrests* is completely batshit. Right?

Enter pissed-off journalist Nic Medic of Presswise:

'As an Eastern European who has sought asylum in the UK, I have to admit that my own feathers had been ruffled by this,' he wrote of his decision to investigate the story further. 'I understand that different cultures have different dietary preferences, yet here was a statement that was not only untrue but also implied a degree of barbarism and savagery.'

Nick took the unheard-of step of checking whether the story was actually true. He rang the police, who informed him there had been no arrests, charges or even cautions for swan-killing or indeed roasting. In fact, after searching some more, there was no evidence, other than conjecture, that any swans were even missing.

After being approached by Medic, the *Sun* printed a small clarification, making clear that there had been no arrests or charges in relation to 'offences against swans' and that '*The Sun* [. . .] referred to asylum seekers being responsible. We have no information at all that supports this contention and indeed when we spoke to [the journalist who wrote up the Swan Bake piece], he agreed that this was a mistake.' As they'd printed 'Swan Bake' on the front page, they ran this correction ~~also on the front page~~ on page 41 – for an audience for whom I would argue getting past page 3 is a bit of a struggle.

The Leveson inquiry – the public hearings into ethics and practices in the British press after the phone-hacking scandal – included 'Swan Bake' as evidence that newspapers 'wilfully' produce stories 'which are factually incorrect' in order to 'fit with a newspaper's adopted viewpoint'. 'Unidentified people were cited as witnesses to the phenomenon, but it seemed there was no basis to the story: the *Sun* was unable to defend the article against a PCC complaint,' they noted.

In essence, imaginary swans had gone missing and some very real asylum seekers took the blame. But, to be fair to the *Sun*, 'swans we aren't sure existed in the first place *may* have died (you don't know!) and one local and potentially racist person we are unwilling to name reckons it's actually the immigrants based on nothing' is a lot more difficult to work into a pun.

BONKERS BRUNO LOCKED UP

23 September 2003

HOW'S IT GOING?

WE'RE STUCK ON THE HEADLINE, SO BOB'S JUST GETTING OUT THE THESAURUS.

THE **BIG** BOOK OF OFFENSIVE TERMS

There are times when you feel like the *Sun* (or the right-wing media in general) is trying to poison the minds of the public, and times when you think that they're just mindless pagan villagers trying to appease an angry god they've created in their own minds.

My impression from reading far more of the *Sun* than I'd like is that they'll run whatever the hell they think their readers want to read, less trying to manipulate them than saying 'We agree with your mad beliefs entirely – please don't go!' Sort of like one of those aeroplane rides outside shopping centres that play music to entice all the kids in, except instead of a mild bounce when you put in 25p, it'll tell you your raging xenophobia is actually fine.

But if your system is trying to guess what your readers want, rather than writing something you think is right and letting people decide if they want to buy it, there are bound to be some missteps. Never was that clearer than in the case of Frank Bruno, where the *Sun* held two strong contrary opinions about the same story on the same day.

In 2003, the former boxer suffered from a bout of mental ill health, and on 22 September was sectioned under the Mental Health Act.

From other papers, sympathy poured in – for example, the *Mirror* went for the headline 'SO SAD'. The *Sun*, however, decided to splash their front page with a picture of him next to the derogatory headline 'BONKERS BRUNO LOCKED UP' in a story that also went on to call him a 'nut'.

Pretty par for the course for a paper that had used language like this around mental health before, although mainly in headlines about murderers going on killing sprees, rather than beloved sports personalities in need of a bit of help.

The mental health charity SANE was quick to condemn the *Sun*, calling the article 'an insult to Mr Bruno and damaging to the many thousands of people who endure mental illness to label him as "bonkers" or "a nutter" and having to be "put in a mental home"'.

When the paper hit the shelves, it was clear they'd not only crossed moral lines and pissed off mental health advocates, they'd badly misjudged their own readers, causing the *Sun* to do one of their U-turn-whiplash specials.

People rang into Radio 5 Live to call for a boycott, and a hundred readers complained about the first edition. I know that doesn't sound like a lot, but this was in 2003, when your options for complaint were enduring the horrors of dialup to access a GeoCities website or sending a messenger boy on a horse, rather than the paradise we have now, where you merely type in the name of the person you wish to speak to and let autocomplete call them a ducking lickhead.

The *Sun* saw their god was displeased and tried to appease it, or a fit of conscience struck. For the second edition that day (note to younger readers: in the olden days you apparently had to wait hours for new news to be delivered on paper – that was the ancient equivalent of refreshing the page), the headline was changed from 'BONKERS BRUNO LOCKED UP' to

'SAD BRUNO IN MENTAL HOME'. Even when they tried to do the right thing they covered it with the emotional dexterity of a dog at its owner's funeral trying to figure out why its other owner is crying. 'SAD? MUM SAD? MUM SAD BECAUSE NO PLAY FETCH INDOORS??'

Bruno also received an upgrade from 'ex-champ' to 'hero' in the subheading. Not bad for a day in which zero facts had changed.

Rebekah Wade, editor at the time, also got in touch with SANE, in an attempt to raise funds for the charity in Bruno's name.

They set a lunch date, in which SANE chief executive Marjorie Wallace recalls Wade asked directly, 'Why can't I use bonkers, and what else would do?' which is a question so basic it's like calling for a meeting with the head of NASA and saying 'Tell me, Mr Spaceman, what call hot thing in sky that make eyes go ouch bad?'

Oddly enough, Wallace says this wasn't even the first conversation she had had where a *Sun* editor had treated the head of the mental health charity like a dummies' thesaurus for the morally bankrupt.

'I remember having the conversation with her predecessor, David Yelland,' Wallace told the BBC. 'He said, "What's a three-letter word I can put in a headline rather than nut or mad?" I said, "What about ill? Because that's what it is – ill. Someone's ill and they go to hospital."'

Next time you have a job interview you feel unqualified for, remember that the *Sun*, with all their hundreds of staff, between them don't know the word 'ill'.

The *Sun*, to be fair to them (and excluding some fairly major slips) did improve their coverage of mental health after finding they'd gone too far even for *Sun* readers. Further coverage of Bruno was more sympathetic, including stories headlined 'Time and space to heal' about his stay in hospital. Although I can't quite decide if this is like a toddler being told for the first time that other people have feelings, and improving, or Dexter learning how better to hide the fact he's a psychopath.

1,200 KILLED BY MENTAL PATIENTS

7 October 2013

WELL ON THE ONE HAND IT'S MISLEADING, BUT ON THE OTHER HAND IT IS VERY PITHY...

You know how in that last piece I said they got a bit better at covering mental health issues? While largely that's true, this piece sort of makes me look like a massive liar, so cheers for that one MURDOCH, you long-past-its-best dishevelled egg.

Anyhow, if there's one thing a person suffering from poor mental health needs, it's people looking at them like they're a potential murderer.

In 2013, the *Sun* published the infamous headline '1,200 killed by mental patients' under the words 'EXCLUSIVE INVESTIGATION', like a cat proudly dragging a half-dead, diseased vole into the lounge for Mummy to find.

The subheading quickly explains the timeframe – this was the figure over ten years – making it seem much less alarming than the massive headline had implied. It's like moaning loudly to colleagues that you've only had an hour's sleep before informing them you meant at lunch.

'The crisis has been highlighted by the killing of 16-year-old Christina Edkins – knifed to death by paranoid schizophrenic Phillip Simelane while heading to school on a bus,' they wrote, before going on to caveat that 'random' killings like this accounted for around ten deaths a year. They included other examples of homicides, along with mugshots of the perpetrators, putting the coverage far into the sensationalist side of things, rather than the 'we're just concerned about mental health services' bracket.

As well as stigmatising people suffering mental health problems, the claim didn't match with the data. A lot of the twelve hundred 'MENTAL PATIENTS' – which the *Sun* said revealed 'disturbing failures in Britain's mental health system' – included people who weren't mental health patients at the time of the offence, but had been experiencing 'an abnormal mental state at the time of the homicide'.

The report the *Sun* had based the piece on hadn't exactly hidden this fact in complex data, but rather spelt it out in easy-to-read sentences like 'During 2001–2011, 615 people convicted of homicide (10% of the total sample) were identified as patients, i.e. the person had been in contact with mental health services in the 12 months prior to the offence, an average of 56 homicides per year' and 'most of these people were not under mental health care; therefore most were not preventable by mental health services.'

The rate had also been falling 'substantially' for years, according to the report; the figures for the most recent years (2009–10) were the lowest since data collection began in 1997.

The *Sun* had seen figures that showed improvement in dealing with mental health, misunderstood the figures or misrepresented them, and used them in a headline that lumped in the '1.2 million people in touch with secondary mental health services' with those who committed homicide in a way that, I'd hazard a guess, doesn't exactly encourage people who need treatment to seek it.

For a bit of wider context, in 2010–11, 95 per cent of murders were committed by people who hadn't been diagnosed with a mental health problem. Of the 728 murder convictions that took place in those years, 666 were of men. They probably have other things in common too, yet we don't have any shock headlines about '1200 killed by people who are shit at judging how much pasta you're supposed to put in the pan'. Although I suspect that figure would be far higher.

RESCUE BOATS? I'D USE GUNSHIPS TO STOP MIGRANTS

17 April 2015

The Apprentice is a bit like a selection system for the worst human beings on the planet. First the contestants self-select, deciding that they're the kind of person who is good at business. This weeds out all but the most virulent of arseholes, who then take part in a sort of middle-class *Takeshi's Castle* where only the direst specimens of humanity get through.

Katie Hopkins was one such candidate, who made it through to the final of the show in Series 3. During the run, she made a number of statements that people would deem controversial. Though causing her problems in her actual work, it soon led to appearances on everything from comedy entertainment shows to *Question Time*, which is the exact opposite of a comedy entertainment show.

From an outsider's perspective – though Hopkins denies it – it looks like somewhere around here she realised she could turn being an absolute penis into a sustainable business model. She began saying the unsayable (note: people who say the unsayable are generally just saying things that are perfectly sayable, you just don't say them because they're (a) horribly offensive, (b) wrong, or (c) horribly offensive and wrong) for money.

The *Sun* hired her as a columnist. Which is like giving a major TV deal to a guy you found in a pub shouting racial slurs at a urinal cake, 'just to see what he'd do'.

When she started saying things people would find controversial, the *Sun* started promoting her as 'Britain's most controversial columnist', which is essentially like saying 'Come and get your column, there's some real heinous shit in here', putting it on the reader if they don't like what they read. 'Look, we told you this was a toilet, you can't complain about what you saw in a toilet if you deliberately took a massive look.'

Lo and behold, hiring someone with a track record of saying bad things then informing her that her role was to say the worst things of all the newspaper columnists in the country turned out to be a bad plan, and eventually led to senior figures in the UN telling the paper to tone down the Nazi shit. On 17 April 2015, Hopkins wrote a column that would result in her getting a visit from the police, who were investigating allegations of inciting racial hatred.

Unless you were hiding under a rock in the 2010s (wouldn't blame you, they were shit), you'll know that in 2011 the Syrian civil war started, which displaced millions and millions of people and caused more than five million more to become refugees. Some European countries were better at stepping up than others. Germany took in over six hundred thousand refugees, for example, and coped just fine, while the UK pissed itself and believed civilisation would collapse if six made it over in a dinghy. For Hopkins and others, any people making it into the country by boat was too many.

Titled 'Rescue boats? I'd use gunships to stop migrants', Hopkins opened by banging out thoughts to hundreds of thousands of people that you'd be embarrassed to tell your priest in case they thought you were Satan himself:

'No, I don't care. Show me pictures of coffins, show me bodies floating in water, play violins and show me skinny people looking sad. I still don't care,' she wrote, presumably whilst punching a kitten. 'Because in the next minute you'll show me pictures of aggressive young men at Calais, spreading like norovirus on a cruise ship.

'Watching them try to clamber on to British lorries and steal their way into the UK, do I feel pity? Only for the British drivers, who get hit with a fine every time one of this plague of feral humans ends up in their truck.'

She went on to compare people to insects, just in case calling them a virus that makes you shit yourself was too subtle.

'Make no mistake, these migrants are like cockroaches. They might look a bit "Bob Geldof's Ethiopia circa 1984", but they are built to survive a nuclear bomb. They are survivors.'

Hopkins was given the opportunity to see more dead bodies floating in the water and feel nothing later that same day, when a fishing vessel with migrants on board capsized off the coast of Libya, with around eight hundred people being killed.

After the column, the UN High Commissioner for Human Rights, Zeid Ra'ad Al Hussein, criticised the paper for printing the column, pointing out: 'The Nazi media described people their masters wanted to eliminate as rats and cockroaches.'

The column did not get Hopkins fired – despite a petition signed by 315,636 people requesting that it should – and she eventually moved on to the *Mail Online* – a fate worse than death for most people who aren't Katie Hopkins.

IT'S LIFE AND DEATH

3 September 2015

It's hard to turn men, women and children fleeing war zones and such into the bogeyman, but the *Sun* have given it a good old go. It might even be their greatest success story, a time when they and their readers truly gelled.

Over the years they've printed a plethora of articles negatively portraying asylum seekers, as well as immigrants. They tend to focus not on typical experiences (it's hard to wail on people fleeing war zones and such without looking like a bit of a dick), instead homing in on outlandish tales of 'bogus' asylum seekers ('Asylum rat left me holding the baby . . . and a £30k debt' – 20 November 2008), perceived abuse of the system ('"DEPRESSED" REFUGEE TO SUE BRITAIN FOR £30,000' – 10 March 2003), or making the number of asylum seekers heading to the UK sound terrifying in some way ('ASYLUM ARMY' – 1 March 2003).

They even made space to begrudge kids, who I really must stress are fleeing from their own countries and *are kids*, for having a few rounds of golf ('Migrant madness: "ASYLUM KIDS GET FREE GOLF LESSONS"' – 3 March 2003) and learning a few circus skills as part of a scheme to engage disadvantaged young people including – but not limited to – asylum seekers and refugees ('REFUGEES' £60,000 TRAPEZE LESSONS' – 22 January 2007).

In the latter half of 2015, the United Nations High Commission for Refugees looked at coverage of the refugee and migrant crisis in Europe. The *Sun* used the word 'illegal' when talking about migrants, refugees and asylum seekers much more frequently than other papers – at 16.3 per cent of the time. The closest other paper looked at was the *Telegraph* (5.9 per cent).

Whether it's the *Sun* correctly guessing how much xenophobia their readers are into, or directly influencing their xenophobia (I'm going to take the boring option here and say both – the *Sun*'s readers aren't fans of asylum seekers and the *Sun* are willing to pump out stories that reinforce that view, making that xenophobia stronger), their readers are on board with the coverage of refugees, as evidenced by signatures on petitions to be tough on asylum seekers (one such campaign received a million signatures in 2003) as well as their letters.

For instance, the *Sun* made room for readers' letters about the 'sheer madness to throw open the asylum doors' the day after 9/11, in an edition otherwise pretty much devoid of any reference to things that weren't 9/11. Then, on 17 February 2003, readers' letters were about how 'Asylum vandals deserve new home – back in Iraq', roughly a month before the Iraq War. Seems a tad on the harsh side to send people to a country we were about to bomb the shite out of, but you do you, *Sun* readers.

The *Sun* constantly pressured governments to keep borders strict and asylum-seeker numbers down. But there are consequences to strict borders: if there's no safe way in, desperate people will take desperate measures. On 2 September 2015, a three-year-old boy, Aylan al-Kurdi, drowned in the Mediterranean Sea. Photos of the child were heartbreaking. The *Sun* printed the photos alongside 'MR CAMERON, SUMMER IS OVER … NOW DEAL WITH THE BIGGEST CRISIS FACING EUROPE SINCE WW2. IT'S LIFE & DEATH'. They called for the Prime Minister to take in people fleeing imminent danger. It showed compassion, was the right move – and was a blip. By 22 October they were back to the usual, splashing 'ILLEGALS HAVE LANDED' across the front page when a boat landed on a British base in Cyprus, in a story that invited outrage about 114 refugees from Syria, who were the 'first to land on British sovereign soil', stating 'Aid staff believe they hoped to claim asylum in Britain via the base'. Which the *Sun* had called for not a month before.

HOLLYWOOD HIV PANIC

10 November 2015

WHO'S TAKING THE HIV STORY?

THEY'VE DEFROSTED GEOFF FOR THAT ONE. FELT IT NEEDED AN EXPERT TOUCH.

In 2015, long after the heights of their terrible 1980s HIV and AIDS coverage, the *Sun* were pulled out of retirement for one last job when it turned out a celebrity was HIV positive.

In the piece, teased on the front page, the *Sun* said that they were choosing not to name the 'womanising A-list actor' who had been diagnosed with the condition, making it look like they were going to take the high road. I say high road – they were still doing a sleazy piece on somebody who'd just been diagnosed with HIV, but at least it was the higher of the incredibly low roads on the way to the sewage works.

While not naming the A-lister directly, the piece gave clues as to who the person might be, specifying his exes include 'an award-winning actress, a religious movie star, a top Hollywood personality with a controversial past, a TV star, a media personality and a glamour model'.

It was sort of a game of *Guess Who?*, but for figuring out which Hollywood star had a health condition they didn't want to publicly disclose.

'Have they got a beard?'

'No.'

[Tiles are flipped down.]

'Then Alan has diabetes!'

If you know enough about 2015 Hollywood, you could probably guess who it was through the clues the *Sun* provided, meaning they were basically outing someone as HIV positive in the form of a puzzle.

As if the piece wasn't stigmatising enough – why draw attention to someone's health in this sensationalised manner at all if you aren't stigmatising their condition, let alone give clues to their identity like it was some sort of scandal to uncover – they made out that Hollywood was 'gripped with fear' by the revelation, as if HIV positive people are something to be terrified of. They even had a 'US showbiz insider' speculate and express disapproval at his actions, stating 'if he's knowingly put women at risk then that's disgusting and it's only a matter of time before that becomes public'. Even though antiretroviral treatments can suppress viral loads in patients to the point that they are uninfectious, condoms do exist, and there's nothing to suggest that the women he slept with hadn't known about his status.

The story noted that the star was distraught at the possibility that his HIV status could come to define his career, but didn't quite note it enough in their own hearts to not write the article in the first place.

Once again, the *Sun* proved that there were very few depths to which they wouldn't sink in order to sell papers. If there wasn't such a backlash from people such as the HIV campaign group the Terrence Higgins Trust, I'd speculate that they'd have introduced a regular *Guess Who Has Rectal Cancer?* cryptic crossword before the month was out.

1 IN 5 BRIT MUSLIMS' SYMPATHY FOR JIHADIS

23 November 2015

...SO YOU TAKE THOSE FACTS, AND THEN YOU IGNORE THEM, AND THAT'S HOW YOU WRITE AN ARTICLE. ANY QUESTIONS?

In 2015, IPSO received more than twelve hundred complaints about a *Sun* article headlined '1 in 5 Brit Muslims' sympathy for jihadis', setting a new record for the number of complaints received.

The article, which came in the wake of a series of coordinated attacks in Paris, claimed that 'NEARLY one in five British Muslims has some sympathy with those who have fled the UK to fight for IS in Syria. The number among young Muslims aged 18–34 is even higher at one in four.' For good measure, this was accompanied by a picture of Mohammed Emwazi, a Brit believed to be involved in several ISIS beheading videos in 2014–15, holding a big old knife above the caption 'Support . . . Brit Jihadi John who went to Syria'.

On pages 4 and 5 a columnist expressed her 'shock, horror, bewilderment, anger and disbelief . . . Surely this can't be true? There cannot possibly be so many Muslims harbouring sympathy for such a murderous twisted ideology? [. . .] a whopping one in five saying they've some, or a lot of sympathy for IS doesn't make any sense to me.'

And she was right, it didn't make sense, because that's not what the survey had found. As I'm sure you're aware, it's possible to feel sympathy for young people who are groomed or misled into fighting for ISIS without even slightly thinking, I SUPPORT ISIS. Sympathy for misguided young people is not in any way 'harbouring sympathy for such a murderous twisted ideology'. In fact, a similar Sky News/Survation poll earlier that year had found that 30 per cent of non-Muslims had sympathy for 'Muslims who join fighters in Syria', but you'll be surprised to learn that didn't result in a 'NON-MUSLIMS LOVE ISIS' edition.

Doubling down, a piece by the *Sun*'s political editor noted that 19 per cent of UK Muslims have 'some sympathy with those like Jihadi John'.

Really taking the piss was the fact that the question posed by the survey did not actually mention jihadis or ISIS, but asked them to rank the statement 'I have a lot of sympathy with young Muslims who leave the UK to join fighters in Syria'. Fighters who participants in the survey could also take to mean a number of groups fighting in Syria, including anti-Assad forces and forces that see ISIS as the main enemy.

It would be like finding that five out of five British people at the time of the Second World War expressed sympathy for those going to Europe to fight, and then assuming they meant 'for Hitler'. The *Sun* said that it was clear that the survey was asking about ISIS from previous questions. Though it would have been a lot clearer if they'd actually mentioned ISIS in the actual question.

The *Sun* also didn't help themselves by arguing they hadn't misrepresented the results, by saying things like 'among British Muslims, a minority – but a substantial one – appear sympathetic to a death cult which is amongst the most evil in history', as if sympathy for young

Muslims who go to fight in Syria (again, we don't know who for) meant supporting ISIS.

It's like saying, 'Oh, I feel a bit sorry for people who've been raised so badly they become murderers,' to be told, 'Oh, I see you endorse the actions of serial killer Fred West. Interesting.'

IPSO ruled that the *Sun*'s coverage of the survey had been misleading, and the paper duly printed a correction (much smaller than the original story) stating that their headline had been misleading.

In fairness to the *Sun*, four out of five *Sun* reporters said that they were incredibly ashamed of what they'd done, in stats I pulled right out of my arse just now.

'6 DAYS TO TERROR'

5 December 2015

In the wake of the November 2015 Paris attacks, which saw 130 dead and 413 injured, the *Sun* published a piece titled '6 days to terror'. It was a story about 'a *Sun* investigator' who had managed to 'smuggle himself 2,000 miles from Turkey to Paris in just six days without showing his passport', which they took to be a 'damning exposure of Europe's lax borders' following a 'similar journey to Paris suicide bombers Ahmad al Mohammad and M al Mahmod who passed most borders without checks before blowing themselves up at the Stade de France just over a month later'.

The story claimed that former Marine Emile Ghessen snuck across the continent thanks to lax security, including incidents where he hid in a toilet to dodge passport control like someone trying to avoid the ticket guy just outside Birmingham New Street.

'I expect to be hauled off by police but am left alone to board,' the story went. 'The train stops about a mile into the journey and border officers come on to check passports. But I hide in the toilets, leaving the door unlocked so it looks unoccupied. After a tense wait I hear the cops leave the train and we move off.'

The story had big implications for international security. As the *Sun* said, 'EU leaders have called for tighter controls and suspension of the freedom of movement agreement over fears more jihadis could creep in'. A Labour MP they quoted called the probe 'very worrying'.

So how did Ghessen manage to get all that way without using a passport? He, uh, used a passport.

Shortly after the story came out, the Croatian government turned into one of those men online who says 'DIDN'T HAPPEN' whenever a woman relays a perfectly believable anecdote or makes what is obviously a joke online. But rather than just being lonely incels with nothing better to do with their time, they were correct and had proof.

The Croatian authorities had a record of Ghessen when they checked his passport at the border, and they then saw his passport again as he left Croatia at Zagreb Airport. It turns out he had flown to Paris. Well, that's one way to dodge a train guard.

Essentially the story, once you've stripped out the lies, was 'man goes on holiday'. Which is nice, but probably doesn't deserve a double-page spread and a headline that implies you should be shitting yourself in fear of terrorism. The *Sun* removed the story from their website and issued a tiny apology on page 2, confirming he'd been twatting around Europe freely due to the magic of having a passport.

The *Sun* was the only paper that took the story, and remains one of the select few newspapers to have 'bullshit' called on them by Croatia.

RAMADAN TRAIN DRIVER IN CRASH

20 August 2016

TOP TIP: IF YOU WRITE A STORY THAT YOU KNOW YOU'LL NEED TO CORRECT AFTER A COMPLAINT IS UPHELD, THAT'S TWO ARTICLES YOU CAN SQUEEZE OUT OF THE SAME STORY.

In June 2016, a train driver ran through a red signal, leading to a derailment and severe delays to and from Paddington. Nobody was injured. By the time it came to the inquiry a few months later, it was a non-story which even trainwatchers would call 'a bit shite' if it was printed in *Modern Locomotives Illustrated* – a real magazine bought by virgins.

The *Sun* ran it on page 2, and essentially assigned blame for the crash to the train driver's religion. They wrote that 'rail accident experts claimed his fast [for Ramadan] caused the rush-hour derailment' in which he sped through 'a double red light'. They went on to give details of the last time the driver had eaten. They then mentioned casually that 'The Rail Accident

Investigation Branch (RAIB) was unable to conclude that fasting was a factor in the crash' before saying that 'not eating can cause "sleepiness and reduction in concentration which can result in safety concerns"' and mentioning that Islam forbids daytime eating and drinking during Ramadan.

That's four mentions of fasting and many other suggestions that Ramadan led to the crash in a story about an investigation that didn't conclude that fasting caused the crash. There could have been any number of factors that caused the crash – the RAIB said it showed the importance of drivers refreshing their knowledge of track layout, if you want to talk facts. Maybe he was thinking too much about tennis, if you want to speculate wildly. The *Sun* just happened to pick the angle that implies that Muslims are unfit to drive trains for a whole month of the year.

Miqdaad Versis, assistant secretary-general of the Muslim Council of Britain, put in a complaint about the article to IPSO. He said:

'Creating a link to the faith of the driver and the Islamic act of fasting without any evidence is totally unacceptable. In today's environment where Islamophobia and bigotry have become more and more normalised, I hope the *Sun* will avoid creating stories that unfairly depict Muslims as the "bad guy" and will introduce safeguards to deter future inaccuracies.'

After IPSO upheld the complaint, the *Sun* apologised and issued a correction, reiterating that the RAIB were unable to conclude that fasting was a factor in the crash. Since everyone who read the story will have seen the correction and contacted all their friends to say, 'You know how I told you Muslims crash trains during Ramadan? Well, don't I feel quite the fool,' we can rest safe in the knowledge that the system works.

TRAN AND WIFE

27 March 2018

Back in November 1978, the *Sun* ran a series of stories about round-the-world sailor Rosie Swale, who fell in love with a trans woman and left her husband so they could be together.

It was sensationalist, with headlines such as 'RUNAWAY ROSIE: Why the nude round the world sailor left her husband for a sex change witch' and 'we even fancy the same men!' Yet, once you look past the headlines, it was actually ... quite good.

The paper had for years been free-talking on issues of sex, featuring sex guides regularly and discussing topics that other papers at the time just wouldn't – often in quite a progressive and positive way. In the series of pieces they ran on the couple, there were details that would be unacceptable today (dropping in photos of Tracey from when she was younger with the caption 'Tracey ... when she was called Bernard' are particularly glaring). But you got the sense that they were genuinely trying to convey to their readers what it's like to be trans, and allowed Tracey and Rosie space to talk about their relationship. Other headlines read 'A VERY SPECIAL KIND OF LOVE' and a piece by Tracey read 'IT'S GREAT BEING A GIRL'. The photos accompanying the stories showed a couple, happy and in love.

In 1978, the *Sun* clearly thought their readers were open minded, at least on issues of gender and sexuality. By the eighties that was shot to bits – there was more homophobia than you'd find inside John Wayne's mind. So what about how they cover trans stories more recently? What does that say about our *Sun* reader today?

Covering a story of a couple's *wedding day* in 2018, they led with the headline 'TRAN AND WIFE', and the subheading 'JAKE WHO USED TO BE A WOMAN WEDS HANNAH WHO WAS A MAN', accompanied with big wedding photos as well as smaller pictures showing 'GROOM Jake as he used to look' and 'BRIDE Hannah's early army days'. They'd somewhat lost their nuance, huh?

The tone of the actual article was better, and was called 'positive' by the couple, despite the Victorian freak show tones to the headline itself. But Hannah said that their wedding had been 'marred' by the 'offensive headlines' put out by the *Sun*. Responding to accusations of transphobia, the *Sun* said that 'Jake and Hannah's is a wonderful story and we hope they have every happiness'.

But that's offset somewhat by the fact they went with 'TRAN AND WIFE' rather than any of the endless headlines you could run about a wedding, such as 'EVERYBODY HAD A LOVELY DAY' or 'NICE CEREMONY BUT THE SHITHEAD FRIENDS OF THE GROOM KEPT LURKING NEAR THE CANAPES AND A LOT OF THE TINY BURGERS DIDN'T MAKE IT TO THE OTHER GUESTS'.

WHAT THE FU—

I'M THE BINGO BUNGLER

21 May 1984

As much as editors at the *Sun* probably like to think the (undeniably impressive but now declining) sales figures are down to their genius, the truth is a lot of their readers were probably only in it for the bingo (and, I would venture, the tits).

In 1981, worried about losing readers to the *Star* with their bingo game, the *Sun* introduced Sun Bingo, like Beyblade ripping off Pokémon. Within three months, circulation had gone up by half a million. Later on, they would compete with the *Mirror* in terms of prizes and a lot of readers vacillated between the two papers, based on how good the winnings were, which must feel great if you're a writer trying your hardest, only to discover your readers mainly see the paper as a large lottery ticket with discardable shit printed all over the side.

Still, you must be thinking, the more space taken up by gambling, the less space for any racism. Not so fast, buddy, let's not jump to any conclusions.

On 22 November 1985 the *New Statesman* published a first-person account from graphic designer Peter Court, who had worked for the *Sun*, of his time at the paper. On 2 August 1985, he said he overheard a sub-editor suggest that for a picture of the winners of the bingo, they use an Asian man with money stuffed into his turban.

'No, I'm not having pictures of darkies on the front page,' Peter Court asserted that the acting editor said, and a night editor had his back: 'That's the last thing our readers want – pictures of blacks raking it in.'

The winners pictured on the front page of the paper the next day were all people so white they find mayonnaise 'too spicy', an absolute Coldplay of honkies.

Once, on 21 May 1984, instead of announcing bingo winners, the *Sun* shamed the guy who ran the bingo numbers after he cocked up one of the results. This led to hundreds of delighted *Sun* readers queuing up outside the offices, all believing themselves to be the one true winner, like a group of pleased children who actually believed their mum when she told them they were all her favourites. I'm sorry, Gregory, but Mamma loves Richard more, it's time to stop kidding yourself and play the cards you were dealt.

When Editor MacKenzie found out, he apparently offered the bungler – Mike Terry – the option of being either fired or faced with a bit of public humiliation. Because he was older, in poor health and unlikely to find another job in media, he chose to stick it out and take the walk of shame.

Mike Terry was literally put in a dunce cap and splashed on the front page, and shamed over several days for the mistake. His dunce-hatted little face was put next to a piece looking at THE WORLD'S GREATEST BLUNDERS. Which I suppose is better than being fired, but probably not the most fun way to spend the last years of your career during a bout of ill health.

BLAZING CURSE OF THE CRYING BOY

5 September 1985

SURELY THE REAL QUESTION IS: WHY WOULD YOU WANT A PAINTING OF A CRYING BOY ON YOUR WALL IN THE FIRST PLACE?

In terms of microcosms of the relationship between the media and the public, you can't do much better than the CURSE OF THE CRYING BOY.

If you're someone who likes to stay up late attempting to scare the shit out of themselves on the internet, there's a good chance you've come across the story already. The legend goes that after a fire or other disastrous event, firefighters go through the rubble of a house and find the only thing that has survived the blaze is a creepy old (but weirdly popular) painting of a crying child, who is staring out at the viewer. The story is that they've found this same painting before, at other burned-down homes, always the only thing that survived. And so, because this is definitely a legitimate and newsworthy story, in 1985 the tale of the cursed painting got popularised by a series of stories in the *Sun*.

'HEARTBROKEN May and Ron Hall were blaming the curse of the crying boy yesterday after their home of 27 years was wrecked by fire,' the batshit story read.

'The couple had laughed off warnings that there was a jinx on their picture of a tot with tears running down his face. Ron's fireman brother Peter told them he and his mates had seen the print too often in houses where there had been blazes. And he claimed the popular picture – an estimated 50,000 have been sold in Britain – always seemed to survive the flames.'

A caption to the photo read 'Tears for fears . . . the portrait that firemen claim is cursed'.

Before you could say 'They didn't actually say it was cursed, though, if you read back his quot—', *Sun* readers started sending in their own tales of incidents involving the Cursed Boy.

They told the paper of basements flooded and the cursed painting being the only surviving item, and others told of fires where nothing remained but the creepy toddler looking up at them at the end of it, still crying despite his massive good fortune, the ungrateful little Antichrist. It turns out there were enough of the paintings out there and enough fires that once you put the thought in their head, plenty of people desperate for an explanation that wasn't 'I fell asleep with the hob on' looked at the picture of a little crying boy and thought, this fire is *your* fault!

As the accounts continued to flood in, the *Sun* were able to continually print stories from readers about a curse they'd magicked from nothing, such as the much-awaited sequel 'CRYING-BOY CURSE STRIKES AGAIN – Print undamaged as home burns' in which a family posed next to their burnt home *and a completely different painting of an unrelated sad child*. One woman claimed that, shortly after getting the painting, her son had died, then her daughter, then her husband and her mother. Thank God the *Sun* had found the explanation for the deaths, lest the police investigate the obvious murderer picking off her family members one by one.

The *Sun*, writing 'enough is enough, folks', invited people to send in the Cursed Painting, which – and this really should have set alarm bells ringing about the gullibility of their audience – *people did in their thousands*.

The paper then burned a massive pile of the paintings, getting yet more mileage from a non-story now that they'd scared the shit out of everyone to the point that they wanted to torch their own possessions. They told readers, '*Sun* nails curse of the weeping boy for good' as they burned them, clearly reasoning that a curse you made up can be destroyed using a solution you pulled out of your arsehole.

They got 'Page Three beauty' Sandra Jane Moore to set the paintings alight. Because why not? There's no reason burning the shit out of a cursed pile of family-killers can't be sexy. Although I've got to say, a picture of 'sexy Sandra' burning a gigantic pile of children made for some very weird optics.

And that was the end of that, with no rational explanation proposed for the 'curse'.

But OK, if you must know, the Radio 4 programme *Punt PI* used scientific experiments to investigate why the paintings might survive. It concluded that they were treated with fire-retardant varnish, and the string that held them up burned first, so the painting would fall, often landing face down and so being protected from the fire.

Though *Punt PI* didn't conclude why this painting in particular was surviving, I'd hazard a guess that it's just that there were a lot of people out there who had it. For some reason, everyone in the godforsaken eighties was mad for a picture of a little boy crying his face off. They were like Andy Warhol with that fucking tin of soup. I'd also hazard a guess that if you find two paintings in your rubble after a fire, and one of them is a nice horse and one of them is a picture of a little child of Satan who everyone thinks is haunted, I've got a pretty good idea which one sticks in your mind. Even if it's a *really* nice horse.

The *Sun* took no notice of this turn in events, and four years later covered the 'RETURN OF THE CRYING BOY CURSE' when the painting was found in the cellar of another man's house which had burned down.

Years later, there are still urban legends about the painting spread around the internet, with extra embellishments, e.g., the boy depicted accidentally burned his parents to death in their home in Spain, and since then wherever he went things would burn down around him, like he was an early prototype of Chris Grayling.

All because the *Sun* had a (I'll admit, quite fun) front-page idea on a slow news day, and weren't too concerned about telling their readers stuff like 'fun fact: curses aren't real'. They didn't even have the integrity to inform them they had crap taste in art.

'ELLO 'ELLO WHAT'S ALL THIS REAR THEN

4 April 1988

A stereotype of right-wing tabloid readers is that they go around saying 'You can't even climb a ladder without filling in a form these days, it's pc gone mad,' confusing political correctness – a way of not using terms that offend or exclude people – with a non-existent ladder form they've made up in their glue-addled minds.

When these kinds of stories appear in a paper it's usually nonsense and a sign you're in a slow news week. Nevertheless, take a breather from anything too serious, as these next two brief articles from the *Sun* lament artforms and activities that have disappeared, noble practices lost to the ages because of that bloody political correctness.

1. You can't even drop your pants in a pub and wiggle your bum around these days, it's pc gone mad.

A page 3 article from 4 April 1988 told the tale of a police officer (so it's a double whammy 'pc gone mad' tale, don't say I don't treat you) who 'twice **DROPPED** his trousers and underpants to his ankles and **WIGGLED** his bottom at a crowd of cheering chums and their wives'.

Don't judge the cheering crowd. Before iPhones and *Shrek 2* there was very little in the way of entertainment; showing your arsehole to a crowd of strangers in a Wetherspoons was basically their version of *Game of Thrones*.

'But unfortunately for him,' the article continued, making it seem like he, the police officer showing his butthole to strangers, was the victim: 'a woman drinker' – sinister, bloody WOMEN again – 'with a camera was there to record the scene for posterity.'

The officer was transferred to another police station following the repeated nudity, while the *Sun* obtained quotes from fellow pub-goers lamenting that 'somebody grassed him up'.

2. You can't even shout racial slurs in bingo halls these days, nor continue to shout racial slurs when they've asked you to stop. It's pc gone mad.

On 7 April 1988, the *Sun* put out the front-page breaking news of a man who was possibly going to get banned from a bingo hall.

Dave – everyone who complains about political correctness is called Dave, these are just the facts – had decided that he didn't like shouting 'housey-housey' whenever he'd won a game, calling it 'daft'. Whilst he's absolutely spot on, instead of leaving the game of bingo in fifties retirement homes for the criminally fucking tedious, his solution was to start yelling out an ethnic slur whenever he got a full house.

A fellow bingo player – an Indian woman – told the committee running the bingo hall that she thought it was racist, and that he had looked at her specifically when shouting his chosen term, 'golly golly'. Dave told the *Sun* it was merely an expression of surprise, and that he wasn't a racist.

The club, siding with a woman who didn't want to hear ethnic slurs over a man who has plenty of other expressions to choose from that aren't also ethnic slurs, told him he had to shout a different expression of surprise or else he wouldn't be able to keep coming back.

And that's how a man too stuck in the past to hang out in a fucking *bingo hall* made it onto page one of the UK's best-selling newspaper as an example of pc gone mad.

BLONDE HOSTAGE IN HIJACK HELL

6 April 1988

One theme that runs through the *Sun*'s stories across the years is that if they could crowbar the word 'blonde' into a headline they would do. And 'nude'. Also 'murder'. *Sun* readers apparently love a nude blonde murder, and the *Sun* are damn well going to give it to them.

This has made for some frankly absurd headlines over the years, including my personal favourite, 'BLONDE HOSTAGE IN HIJACK HELL' to lead a story about how a terrorist had taken twenty-two people hostage on a plane bound for Kuwait and forced the plane to land in Iran. Blonde. Of all the details that could have gone on the front page about a terrorist taking a *planeload of hostages* with a hand grenade, they went for the angle that one of the hostages was not a brunette.

Another classic of what I've started to call 'sexy crime' (in my head) is 'MURDER MYSTERY OF THE NUDE WITH THE SILVER NAILS'. I know what you're thinking, and yes, the first three words of the article did specify she was 'a naked blonde'. Then, cutting straight to the point on 4 July 1972, they went with 'RIDDLE OF NUDE BLONDE'S MURDER', giving you all the details you need of how dressed and blonde she was up front.

It's an odd trend and makes me wonder what their process was like on the crime desk.

'There's been a murder.'

'Love it, the readers love a good murder. You know what I'm going to ask you, don't you?'

'She is blonde, yes.'

'Fantastic, a dead blonde, perfect. Now, it all rides on this next question—'

'Yes, she is nude.'

'A nude blonde murder?'

'Yes.'

'Ring the nude blonde murder bell for Christ's sake, man. Look into my eyes – you see that? Actual dollar signs. STOP THE PRESSES, WE'VE GOT A NUDE BLONDE MONEYMAKING MURDERAMA!'

The trend of crowbarring in a detail of how the victim was in some way attractive was clearly to elicit sympathy for the victim. But reading back through it, it strikes me as weird (though not completely out of the ordinary compared to other newspapers at the time) that they seem to think, why should they care? Because the victim was total hotty, that's why, on so many occasions.

DIVORCE FOR VIRGIN WIFE

22 April 1988

For several days from 22 April 1988, the *Sun* dedicated their front pages to a pair of married nineteen-year-olds – because the husband wasn't banging his wife.

'TWO teenage toffs who sneaked out of classes to get married were divorced yesterday – because the boy REFUSED to make love to his new wife,' the frankly fucking baffling story read.

The couple had been childhood sweethearts and had skived off their respective schools to have the ceremony in a register office. Afterwards, the couple had a drink together, before she returned to her boarding school and he returned to his home, REFUSING at any point to pork.

After several months of not going to Pound Town, the couple had the marriage annulled.

So far, so 'why in shitting hell is this front-page news?' Well, the *Sun* was about to crank it up a notch. The following day, they published a photograph of the teenager – again on the front page of the most-read national newspaper in the country – under the title 'BRIDEGROOM WHO NEVER MADE LOVE. He goes into hiding'. The only new details today's story revealed was that the boy, who was shy, had hidden away from the press. Baffling. You'd have thought he, a random person, would have loved to address a baying mob of journalists holding up a picture of his ex-wife and demanding to know 'WHY WON'T YOU FUCK HER?'

No matter. He refused to talk to them, but the *Sun* weren't done solving the mystery of why a regular teenage couple refused to bone just yet; there was journalism to be done. Their eyes were firmly on that sweet Pulitzer Prize.

A few days later, they found out more details. It emerged that 'the divorce mystery of the virgin bride and groom deepened when their landlady revealed they shared a double bed'. They had been living together for several months in a flat in Oxford. The story had turned from a 'couple didn't bang' scoop into 'yeah, OK, they might have banged' filler.

Following the *Sun*'s absurd obsession with what these teenagers had done with their genitals, the couple were investigated by a divorce watchdog, with the possibility that their annulment would be reversed if it turned out they'd had sex.

This story, and its inclusion as front-page news, is batshit. I wish I could put this in some kind of context or make some wider point about the media, but in all honesty it seems like the *Sun* just found it so outrageously perverse that a teenager wouldn't immediately boff his wife that they thought it was front-page news.

The Pulitzer Prize for investigative reporting that year went to Bill Dedman of the *Atlanta Journal and Constitution* for his report of the racial discrimination practised by lending institutions in Atlanta. May I be the first to say the *Sun* were fucking robbed.

THE TART

30 April 1988

You're probably aware of the Troubles (and if not, I highly recommend Google and the trait of basic curiosity about our world), the often violent conflict that took place between loyalists, who wanted Northern Ireland to remain part of the UK, and republicans, who wanted a united Ireland. The IRA (on the republican side) conducted a paramilitary campaign in Northern Ireland, with some violence also taking place in England, and the British Overseas Territory of Gibraltar, where this story took place.

On 6 March 1988, three members of the IRA were killed in Gibraltar by the SAS, who believed them to be about to attack British military in the territory, using car bombs.

The SAS approached them in the forecourt of a petrol station and shot them. After the killings, Seán Savage, Daniel McCann and Mairéad Farrell were all found to be unarmed. Witnesses emerged, alleging that the soldiers had fired without warning.

'They didn't do anything,' Carmen Proetta said in the 'Death on the Rock' episode of the flagship ITV current affairs programme *This Week*.

'They just went and shot these people. That's all. They didn't say anything, they didn't scream, they didn't shout, they didn't do anything. These people were turning their heads back to see what was happening and when they saw these men had guns in their hands, they put their hands up. It looked like the man was protecting the girl because he stood in front of her, but there was no chance. I mean they went to the floor immediately, they dropped.'

After the programme aired, the *Sun* printed its famous 'shock truth' about Proetta. In a piece titled 'THE TART', they alleged in large type that she was 'an ex prostitute, runs an escort agency, and is married to a sleazy drug peddler'.

They also had quotes that 'she was very beautiful – and very good at her job'. Hey, if they're falsely claiming somebody is a prostitute at least they have the decency to say she was good at it.

Though these things wouldn't have any bearing on anything – newsflash: someone who worked as a prostitute can still witness a crime – the piece was clearly meant to make people doubt her testimony, which contradicted the government's version of events. It alleged that 'her neighbours say she and her husband both **HATE** the British', and that she had been one of forty-four Gibraltar residents to vote for the Rock to become Spanish in the 1967 referendum. Casting doubt on her evidence more directly, they carried quotes from a teenage boy who said, 'I can't even remember seeing Carmen here at the time of the shooting.'

Making it easier for her to sue, the *Sun* wrote that police had said Proetta had a criminal record, which she just didn't. She hadn't worked as a prostitute or run an escort agency either, though she had worked for a short time as a director of a Spanish tour company, so you can see why they'd be confused. Potato – potahto, tomato – tomahto, holiday booker – someone who has sex with strangers for a pre-agreed sum.

She also didn't hold anti-British views. She just happened to have witnessed something that was at odds with the British government's account and so ended up being called a prostitute on the front page of the paper. Which probably isn't the doctor-recommended way to recover from the stress of seeing people die in front of you.

The *Sun* and the *Sunday Times*, who also published stories about Proetta – and is also owned by Rupert Murdoch's News International – together ended up paying her over £300,000 in an out-of-court settlement after she launched a libel case against the publications.

Even though they'd said she was good at being a prostitute. As smears go, 'James Felton is an excellent prostitute, just absolutely fantastic at it – I'm telling you, you've got to buy sex from this guy' is one I'd be at least a little conflicted about fighting in the courts.

WORST BRAT IN BRITAIN

July 1989

In 1991, the *Sun* made history by losing a case to the first child in the UK ever to sue for defamation.

In 1989, a mother called Josephine Hunt had approached newspapers in order to talk about her five-year-old son Jonathan. He had suffered from acute neo-meningitis and septicaemia at birth, and as a result was disabled and had behavioural problems, including that he had no real sense of danger and was accident prone, and also had ADHD.

The *Sun* did print an article about her boy, but it wasn't the sympathetic piece you'd expect to be published about your day-to-day life with your disabled son. The *Sun* ran an absolute hatchet job titled 'WORST BRAT IN BRITAIN'.

The story alleged that 'terror tot Jonathan Hunt was last night dubbed

Britain's naughtiest kid after WRECKING his parents' home, CUTTING off his ear, KILLING the cat by putting it in the washing machine', smashing two video recorders, swallowing insecticide and 'PAINTING the dog Jessie with blue emulsion paint'.

The article – which was accompanied by a picture of the boy scrunching up his face and making a little 'naughty boy' fist – went on to report that a child expert had said he was 'the worst-behaved boy he had ever come across'.

Later, Hunt would explain to Channel 4's show *Hard News* that their home had not been wrecked by her son, his ear had been severed not by him cutting it off but because he'd fallen onto a coffee table, detaching his earlobe, the dog was painted blue after a paintbrush fell off a freezer onto it, and the cat had died of feline leukaemia, according to a post-mortem.

The child psychologist in question told the show that he hadn't met Jonathan, had spoken to the *Sun* over the phone, and would never have called Jonathan the worst-behaved child he'd ever come across if he had known about the his conditions.

The picture – *Hard News* said – was obtained by getting the child to sing a song that involved pulling faces, then publishing the worst one. In this case, the one where it looked like he'd punch every last one of the *Sun*'s readers in the face.

What's more, the article didn't even mention Jonathan's health problems, making it sound like he was merely doing all these things (which he didn't actually do) because he was some sort of dickhead rather than because he had behavioural problems as a result of poor health.

Following the published piece, Josephine received an angry letter telling her 'I CAN TELL YOU WHAT TO DO WITH THE LITTLE BASTARD, BELT HIS ARSE OFF' and death threats over the phone because of the dead cat, which again, had died of leukaemia.

When Hunt initially complained about the article, the *Sun* tried to make amends by running a second piece, written by a features writer rather than as a news piece, but this ran under the headline 'LIVING WITH BRITAIN'S

NAUGHTIEST BOY', and though it mentioned his health problems, according to Hunt it just reinforced the factual errors of the first story.

Finally, in 1991, after being sued, the *Sun* agreed to pay 'substantial' damages, and money to help with Jonathan's condition, as well as all legal costs. All's well that ends well. Although you'd hope their image of themselves as the defender of the underdog took a bit of a knock when they were being successfully sued for defamation by a six-year-old disabled child they had libelled.

PSYCHIC WAVE ENDED MY 30 YEAR AGONY

17 July 1989

On 6 July 1989, at 12:34:05, if you ignore the 19 and then the 0, the time and date read 12:34:5 6/7/89. I shall pause briefly whilst your mind is blown.

The *Sun* went big on this arbitrary point in time, pulling their retired psychic Doris Collins out for one last job, like a con artist in a film, except with a con artist in real life. Because psychics aren't real.

After trailing it for a week, readers were instructed to look at a picture of Collins's face at precisely 12:34:05 and empty their minds, as if the minds of people who'd go through with this were particularly full in the first place. They then had to think of something they wanted help with, or say it out loud. And then, crucially, dial the *Sun* psychic hotline if something happened.

They'd done a similar stunt the year before, when 'a crippled farmer threw away his crutches' and a woman 'was reassured by the sight of her dead son'. This year, they claimed that a woman with spina bifida had been cured of all her pain.

'I can even touch my toes,' she told the psychic hotline. 'It is truly astounding, the sort of thing you read about in books, but it's true.'

All this was reported with the same factual authority as if they were covering normal events. Here's a crime, here's what's happening in politics, here, against all evidence of how science and physics work, is a woman was healed by looking at a photograph of a psychic gran, and now here are some tits.

They also had anecdotes from people attributing normal life events to Doris's powers, from someone who was injured in a bike accident and suddenly didn't limp, to someone who got an interview for a job she'd applied for.

The effect worked in the same way that faith healing works, in that it's a massive placebo effect, or people just happened to get better at roughly the same time and attributed it to the guy in the fancy costume screaming 'THE LORD COMPELS YOU TO HEAL' rather than the insulin. When you have an audience of about four million, like the *Sun* did, it's even easier to find people who happen to have a slightly better ankle that day, or the virtually unheard-of scenario of receiving an interview after applying for many jobs.

You could judge the *Sun* harshly and say that this kind of positive coverage of charlatans is what leads to people seeking out faith healers and, e.g., discontinuing their cancer treatment in the hope that the magic voodoo man's sugar pills cure it rather than chemo (I like those odds!), or you can be kind, give them the benefit of the doubt, and just call it wank.

BABY'S GHOST IS HAUNTING US

10 November 1989

In trying to focus the book on larger events in history, it's difficult to get across the endless streams of shite that have appeared in the *Sun* over the years. But to give you an example, here's one I plucked at random from 10 November 1989, about a family being haunted by a dead baby.

The *Sun* had asked their readers if they had ever been 'victims of revenge from beyond the grave', and then printed some of the drivel that question deserves. First up was the story of a stillborn baby who launched a 'campaign of mayhem and menace'. A family who'd sadly had a stillbirth told the paper that the baby's ghost had come back to 'claim the nursery that was prepared for him' from their fifteen-month-old daughter who was living in there. I can't imagine what they were going through at the time, although their belief that their son was haunting them is probably a good indication that it was a lot, and that a newspaper shouldn't be exploiting their story while they were still going through it.

The evidence the parents presented included that toys had been moved around, drawers opened and closed and lights switched on and off.

'Things started to go missing, including Samantha's dummy. We searched the bedroom but found nothing. Six weeks later the dummy turned up on a shelf.'

Sure, this could be evidence that everything we know about the universe is wrong and ghosts exist but – crucially – *it's also evidence of having a fifteen-month-old child*. Really adding weight to the claims, they told the *Sun* that the daughter had occasionally woken up crying, 'as if she was having nightmares'. WHICH ALL CHILDREN DO.

The *Sun* printed the claims with no caveat or scepticism. These were the facts as far as anyone reading the paper was concerned: the ghost of a dead baby was haunting a couple by doing ordinary toddler shit in order to make its sister fuck off out his room. Ghosts exist, and they put it on page 27. Rather than doing the right thing and gently suggesting therapy (the family had just gone through something extremely traumatic, after all) or saying, 'I regret to inform you that you have an ordinary child,' the *Sun* gave them validation and a double-page spread.

Stories like this aren't uncommon in the *Sun*, which once printed a story of a 'DISHY divorcee' who was 'haunted by something going bonk in the night . . . a groping ghost who makes love to her!' They included details about how sexy and blonde the woman was, so that you could properly picture the clearly unwell woman having sex with the 'sexy spook' (3 June 1989). Alternatively, she was just someone who fancied a holiday and was willing to claim she was having a house share with Casper if it meant it would be paid for by the *Sun*, or merely bored and thought the wind-up was funny.

OK, it's harmless guff and at least it wasn't yet another column about Barry from *EastEnders* (you won't believe how much this paper wrote about the East Enders from *EastEnders*). But I worry that if this is the level of bullshit their readers are accustomed to swallowing – 'Says here dead babies are seeking revenge from beyond the grave.' 'That's interesting, Sheila' – how much critical thought are they putting in when the *Sun* tells them that asylum seekers both bake swans and are going to steal their jobs?

THE MEASLES DEBATE

5 January 2001

The *Sun* used the MMR autism scare as an excuse to conduct an absolute masterclass in false balance.

In 1998, a study (based on twelve children) was published that linked the measles, mumps and rubella (MMR) vaccine to autism. The results have not been replicated, and the lead author on the paper had their medical licence revoked when it transpired that they had falsified data.

Nevertheless, you're probably aware that the rumour persists everywhere, from Mumsnet to your dad's Facebook feed, that vaccines cause autism and you're better off [squints] letting your children die of a long-preventable disease. The media had their part to play in this of course, particularly the *Daily Mail* but also the *Sun*.

In a piece titled 'THE MEASLES DEBATE: Should kids have the

MMR jab?' they pitted Dr Robert Aston, adviser on vaccinations for the Department of Health, against a reflexologist, i.e. someone completely unqualified who reckons jabbing at your palms can cure vag pain.

You see it all the time in climate change debates today. It's your classic 'on the one hand, we have a climate scientist who is backed up by all the science and stats, but for balance we've got some complete fucking potato who's here to ask, "If global warming is real, how come it's so cold when I get out the bath? Answer me that, science boy."' To the audience, it looks like the split between opinions is fifty-fifty, when really 99.9 per cent of experts agree with the scientist rather than the potato.

Also like climate change, there was of course no real debate, just a few people with an incorrect opinion and a consensus of scientists looking on, asking 'What the fuck are you talking about?' and hunting around for the source of glue belonging to the holders of the incorrect opinion.

The doctor patiently explained – in plenty of space, to be fair to the *Sun* – that vaccines had reduced suffering and death, and that 'myths are being bandied about'. He added a pertinent example: 'In the sixties, an eminent professor announced there was a risk of encephalitis with the whooping cough vaccine', and as a result immunisation rates went down. '300,000 children got whooping cough and 70 died.'

It was persuasive, factual stuff. And then, on the opposite page, someone who ran three 'complementary therapy' clinics started cranking out anecdotes and asserting her superior knowledge, such as that she went to a lecture where people were arguing for and against (indicating she might also be a victim of false equivalence, by the way) and 'we also read lots of books'. Her section quickly strayed into talking about how the immune system should be left to its natural devices, and how she treated her own kids with homeopathy.

She also cited there being much less disease these days as a reason why you shouldn't need vaccines: 'We are living in the 21st century here. We do not have bad sanitation which is the cause of so many diseases.' You're talking about diseases, Yvonne, *that were eradicated by vaccines.*

All this took place in the context of vaccination rates going down. It got to the point that the government were forced to take out newspaper ads as part of a £3 million campaign to dispel vaccine myths, many of which were being propagated by . . . newspapers.

You couldn't have planned a more perfect scam if you'd tried.* You make people question the fuck out of vaccines to the point where the government are willing to spend money in your paper to properly inform your readers. It was like getting the government to pay to be science reporters for the *Sun* and the *Daily Mail*.

---

* They didn't plan it as a scam. See how easy it is to correct a conspiracy theory if you just put in a little bit of effort?

MMR JABS DAMAGED FIVE OF MY CHILDREN

26 January 2001

AS THERE'S NO REAL PROOF MMR JABS CAUSE DAMAGE, I GUESS THE HEADLINE IS SUPPOSED TO BE... IRONIC?

LOL, YES. VERY, ERM, FUNNY.

The MMR-gives-kids-autism rumour machine was still churning its way through the population like measles through an anti-vaxxer's face. Vaccination rates were by this point below the 95 per cent you need for herd immunity. Cue some more irresponsible reporting from the UK's number-one newspaper.

The *Sun*, for their part, ran articles giving far too much prominence to the supposed risks of the jab and space to people questioning the safety. They had a piece on how Carol Vorderman was calling for the vaccine to be broken up into three separate jabs again (8 January 2001). While she's really goddamn good at adding up, knowing what is and isn't dangerous for kids didn't appear to be Carol's strong point. To its credit, the article at least ended with the *Sun*'s GP explaining that getting immunised is preferable to the effects of measles, including 'blindness, permanent brain damage or even death'. But then covering the rumour gave it more credibility and the headline 'GIVE OUR KIDS SAFE JABS FOR MEASLES' heavily and falsely implied that the current jabs weren't safe.

One particularly bad article focused on a mother's claim that five of her children were 'damaged by the controversial MMR jab' and how she was attempting to sue for £250,000, along with hundreds of others.

Mary claimed that four of her kids had shown signs of autism within weeks of being vaccinated, and a fifth went on to develop behavioural problems. This is either a coincidence or an example of confirmation bias, because countless studies (some involving millions of people) since that initial bad study of twelve have shown that there is no link whatsoever. In fact, the *Sun* knew about one of these studies – a fourteen-year study involving two million children, which had found no link whatsoever – and had even written about it, but they clearly didn't want to come across as eggheads as they suddenly went all shy about mentioning it.

A responsible paper would jump in at this point and explain the dangers of extrapolating from one twelve-person study with non-replicable results and basing decisions on anecdotal evidence, or maybe just casually slip in 'Yeah, signs of autism happen to start to show themselves around that age; what we're looking at here is some sort of coincidence.' Or, if they weren't willing to do any of those, they could have taken a big old injection of STFU and not run an article at all. All the *Sun* did was a quick note to say that the Department of Health was warning about the possibility of another measles outbreak, as if there were established risks associated with both courses of action, rather than big risks being involved in not vaccinating and virtually no risk involved in vaccinating.

It was like they had teamed up with measles, or were taking money from Big Mumps. Which sounds mad, and it is, but is based on far more credible evidence than the claim that the MMR jab causes autism.

CURSE OF DEVIL DRUG MONKEY

2 September 2001

I KNOW EVERYONE'S FEELING ALARMED THAT WE'VE RUN OUT OF NEWS TO REPORT, BUT I HAVE FAITH IN YOU. MAKING UP NEWS IS WHAT WE DO BEST!

The few weeks leading up to the 'day that changed the world' were pretty slow in terms of news, it seems, because the *Sun*'s front page featured a story about the 'CURSE OF DEVIL DRUG MONKEY', a story not grounded in any kind of reality.

'SCORES of customs officers have been hurt by a wooden "devil monkey" cursed by an African witch doctor, it was revealed yesterday,' the story read, pushing the words 'scores', 'revealed' and 'devil monkey' to breaking point.

It was claimed that customs staff had found a monkey statue jammed full of cannabis, which had since caused countless injuries including:

Painful splinters – so uncommon in things made of wood.

Hitting somebody on the head after falling off a shelf – which famously can only be done by a curse.

Somebody tripping over it – presumably after the guy who got hit on the head forgot to pick it up again.

The following week, on 8 September 2001, they ran a front-page story that 'BOB THE BUILDER IS A GIRL', a sensational story that revealed that the person who occupied the Bob the Builder costume didn't have a penis of their own. Children's TV will never be the same again.

This wasn't even the first time the *Sun* had completely run out of news and so did an exposé of who was underneath kids' TV costumes. They once outed Laa Laa as a 'shaven headed hippy' who 'lives alongside squatters', Dipsy as someone who enjoys rap music, and Po as a 'left-winger who wore bovver boots in [an] adult panto', like kids were going to catch commie sympathies through the costumes. Tinky Winky, you won't be surprised to hear, was just someone dull, an absolute accountant.

This all pales in comparison to the front page of 19 February 1993, in which they reported the story of a 'MAN WHO MADE LOVE TO PAVEMENT' and 'even had a go at an underpass' (which was quite an irresponsible and surprisingly upbeat reporting of a man who clearly had a mental illness of some sort exposing himself in front of minors) or 5 January 2001, when they clearly ran out of news and made a quiz titled 'WHOSE PANTYLINE IS IT ANYWAY', in which they showed readers pictures of celebrity arses and heads and got them to guess which arse matched which head (sort of like the closest they've ever gotten to printing a crossword).

DID THEY LEARN ON £50 CD ROM

13 September 2001

In August 2005, the *Sun* discovered an online game where you're tasked with stopping bombs exploding on the London Underground.

In the article, they quoted London Transport as saying, 'Passengers on the Underground and their staff were faced with horrific scenes on July 7. Anybody involved in the making or viewing of this game would do well to stop and think about that. We will never forget those who were killed and injured in the attacks.'

The *Sun* condemned the game as 'sick' and 'twisted'. Which is a fair comment, if they hadn't slammed a plane into the Twin Towers on a flight simulator two days after 9/11.

'Within minutes of taking the controls yesterday I had mastered them sufficiently to keep the plane in the air,' the *Sun* journalist writing the article bragged, 'and then crash it into the World Trade Center.'

The bizarre piece juxtaposed images of the actual 9/11 with the 9/11 they committed on a computer, showing multiple angles of their own atrocity. They even included an image of the reporter, Tim, looking disapprovingly at the screen, to show that he was 'able to smash into it about a third of the way down', *but he didn't enjoy it.*

'The tell-tale skyscrapers of New York City soon came into view,' Tim wrote of his time trying to smash a plane into the World Trade Center. 'At first I could not make out the World Trade Center' – ah, disappointing – 'but then, as I approached closer and started to circle the city, I could see the Twin Towers. I felt an involuntary shudder as I lined up the airliner on one of them.'

The piece posed the question, 'Did they learn on £50 CD ROM?' but didn't answer it, or offer any evidence that the flight simulator was actually used by the hijackers to train, beyond saying that their demonstration 'showed how it might have been used by the terrorists to train for Tuesday's devastating doomsday attacks'.

Which is like making a person out of pig meat and then attacking it, speculating 'THIS IS HOW MURDERERS COULD TRAIN', or – to use the weirdest and most tasteless example I can possibly think of – like smashing a plane into the Twin Towers on a flight simulator two days after 9/11.

78-YEAR-OLD MAN BEATS HIS WIFE TO DEATH BEFORE DUMPING HER IN A GRAVE – AND YOU WON'T BELIEVE WHAT HE USES

19 July 2017

Clickbait is the most annoying thing about being online, apart from all the people. It's been around longer than you think (how long? It will shock you). For instance, on 28 October 1977, when MP Jeremy Thorpe was caught up in a scandal about an attempted murder, the *Sun*'s front page carried a story about him with the teaser 'THE PRIVATE QUESTION HE DIDN'T

ANSWER – Pages 4 and 5' to make you buy the thing and find out it was the obvious question, about whether he was in a relationship with the victim.

Online, the formula is roughly the same.

The first part – the plot set-up – tells you some of the story to draw you in. The second part is designed to make you curious about some other detail of the story, that you can only get if you do the last resort of the internetter and actually click on the link. This usually begins with an iteration of 'what happened next will blow your tiny mind'.

For example, create your own 2008-era clickbait by combining the below:

First part: Plot set-up

This eighty-year-old man came back home from the duck pond and found his wife porking the milkman.

This puppy thought her favourite companion – a lonely stray cat – was dying.

This war vet returned after serving for five years in Iraq to find his dog living with another owner.

Second part: Get curious

What happened next . . .

. . . will make your jaw drop

. . . will make you shit yourself with glee

. . . will melt your heart

. . . will make you puke your guts out in feelings of disgust, but also there'll be some horniness in there. We're not here to judge: just click the link.

It's irritating, and if you actually click on the story it's generally disappointing – that's why they clickbaited it in the first place. The story wasn't quite interesting enough on its own to make you want to learn more. Sorry to break it to you, but the dog has no fucking clue who the army man is, it's just happy because it's a dog. I know, because I click on the bastards every damn time.

But, annoying as it is, ultimately it's harmless.

And, as someone who has worked a lot in social media in my time, let me tell you: it works. No matter how annoying the title, people just can't help clicking on clickbait. For a reasonably sized publication, a title that gives away the main information could expect to get (for example) twenty thousand clicks. If you hold back the right info and build intrigue, you could easily increase this ten- or a hundred-fold, especially during the heyday of clickbait, before Facebook and others (rightly) started cracking down.

In 2017, the *Sun* applied the science of clickbait to a pensioner bludgeoning his wife to death with a walking stick. In 2015, Charlie Bevill-Warcup had killed his wife, before burying her and joining the police search for her body. He was convicted of her murder two years later, at which point the *Sun* – whether it was the initial journalist, or the social media folks – saw the story and thought, ah, I reckon I could get a few clicks out of that.

So, they made the plot set-up pretty straightforward: the seventy-eight-year-old man had beaten his wife to death. Classic. Then, in a baffling decision, they decided that the 'get curious' part was that you had to guess what weapon she'd been bludgeoned with. Which (AND IT WILL SHOCK YOU) turned out to be a widely available blunt instrument.

The tweet where they put this out was deleted, presumably in some flash of having a bit of a conscience, or maybe in fear of getting the piss taken out of them on the internet. But for a moment the *Sun* made it a little *too* clear how they saw an old man beating to death an old woman: not as a tragedy but an opportunity for a bit of ad revenue. In a weird way, it was quite refreshing.

GLOBAL THREAT WARNING TO PARENTS OVER MOMO 'SUICIDE GAME'

3 September 2018

HI THERE.
I'M LOOKING FOR
A LAWYER: I'VE
BEEN FALSELY AND
CRUELLY VILIFIED.

In 2018, the story of a bug-eyed chicken woman encouraging child suicide started to spread around social media.

Accounts varied. Some said that 'Momo', a freaky model, a distorted half human half animal, would WhatsApp children and ask them to complete various escalating challenges, before telling the child to kill themselves as a final challenge (well, it wouldn't make sense to have two further challenges afterwards, I guess). Others suggested that Momo was being inserted into *Peppa Pig* videos on YouTube. Halfway through the video of *Peppa Pig* (herself a grotesque, freaky half-human half-animal monster), Momo would pop up to tell the viewer to kill themselves, thus relieving them of having to watch *Peppa Pig*.

Your bullshit meter should of course be all the way up to the 'Boris Johnson is saying a sentence' setting. It has tech, it has a creepy figure talking to you from your device, it has suicide. The whole thing smacks of a bad urban legend. Yet by the time the media was done, the police would be issuing statements about it and kids were being told about it in schools, like there was actually some mad chicken woman taking control of the YouTubes. Like that's just a thing that happens in real life.

In August 2018, it was reported in Argentinian news outlets that someone had killed themselves and it was 'linked' to the Momo challenge (though no connection was actually ever found). Media in the UK picked it up and ran with it, largely treating it with a hell of a lot less cynicism than you'd like for stories involving a talking chicken mermaid.

The first trace in the *Sun* warned of Momo mods adding the character to Minecraft, and reported the rest of the hoax as if it was established fact, under the headline: 'SICK SPREAD Momo "suicide game" now targeting kids via Minecraft and Youtube[:] US cop fears after it was linked to death of 12-year-old girl in Argentina'.

Then another story cropped up, linking a death in India to the 'game':

'GAME OF DEATH Teen death linked to Momo WhatsApp "suicide game" as boy is found hanged with "Illuminati" and "Devil's one eye" scrawled on wall', the *Sun*'s online coverage read (25 August 2018).

Again, no actual link was found and the Criminal Investigation Department of West Bengal called the claims 'far fetched and devoid of any evidence'.

The stories – weird though they were – didn't receive much attention in the UK until the following year, when adults here started pretending it was real too.

In February 2019, a boy in Bolton was told about Momo by a classmate.

As is the law, the mother then posted a warning about Momo on Facebook. In the warning, she claimed one of the boys in the school had watched a video of Momo who told him to inform everybody they should fear Momo or it would kill him in his sleep.

In an article from 21 February 2019, titled 'MUM'S MOMO WARNING: Momo "suicide game" warning after schoolboy, seven, told pals the creepy character would kill them in their beds', the *Sun* online said 'the sick suicide game has swept the web and is already believed to have caused the tragic deaths of two teenagers in Colombia' and linked to a previous *Sun* article as evidence for the Colombian death, which had no links to Momo because – and I really must stress this – it was a hoax.

The *Sun* then continued the story the following day, with a helpful explainer:

'Momo is a disturbing "suicide" game that has spread through social media platforms such as WhatsApp and Facebook [. . .] She sends violent images [to] victims and then threatens the player if they refuse to follow the game's orders.'

Ah, facts.

This story took off much more in 2019 than in the efforts from the previous year. To make things worse, the police got involved. The Police Service Northern Ireland put out a statement saying that they had received no official reports of Momo, before going on to describe it like it was a real thing, recounting details from the media that it contacts you through games, video or WhatsApp, and 'it is at this point that children are threatened that they will be cursed or their family will be hurt if they do not self-harm'. Detective Sergeant Elaine McCormill said, 'I am disgusted that a so-called game is targeting our young children.'

We were now in a horrible feedback loop where the police saw the media as confirmation of veracity and the media could point to the police talking about it and go, 'See? There's something to this, it's a police matter.' Schools also issued their own warnings to pupils, which would then get written about, and psychologists warned that 'just a few seconds glimpse of sick Momo meme could haunt kid's lives and control their behaviour', at least according to a *Sun* headline (27 February 2019) that makes me want to throw my phone away and live out the rest of my life with the Amish.

Very few kids had actually seen anything about Momo before the media got involved. Now they were being warned in schools, e.g., 'Listen up, kiddos, you're going to be hearing a lot about a deformed chicken woman telling you to kill yourself with a knife over the next few weeks and I'm here to tell you, you do not have to do what she says.'

'These stories being highly publicised and starting a panic means vulnerable people get to know about it and that creates a risk,' the Samaritans pointed out in a statement.

The *Sun* wrote several more articles, including a how-to guide on keeping your child safe from Momo and blocking it on WhatsApp. Might as well have had a how-to guide on keeping your child safe from the dangers of Lord Voldemort or receiving texts from Satan.

By the time it was forgotten about, an urban legend had generated more than thirty pages of content for the *Sun*.

FOREIGN AFFAIRS

STICK IT UP YOUR JUNTA

20 April 1982

The Falklands War was a complicated and messy affair that led to a tragic (and unnecessary) loss of life. Argentina had been claiming sovereignty over the Falkland Islands from the nineteenth century, after it had been seized by Britain in 1833, before the dispute escalated in the late seventies. Negotiations took place between the UK and Argentina through third parties, with Switzerland representing British interests and Peru Argentinian. In 1982 the Argentine military junta launched an invasion of the islands, believing that Britain wouldn't defend them using force. They'd underestimated Britain – a nation that (if you merely glance in one of our museums) would rather die a thousand deaths than give stuff back to its owners – and soon they were met with the might of the British Navy.

Before the conflict turned violent, when possible peaceful solutions for the claims over the Falkland Islands were being talked about, the *Sun* famously tried to encourage the British government to tell Argentina to 'STICK IT UP YOUR JUNTA'. I should explain that Argentina was controlled by a military junta at the time, but the *Sun* were also clearly hoping that readers would take it to mean 'arsehole' in this context, which is more than meeting them halfway.

As the talks broke down and the reality of what war means sank in, instead of switching to a more sombre tone, the *Sun* went on to produce and sell thousands of T-shirts with their 'stick it up your junta' slogan printed on the front, and on the first day of the conflict chose the headline 'WE'LL SMASH 'EM', like a football fan talking about a friendly where there is zero chance of anybody actually dying a horrible death. They ran opinion columns titled 'I am getting pretty twitchy waiting for this so-called war', like a cowboy in a western complaining about how his 'itchy trigger finger needs feedin''.

This was just the springboard to how full 'Tom Cruise jumping on Oprah's sofa' enthusiastic the *Sun* would become about killing people to death with bombs in a war. They even sent shipments of fizzy drinks to the troops (reported under the headline 'The Sun puts the fizz in fizzical' (12 May 1982)) like it was a fucking children's birthday party. Before the conflict was over, they would ask their readers to sponsor a *missile* to be used on the 'Argies' in the same way a charity worker might ask you to donate a few pounds a month to a slightly injured donkey.

A few days earlier, on 3 May 1982, they ran the headline 'STICK THIS UP YOUR JUNTA: A Sun missile for Galtieri's gauchos' – Leopoldo Galtieri was president of Argentina, just for context – above a picture of an actual missile they'd sponsored. Somehow it got worse, as they added:

'Here it comes Señors. The first missile to hit Galtieri's gauchos will come with love from the Sun. And just in case he doesn't get the message it will have "Up Yours Galtieri" painted on the side, signed by our man aboard HMS Invincible,' as if their problem was they were being too subtle.

A *Sun* journalist reported its deployment: 'I saw my missile hit the back of the enemy aircraft. It exploded as advertised. His plane was in flames.'

As the conflict continued and other newspapers watched in horror, the *Sun* went full *Match of the Day*, writing headlines like 'BRITAIN 6 [referring to six victories in the war, including the destruction of planes], ARGENTINA 0'.

The mystery of why they think 'junta' works as an acceptable substitute for 'bumhole' remains to this day.

GOTCHA

4 May 1982

WHAT'S THE *THESAURUS FOR CLASSY HEADLINES* DOING RIGHT AT THE BACK OF THE CUPBOARD?

On 3 May 1982, the Argentine cruiser *Belgrano* entered the 200-mile Total Exclusion Zone around the Falkland Islands, as declared by the British. In one of the most controversial acts of the war, it was ordered to be sunk by British nuclear-powered submarine *Conqueror*. It wasn't immediately clear, but 323 Argentinian sailors died as the ship went down. Critics believe the *Belgrano* may have been leaving the exclusion zone at the time, and many think this constitutes a war crime by the British.

When the *Sun* first heard of the sinking they put out an early edition of the paper with the tasteful headline 'GOTCHA', a headline they still include in lists of their best today.

As if that wasn't bad enough, they settled on the subheading 'our lads sink gunboat and hole cruiser', making the potential war crime sound like laddy bantz that got out of hand. Contrast this with how the (far fewer) deaths of British troops were treated – 'GRIEF OF HERO PILOT'S PREGNANT WIDOW' (8 May 1982) or 'MY SON – I'm proud to have a son who died doing a job he loved for the country' (6 May 1982) – and it seems even more crass.

When more details of potential deaths came in, the *Sun* realised the tone was a tad Bond-villain-laughs-as-he-murders-minor-character-using-sharks. Even the *Daily Express* went with 'Fears for 1,042 on Argentine warship sunk!', whilst the *Mirror* had the factual 'ATTACKED CRUISER "SUNK"', and also used the front page to express concern for the crew. The *Sun* changed subsequent editions to read 'Did 1,200 Argies drown?', but still not finding the space (or respect) to use the slightly more formal 'Argentinians'. It's like if you died and your killer insisted on putting your 'wacky' nickname 'Dickhead Jeff' on your tombstone, against the wishes of your widow.

Perhaps sensing they'd still not made enough reparations, the *Sun* printed the headline 'ALIVE! Hundreds of Argies saved from Atlantic' the following day, welcoming that fewer lives may have been lost than feared. They weren't that bothered by their initial error of judgement, though, as demonstrated by their playful use of it for other headlines, such as 'BOTCHA!', when they found someone who had flashed their bum at a navy ship (7 June 1989). They might not do a lot of investigative journalism of the type that brought down Nixon, but to be fair to them, they are the Sherlock Holmes of 'who got their arse out?' mysteries.

The *Sun* doesn't have a penis, yet during the build-up to the war somehow they had managed to wave it around with the enthusiasm of a rugby player during freshers' week. Pieces were printed like the 'Mighty punch of the Vulcan' (3 May 1982), just straight-up bragging about how bomby our planes were. On the day they celebrated that hundreds of Argentinians had been saved from the Atlantic, they ran a two-page spread on 'the "nuclear shark" that strikes from 30 miles away', which, considering hundreds of people died in the attack on the *Belgrano*, is a bit like running a piece on how buff a serial killer is shortly after a spree.

On 22 May 1982 the entire front page was just the headline 'WAR', followed by four bullet points, one of which was 'SAS men smash them' – 'them' being people. They would have other one-word headlines, including 'BLITZED' (8 May 1982) and 'WALLOP' (10 May 1982) after a shelling raid.

Despite the controversy surrounding the 'GOTCHA' headline, the *Sun* didn't appear to learn that complex issues such as war need more detail in a headline than a word UKIP members shout when they come.

Nevertheless – according to Ipsos MORI polls conducted at the time – they managed to judge the mood of the nation correctly. At the start of the war Thatcher and the Tories were polling below Labour, but by the end they had a 27-point lead, and support for various military interventions (by boat or by air, sea or land) went up as the conflict went on. Who'd have guessed that the people who took over a third of the planet through war and never shut up about war love a war?

THE *SUN* SAYS DARE CALL IT TREASON

7 May 1982

...AND HERE'S OUR MAGGIE THATCHER SHRINE.

As well as loving the idea of mass enemy casualties, the *Sun*, during the course of the Falklands War, appeared to come out in favour of not doing a journalism.

On 6 May 1982, Margaret Thatcher gave a speech in the House of Commons, a coded attack on BBC *Newsnight*'s coverage of the war, which had dared to caveat its reports with 'if we believe the British [account]' and 'damage the British admitted', implying that one side's accounts of the war during a war might not be 100 per cent objective truth.

Thatcher said, 'Judging by many of the comments that I have heard from those who watch and listen more than I do, many people are very concerned indeed that the case for our British forces is not being put over fully and effectively.

'I understand that there are times when it seems that we and the Argentines are being treated almost as equals and almost on a neutral basis. I understand that there are occasions when some commentators will say that the Argentines did something and then "the British" did something. I can only say that if this is so it gives offence and causes great emotion among many people.'

So far, so Donald Trump. As sure as the pope is Catholic and Nigel Farage is a wanker, politicians will moan about the media being biased against them.

What makes this stand out is how the *Sun* – a newspaper – reacted to being told by a prime minister to prioritise patriotism over, you know, accurate reporting of facts.

In their breathless report of her words, they told how she 'launched a furious attack' on the 'lack of loyalty and patriotism being shown by some commentators' and how she 'poured scorn on the wishy-washy even-handed approach of many news programmes'. Or 'trying to be as accurate as possible', as it's otherwise known.

In a Sun Says column they were more explicit, saying '**There are traitors in our midst**' long before the word 'traitor' became a fashionable thing to shout at someone who disagreed with you slightly about, e.g., how bendy a banana should be.

'The Prime Minister did not speak of treason. The *Sun* does not hesitate to use the word.

'We regard the freedom of opinion and speech as among our most ancient and precious rights. *But with rights go responsibility and a duty to one's country,*' they continued, like Uncle Ben from *Spider-Man*, but huffing patriotism whilst dry-humping a flag.

'What is it but treason to talk on TV, as Peter Snow talked, questioning whether the Government's version of the sea battles was to be believed.'

Journalism. The word you're looking for is journalism.

The *Sun*, as ever, didn't appear to be looking for journalism awards but for readers. In the column they went on to attack the *Mirror* – their main rival – for daring to suggest that 'the killing has got to stop . . . if that means Britain and Argentina need to compromise, then compromise they must'.

'What is it but treason for this timorous, whining publication to plead day after day for appeasing the Argentine dictators because they do not believe the British have the stomach for a fight.'

The *Mirror* retaliated, taking the high road and saying, 'The *Sun* today is to journalism what Dr Joseph Goebbels was to truth,' but also losing the high ground slightly by calling them 'demented'.

Nevertheless, the *Sun* went on to win the much-coveted (and entirely self-proclaimed) title 'The Paper That Supports Our Boys', though there's evidence that the 'boys' thought differently. According to one soldier, the *Sun*'s headlines 'often made us feel sick' and they conducted 'ritual burnings of the *Sun*'.

Whilst the *Sun* was out of step with other papers, they were perhaps more in tune with the public. Before the war, Thatcher's popularity was lower than her eventual grave. By the end of the war, with the *Sun* cheering her on the whole way, she added ten points to her poll rating.

L'AMBUSH

12 January 1984

The *Sun* loves a war, and gets a bit twitchy when the government occasionally doesn't fancy bombing the shit out of some regime they aren't a fan of. The Falklands had ended two years prior, and the blood lust was beginning to show.

As luck would have it, there are plenty of other things going on in other countries that they can blow out of proportion and use as an excuse to be xenophobic dickheads for a while. In 1984 they were handed one such excuse when French farmers began protesting at levels of imports of foreign meat to France. The protestors had burned the lorries of some British drivers (who were not in the vehicles), resulting in another headline that always shows up in the *Sun*'s round-ups of their own favourite one-liners: 'L'AMBUSH'.

The farmers, regardless of whether they had a valid point, were being what's known as 'arseholes'. The *Sun*, like soldiers finding it difficult to return to civilian life twatting innocent members of the public in a kebab shop, responded by trying to escalate the issue, and laying into the nation of France and the French rather than just the farmers. God knows the Brits love a bit of French-bashing, and the *Sun* were more than happy to oblige.

A few days after the initial 'L'AMBUSH' they were giving away *Sun*-branded 'HOP OFF YOU FROGS' badges to any readers with little enough self-respect to send a self-addressed envelope to get one. They were also offering a prize to whichever reader could send in the best 'anti-French joke'. It sounds bad, but to be fair the prize was a 'super case of fruity ENGLISH wine', so perhaps it was meant to be a punishment for being a horrendous xenophobe. Fun trivia: the best thing you could say about English wine in the eighties is that it did technically qualify as wine, legally speaking.

Next to a picture of a man dressed in a stripy top with a beret and a massive moustache, they printed jokes like you're imagining ('Why do surgeons hate operating on Frenchmen? They have only two moving parts, their mouth and their bottoms, and they're both interchangeable.') The Press Council called them 'wholly tasteless and puerile', following several complaints – likely from stuck-up liberal types who think you shouldn't use your massive platform to do a xenophobia on a whole nation – but 'cannot agree that the newspaper should have been inhibited by ethical consideration from publishing [them]'. Which is a long-winded way of saying they thought they were shit.

Still trying to stir up some manufactured argument with the French, the *Sun* flew some of their staff, as well as models, all dressed as stereotypically British things such as a town crier, butchers, milkmen and miscellaneous twats, to Calais. The 'Sun's fun invaders', in what they embarrassingly called the 'the great oo-la-laugh invasion', went to plant a flag as 'the wartime spirit shone through', before getting the town crier to tell some more jokes.

Before they got bored of their own zany antics, the *Sun* found some industry survey that said the French use less soap than Brits do, and had some Page 3 models – who were beginning to just be seen as extremely expensive couriers at this point, like Hermes, but in the nip and actually reliable – deliver toothbrushes and soap to the French embassy. They printed this under the headline 'ZEE FRENCH ARE FEEL-THY – OFFICIAL'. And then, having done what would probably, in more recent times, get a non-newspaper banged up for a hate crime, they ran out of ways to piss off the French and forgot about it.

UP YOURS DELORS

1 November 1990

In 1990, the *Sun* invited their readers to take part in a stunt that would make even Donald Trump's hairdresser die of embarrassment: going outside at an allotted time and swearing in the direction of France.

The *Sun* didn't like closer ties to Europe, and were worried about the European Currency Unit, a precursor to the Euro, which they'd twat on about for years but we wouldn't actually join. In particular, they were against European Commission President Jacques Delors, who they saw as wanting to promote closer and closer ties between European nations (can you think of anything so ghastly as a group of nations getting along just famously?). Keeping things in proportion, they wanted their millions of readers to tell France to go fuck itself.

Next to a picture of a hand sticking its fingers up at the reader in a Union

Jack jacket (the kind only worn by someone who'd get kicked out of a Brexit Party conference for being *too* Brexity), the *Sun* led with the headline 'UP YOURS DELORS'. 'The *Sun* today calls on its patriotic family of readers to tell the feelthy French to FROG OFF!' the infamous front page began.

'At the stroke of noon tomorrow we invite all true blue Brits to face France and yell "Up Yours, Delors."' This painted 'true' Brits as petty vindictive xenophobic wankers willing to make a pointless gesture at short notice, which later turned out to be entirely accurate.

'The ear-bashing from our millions of readers will wake the EC President up to the fact that he will **NEVER** run our country.' In actual fact – bit of trivia for you – if he had ever heard it, it would only alert him to the fact that a lot of dads were going through a tough divorce.

'[Delors's] bid to replace the £ with the faceless ECU is the last straw after centuries of Froggy brit baiting,' the piece continued. It was the early days of euroscepticism, and the press hadn't quite got the hang of claiming they 'love Europe, hate EU' just yet and therefore erred a bit too much on the side of repeatedly calling the French 'froggies' and throwing around terms like 'garlic-breathed' to claim their concerns were about European institutions.

The *Sun* listed the crimes of the French, for which they were receiving this ear-bashing, including that they:

'**JEERED** Mrs Thatcher when she visited Paris'. Can you imagine, booing Satan of all people? '**BANNED** British beef after falsely claiming it had mad cow disease', even though it did have mad cow disease, and '**GAVE IN** to the Nazis during the Second World War when we stood firm', like being brutally overwhelmed by Nazi Germany was a scheme they hatched merely to piss off the Brits. I know it makes me sound like a dick for saying it, Joan, but France got invaded *at* us.

The *Sun* printed details of where you could go to embarrass yourself by yelling at the wind, accompanied by a picture of a bearded man with a pint and a flag yelling off a cliff. I presume it was meant to look patriotic, but my first instinct was to look for a number to call if I'd seen this reprobate on the loose.

SQUIRM, WORM

21 February 2003

ANYONE KNOW THE FRENCH FOR 'PRESIDENT'?

SURE THING, IT'S: JE SUIS GÊNÉ DE TRAVAILLER ICI.

Disaster struck war fans when France wasn't as horny for war as the *Sun* were, and President Jacques Chirac threatened to veto a United Nations resolution authorising military action. Cue accusations of disloyalty and your classic cries of 'SHAME ON YOU CHIRAC French repay WW2 Allies with betrayal' (11 February 2003). Considering we'd been friendly nations for decades since the war, helping each other out and getting along like gangbusters, this is like you, an eighty-year-old, asking someone for 'that quid I lent you when we were two', right after they'd given you an Xbox. This headline was accompanied by a photograph of Normandy graves of soldiers killed in World War Two, by the way, just to let you know what level of emotional sucker punches they were landing.

To be fair to the *Sun*, they were clearly torn on the issue, and that issue was whether to portray Chirac as a worm, or as Saddam Hussein. They went for both, believing him to be one of those Saddam Hussein-y worms you were constantly finding in early 2003. He was given the nickname 'Le Worm' and a picture of Chirac's head on a worm's body made its way into the paper, for the unimaginative xenophobe market.

One edition, from 14 March 2003, featured a picture of Hussein and Chirac with the caption 'One is a corrupt bully who is risking the lives of our troops. He is sneering at Britain, destroying democracy and endangering world peace. The other is Saddam Hussein.' I know this seems shit now, but they'd have pissed themselves laughing at this back in the *Bruce Almighty* days of 2003. On page 8 they followed it up with Chirac slowly transforming into Hussein in a series of photographs, in case you missed the subtlety of the front page.

As well as the Worm Content, the *Sun* asked France, 'Are you not ashamed of your president today?' This they translated into French and delivered to Paris.

As well as being a dick move – and not the baller power move of, e.g., encouraging their readers to send Chirac cut-out white feathers, which they also did – it actually broke French law at the time, which said it was a criminal offence to insult the president. Which is a shit law, but I imagine this is what it must have felt like for a sixteenth-century peasant to watch an annoying colleague get prosecuted for witchcraft. Sure it was unjust, but Janice did sniff up her boogers far too often, rather than blow her nose.

Unfortunately they didn't get into trouble for breaking this law, and so would go on to insult the president on the streets of France again, calling him a 'harlot' on 21 March, and flying to France, where they delivered copies of a French edition of the paper to individual members of the public. They reported that '*sadly but predictably, the poor, misled French people backed their spineless president to the hilt*' alongside a bit of light Francophobia ('[one French person] nearly choked on their baguette when they saw our headline') (21 March 2003), like a prototype of an internet basement-dweller yelling 'HA, TRIGGERED!' when you politely say his joke wasn't very good.

WEAPONS OF MASS SEDUCTION

4 March 2003

IT WAS JUST TOO GOOD A PUN NOT TO GO WITH.

By the time the second Iraq War came around, a short and sweet twelve years after the first one ended, the *Sun* was having another Normal One. Like the Falklands War, they were absolutely pumped, filled with Mr Motivator-esque enthusiasm for bombing the absolute shit out of foreign countries. Headlines along the lines of 'LET'S ROLL' (15 March 2003) accompanied pictures of soldiers being addressed by US generals with flags waving in the background and tanks looking a bit menacing on the side.

They also echoed and gave prominence to the government line that the – infamously messy – war was going to be a piece of piss. They started sharting out headlines which from our vantage point of the future would make you give them a little head rub and say 'OK, buddy, that's nice, can you put Papa Sun on the phone?' like they just confessed they still believed in Santa. Stuff like 'THE FIRST CLEAN WAR Civilian deaths could be zero, MoD claims' (20 March 2003) and 'FIGHTING WILL BE OVER BY APRIL 10' (6 March 2003), as well as the usual brags about how our weapons are so good they will destroy you then loop back around for the orphans. The *Mirror*, the *Sun*'s old rival, meanwhile, wrote headlines like 'Shocking and awful' and 'Still anti-war? Yes, bloody right we are' (24 March 2003) which would age like fine wine to the *Sun*'s unpasteurised milk.

Then there were times that the *Sun* would print headlines designed to scare the crap out of Saddam Hussein. Stuff like 'TIME TO BE VERY AFRAID, SADDAM' (12 March 2003) next to a picture of a gigantic explosion, 'THEY'RE COMING FOR YOU, SADDAM' (15 March 2003) and 'GET OUT ... OR DIE' (18 March 2003). Which, sure, is all true, but for *Sun* fans it must have been like reading the letters from an increasingly aggressive stalker.

The tone differed from the Falklands mainly in terms of horniness. The 'JUST FOR YOU LADS' Page 3 models of 1982 now gave way to pull-outs with several models under the title 'WEAPONS OF MASS SEDUCTION' and the less imaginatively titled 'WEAPONS OF MASS SEDUCTION PART 2' sixteen days later. Nothing says 'war is a deadly serious matter' like the sentence 'Presenting arms – and a bit more – for the phwoar effort' on a page containing [bear with me while I do a quick boob tally] thirteen boobs, on the day the Iraq War began.

The *Sun* seemed pretty psyched about the whole thing (until British troops began to die, of course), even saying the quiet part loud on 1 March in a piece headlined 'BAD NEWS Petrol to rocket to 10p a gallon GOOD NEWS Short war will slash price of oil'. War: bad for people who don't want to die, good for knocking a penny off a gallon at Esso.

But all was not well. As usual, those TRAITORS were trying to ruin our fun war (on petrol prices) ...

OPEN FIRE ON TRAITORS

11 April 2003

As well as those pesky French traitors who refused to join us in a potentially illegal war, we even had our own traitors saying traitor things like 'Woah now, I'm not so sure about this war thing. Can't we all just cool our jets?'

On 11 April 2003, less than a month after we invaded, Saddam Hussein looked completely defeated despite all those weapons of mass destruction he had supposedly learned to crap out. The *Sun* used this opportunity to rub it in the faces of opponents of the Iraq War, with a cut-out dartboard with their faces on it, under the title 'OPEN FIRE ON THE TRAITORS'.

It was basically just a bunch of faces you were invited to throw spikes at for saying mainstream opinions from ten years down the line (opinions that weren't 'LET'S KILL SADDAM AND KNOB THE CORPSE'), or just some facts.

'You can aim your own missiles at the cowards and traitors who opted to support Saddam Hussein rather than the brave troops who laid down their lives for freedom,' the *Sun* wrote, in their classic these-are-the-only-two-options-available approach.

'These are the people who wrongly told us that war would last months' – the war would officially end in 2011 and violence would escalate in the country afterwards – 'and many thousands of civilian and coalition soldiers would die.' An independent UK/US group, the Iraq Body Count project, estimates that there have been between 184,868 and 207,759 documented civilian deaths resulting from the invasion of Iraq, as of January 2020. The project has been criticised by academics for underestimating the body count.

The 'traitor' dartboard included Robin Cook, who resigned as Leader of the House of Commons over the war, with a speech in which he said 'Iraq probably has no weapons of mass destruction', which turned out to be just a fact.

George Galloway, then a Labour MP, also made the board. On 1 April the *Sun* had called him a 'TRAITOR' on the front page and an 'ENEMY OF THE STATE', as well as asking people to email him 'what you think of his treachery'. To be fair, he had made comments such as 'Where are the Arab armies? [...] When are they going to stand by the Iraqi people?', arguably attempting to get forces to fight British troops, which is a bit textbook treason. Even stopped clocks are right twice a day, but they don't need to be loud braying 'THROW DARTS AT HIM' dickheads about it.

Charles Kennedy, the leader of the Liberal Democrats, also earned a place on the board with Saddam supporters such as Vladimir Putin and [rubs eyes in disbelief like a cartoon dog] Secretary-General of the United Nations Kofi Annan, who made the board because he had 'called the war "illegal" then did a U-turn and backed our troops'. For this he was also bequeathed a front page, on which they placed his head next to a cobra with the title 'SPOT THE DIFFERENCE: One is a spineless reptile that spits venom . . . the other's a poisonous snake'.

In 2016, the Chilcot inquiry published its findings on Tony Blair's decision to join the US in the war on Iraq, vindicating a lot of the opponents of the war and the grounds on which they opposed it. At which point, on 2 July, the *Sun* published the front page 'WEAPONS OF MASS DECEPTION' and it was discovered that they had deleted the traitor dartboard from their website, thus erasing it from everyone's memory for all time.

TYRANT'S IN HIS PANTS

20 May 2005

In 2005, the *Sun* were investigated by the US military after obtaining and publishing a photograph of Saddam Hussein in his pants.

Saddam had been captured in 2003 and was awaiting trial when, two years later – if he had access to newspapers – he could have bought a copy of the *Sun* or Murdoch's US paper, the *New York Post*, and seen a picture of himself semi-nude in prison staring back at him.

The *Sun* went for the title 'Tyrant's in his pants', and the *New York Post* for 'Butcher of Sagdad'. Now I'm not saying you should go full body positive and all 'yass kween, work those curves' about a man with his kill count, but maybe given how he was partial to a spot of mass murder, state terrorism and genocide, there are other angles to attack him with than fat-shaming.

Speaking of people who broke the Geneva Convention, the *Sun* would soon find out that they could have been up there with Saddam's allies. The international treaty has rules on the humane treatment of prisoners of war, including that they must be protected against 'insults and public curiosity'. By obtaining the photos from Saddam's captors, the *Sun* may have participated in breaking that rule, and thus the Convention itself. Let he who has not tried to obtain nudes of a brutal dictator while he awaits trial cast the first stone.

In a sentence that probably made someone at the *Sun* urgently need to wash their own trousers, the US military said they would 'aggressively investigate' how the pictures came to be leaked to the paper. The *Sun* claimed that 'military sources said they handed over the photos in the hope of dealing a body blow to the resistance in Iraq'. Because nothing crushes the resistance like a picture of the former boss being printed in an English-language paper thousands of miles away.

After initially refusing to reveal how they came by the photographs, the *Sun*'s managing editor Graham Dudman soon revealed that they had obtained the photos by 'professional journalistic methods', before saying they paid a 'small sum' of money (which was over five hundred pounds) for the photographs. In 2012, the *Daily Beast* printed allegations that News Corporation (the parent company of the *Sun* and the *New York Post*) had bribed a member of the US military for the photographs, which if it was true and the executives at News Corporation knew about it, could have led to fines or even prison time under US law.

A spokesperson for News Corporation responded that it was 'just a lame attempt to regurgitate old news', which is like pleading 'I find the murder charge brought against me to be a real bummer' to a judge. They reiterated that they thought they were right to publish the pictures of the war criminal, but declined to say whether the pictures had been obtained by bribery. The investigation went quiet after that, though the *Sun* had caused quite a bit of trouble for themselves merely to get a picture of a brutal dictator in his panties. And he wasn't even that hot.

HANDS OFF OUR BARMAIDS' BOOBS

4 August 2005

WE'VE LEFT THE EU NOW, SO YOU CAN WEAR LOW-CUT TOPS AGAIN IF YOU LIKE?

In 2016 a narrow majority voted for the UK to leave the European Union. There's a chance a number greater than zero of those voters voted because they believed that, ten years earlier, the EU had banned them from leering without consent at tits.

In 2005, the *Sun* reported that 'the EU has declared a crackpot war on busty barmaids', claiming that the 'po-faced pen-pushers have deemed it a HEALTH HAZARD for bar girls to show too much cleavage'. Henceforth, the EU NAZIS had – the article claimed – 'ordered a cover-up' after deeming it 'dangerous' to show too much cleavage.

'They say barmaids run a skin cancer risk if they expose themselves to the sun when they go outside to collect glasses. Last night the move was blasted as an affront. Annie Powell, of real ale group Camra, raged: "It's just another blatant example of Europe gone mad.'"

Of course, the EU directive they were talking of was absolutely nothing to do with breasts. You hopefully won't be surprised to learn that twenty-eight of the world's most powerful nations don't sit around discussing how much cleavage is too much cleavage, nor call for a motion to move on to the more pressing topic of sideboob.

The directive was actually … just about protecting workers from skin cancer. It suggested that those who work outdoors should be given the option to cover themselves properly, or maybe be provided with a bit of sun cream so they don't roast their skin off.

Nowhere – and I really must stress this – did any of the legislation mention bazungas.

I can only imagine the *Sun* thought, well, this EU directive seems a bit dry: it essentially just wants people to not get cancer – how can we get our readers outraged?, before leaping up and exclaiming – probably for around the seventh time that day – 'They're trying to ban tits!'

The *Sun* seems to live in a world where they think their readers are heading to seventies *Carry On* pubs, asking for peanuts from the bar staff – not those ones, *the low ones* – then making a noise implying they've got an erection on their swanny whistles. And so, a story about the EU thinking maybe it would be nice if outdoor workers didn't get skin cancer became an opportunity for the *Sun* to convince their readers that the crazy EU were attempting to ban them from leering at breasts like creeps.

The EU eventually took out the part about sun damage to skin from the directive, and the *Sun* celebrated as if they had something to do with it, by telling their readers to 'lift their jugs to the *Sun*' for rescuing 'Britain's busty barmaids' who were never really at risk, and even if they were it was only at risk of not being required to get cancer by their employers.

EU ARE KIDDING

21 October 2013

IT'S CORRECTION TIME, KIDS! WHICH STORY DO YOU THINK WE NEED TO RETRACT TODAY? I'LL GIVE YOU A CLUE: IT INVOLVES MISTRUTHS ABOUT MIGRANTS.

THAT HARDLY NARROWS IT DOWN.

In an infamous front page in 2013, the *Sun* falsely claimed that six hundred thousand benefit tourists were in the UK and implied that the EU had said 'Yes, that's no problem.'

'EURO bosses have been accused of trying to hide the negative impact of benefit tourism to the UK,' the story read. 'A European Commission report revealed more than 600,000 "non-active" migrants are currently living here. They include the unemployed, students and OAPs.'

You'll notice that the headline is saying something completely different to the story. It's like someone shouting 'FACT: ALL CATS ARE SHIT' in your face before going on to list several subcategories of cats with whom they – the hater of cats who wants you to hate cats too – have no beef.

The report went on to say that 'the cost to the NHS alone could be £1.5

billion a year. But it also concluded the impact on public services was "incredibly low".' They then quoted Tory MP Douglas Carswell, who accused the EU Commission of downplaying benefit tourism, without evidence.

Following widespread criticism online, the *Sun* clarified on 31 October that 'OUR 21 October headline "Brussels: UK's 600,000 benefit tourists is no problem" was not accurate.

'There is no evidence of 600,000 "benefit tourists" in the UK. Neither has the European Commission said this would be no problem.'

Well, that clears that up.

The problem appears to be that a headline writer who can't parse text saw the six hundred thousand figure and reckoned it was to do with benefit tourists. No need to do anything other than skim-read, it's only a front-page splash. Over a million people think that there are six hundred thousand benefit tourists, plus anyone who happened to glance at the headline without seeing the accompanying text, but I'm sure they all saw the tiny correction on page 2. Or, to be fair, in the thousands of social media posts along the lines of 'The *Sun* doesn't want you to see this ... It would be a shame if you all retweeted it' that sprang up shortly afterwards. As well as tarnishing hundreds of thousands of migrants as benefit cheats, they also generated a lot of shit tweets.

In defence of the article, the *Sun* said at the London Press Club, 'I think the *Sun* is pro-immigration. Pro positive immigration,' adding, 'What we want to see is people coming here, contributing to society, getting jobs, building business and that sort of thing.'

The paper went on to write stories titled 'ONE MILLION MIGRANTS HEADING THIS WAY' (22 September 2015) and an editorial 'YOUR BRUSSELS DEAL HAS DONE NOTHING TO HALT MIGRANTS, NOTHING TO WIN POWERS BACK FOR BRITAIN. SORRY PRIME MINISTER, BUT ... IT STINKS' (3 February 2016). Which, I'm surprised to learn, were all pro-immigration.

MYTH BUSTING EU DEBATE LEAVES 15% OF BRITS BELIEVING BRUSSELS HAS BANNED BENT BANANAS AND BUSTY BARMAIDS

10 June 2016

Of all the stories I've stumbled across on the *Sun* online, this is the one that really takes the piss out of its own audience the most.

On 10 June 2016, they published an article pointing out some of the 'more bizarre Brussels myths' that people believed about the EU, according to an Ipsos MORI poll. They included stuff like how the EU banned bendy bananas, that children under twelve or below a certain height must use a booster seat, and that the EU wanted to change the name of Bombay Mix to 'Mumbai Mix'.

The *Sun* neglected to mention that many of these were myths that they themselves had peddled. On 21 September 1994, they ran an article, 'NOW THEY'VE REALLY GONE BANANAS', in which they described the 'crazy laws' drawn up by 'thumb-twiddling EU chiefs' that had seen any bananas which are 'too bendy' banned. They even got a quote from an outraged importer claiming 'this means all our bananas must almost be straight before they come into the country', before asking readers to dial in if they'd come across any bananas which were too bendy. (They have of course never been banned, though a line in the regulations says bananas must be free from 'abnormal curvature'. They can still be sold, though, they're just deemed to have 'defects of shape'. There's no real reason to this, I guess it's a bit like how Penguin bars always include a joke. And no, I have no idea why.)

On 18 July 2006, they claimed that the 'nutty' EU wanted to change the name of Bombay Mix to Mumbai Mix 'to make the snack politically correct'. The *Telegraph*'s Brussels correspondent tracked the source of this story to a small regional news agency, who told them it 'came from a mate at the Home Office, who had heard it being talked about'. When pushed, he said, 'Look, this is just meant to be funny for the tabloids,' which is another way of saying, 'OK, you got me: it's bollocks.'

Having peddled these myths and then published an article about the mad things Brits believed, including said myths, the *Sun* weren't quite done yet. They published an article on 25 June 2016 titled 'BENDY BANANAS AND CROOKED CUCUMBERS The barmy EU rules we can now free ourselves from', and included the banana myth again. Then, seven months later, on 3 February 2017, they published 'BREXIT GOES BANANAS: Bizarre moment Question Time audience member says she voted Leave because she saw a straight banana in Aldi', with many mocking tweets about a woman who believed the kind of myths they'd repeatedly pushed as fact.

Look, I'm as keen as the next guy to take the piss out of people who think the EU have banned curvy fruit (even though you can dispel this myth yourself by *looking at a fucking banana*). But when the *Sun* do it they're like a teacher telling your kids that 'cats are a type of dog' before calling them up in front of the school assembly, goading them – 'Go on then, tell us all what you believe' – before saying, 'Ahaha, look at this this fucking melon, he thinks *cats* are a type of *dog*.' OK, on the one hand well played, but we've placed you in a position of trust and you've really fucked them over here.

CAMPAIGNS
AND VENDETTAS

MEMBERS OF ALL THE
SUN PRODUCTION CHAPELS
REFUSED TO HANDLE THE
ARTHUR SCARGILL PICTURE
AND MAJOR HEADLINE ON
OUR LEAD STORY. THE *SUN*
HAS DECIDED, RELUCTANTLY,
TO PRINT THE PAPER
WITHOUT EITHER.

15 May 1984

235

You'll notice this isn't the usual snappy headline the *Sun* are known for. I've scanned it three times for a pun and found zero, but feel free to check my work.

During the 1984–5 miners' strike, and the violent clashes that occurred as it dragged on, all quarters of the media, be it the *Mirror* or even lefty snowflake broadsheet the *Guardian*, *eventually*, covered the strike with some level of hostility. The *Sun*, however, at times wrote about the striking miners like they were scabs trying to break the unions.

Their coverage focused mainly on conflicts between the miners and strike-breakers, slamming the tactics of strikers and lauding the police officers. Police had a 'LOTTA BOTTLE'; they were 'brave cops [who] defy thugs in pit riot' (8 May 1984), whereas strikers were portrayed as a 'mob'.

As a backdrop to this, there was also ongoing friction between the *Sun* and the print unions that printed the paper. The print unions held power that wasn't to be underestimated. If they downed tools, the next day you wouldn't have a paper. It wasn't like other industries, where time could be made up; if you lost the Friday edition you couldn't print it the following Wednesday and casually act like world events just happened to happen twice.

One day, in covering a strike rally, the *Sun* went beyond what the printers would willingly print, forcing them to act like a printer belonging to a nineties observational comedian ('What is the deal with printers?? Why won't you print things?') and refuse to print anything at all.

During the rally, Arthur Scargill – president of the National Union of Mineworkers at the time, and someone with whom the *Sun* had major beef – had raised his hand, and had been photographed making what looked like (but wasn't) a Nazi salute. The *Sun* had wanted to print the picture on the front page, under the headline 'Mine Fuhrer'. As massive smears go, it wasn't a bad pun. Despite this, the printers refused to print it, and the *Sun* had to print an embarrassing explanation about their own internal dispute on the front page.

The accompanying text explains what the readers would have seen: 'MINERS' leader Arthur Scargill gives a Hitler-style salute as he addresses his supporters,' the story went. 'The gesture, a favourite of the German

Fuhrer, was made by Mr Scargill as thousands of striking pitmen poured in.' Having people *imagine* a Hitler salute isn't quite the same, is it? It sort of makes it so the reader is doing the dirty, Hitlery work.

A few years later, by moving to new printing methods and physically moving the printing process from Fleet Street to Wapping in order to get around the unions, and breaking the striking printers with support from the government, Murdoch's papers took this power away from the print unions. But with Hillsborough a few years after that, who knows if they could have saved the *Sun* from their biggest mistake.

SUN TO SUE GRAN

17 May 1988

The *Sun* once announced that they were going to sue a little old lady on their front page.

'The *Sun* last night vowed to sue £1 million granny Phyllis Hanlon – cleared yesterday of being part of a plot to swindle our Bingo games.'

Phyllis – who has the granniest of names – had been on trial for her part in 'the great *Sun* Bingo fraud'. Two fraudsters who worked where the *Sun* Bingo cards were produced had been taking winning cards from the factory and distributing them at the local pub, in return for a cut of the winnings. These were generally for smaller amounts, but Phyllis – who maintained throughout the trial that she had been given winning cards by her son-in-law, and hadn't known that they were stolen – then won a cool one mil.

The swindle was eventually discovered and went to court, where the jury believed her version of events – she is regularly described as 'everyone's favourite granny' in the coverage – and she was found not guilty. She had been conned, and as the *Sun* reported, she 'broke down in tears' as she left court, nerves shot and wanting to get back to her normal life. At which point the *Sun* announced to their readers they were going to sue the fuck out of her.

'Even though she was acquitted, we will be taking action against her through the civil courts,' they wrote, explaining that they wanted the money back 'because it rightly belongs to our readers'.

It was like a modern-day Robin Hood story where a mind-bogglingly, insanely rich corporation tried to take a little old conned gran to the cleaners in order to give the money back to the people (somehow).

Look, I guess you could argue trying to get back your money is OK. Even if you have an absolute buttload of the stuff. Although, to be honest, if I were the *Sun*'s PR guy I'd be meekly trying to have a quiet word with the owners: 'Are … are we absolutely sure we want to sue "everyone's favourite granny" after she just escaped jail for being conned?'

But it'll never cease to amaze me how willing the *Sun* are to bore the crap out of their audience by telling their readers of their court proceedings. For a paper that has a reputation for being fun, they sure do like to twat on about the backend side of things, like a friend you like but aren't sure you want to arrange stuff with because most of the time he's a riot but he also enjoys telling you lengthy, tedious anecdotes about the system he's got for mortgage payments.

Grans got their own back five years later, when, on 23 December 1992, the *Sun* published the Queen's Christmas speech a few days early, breaking the embargo, and were forced to use the front page to try to persuade her to drop legal action. Their front-page open letter of apology to the Queen (14 February 1993) was enough to make her drop the case, and the next day they announced – on the front page again – that everything was resolved, subject to them donating £200,000 to charity.

BURN THIS EVIL VIDEO

26 November 1993

If you don't want to read the *Sun*, you can get a pretty good impression of their view on crime in years gone by, by picturing what Mark Francois yells out when he comes. Once you edit out the Brexit stuff you'll be left with key phrases like 'BRING BACK HANGING' and 'LIFE MEANS LIFE', which is pretty much bang on what the *Sun* have hinted at quite a bit.

They peddle easy answers to complex questions.

'No one will ever admit that the simple reason most people commit crime is because they are worthless scum and they think they can get away with it,' columnist Richard Littlejohn (picture an estate agent going through a horrifying realisation that he's always going to be an estate agent before deciding to take out that anger on the world) wrote after toddler Jamie Bulger was brutally murdered in February 1993. In a piece titled 'Murderers must never be freed ... help them commit suicide if they can't take it' (19 February 1993) he argued that rapists and violent criminals should be flogged, and murderers should be flogged then die in jail, one way or the other.

The killers of Bulger, when they were known to be two young boys, were at the same time called 'evil' and 'monsters' like it was innate, and used as proof that Britain was fundamentally broken: something the *Sun* kept highlighting at the time through the gimmick of having a jagged black line through pages on crime, giving the effect of a crack.

The simple answers to complex questions kept coming, and before you knew it the *Sun* were having a full-blown, good old-fashioned moral panic to keep their readers from having to think about societal issues on a deeper level than 'CRIME BAD'.

During the investigation into the Bulger murder, police found that the father of Jon Venables, one of the killers, had rented the film *Child's Play 3*, which inevitably led to the *Sun* headline, 'For the sake of ALL our kids ... BURN YOUR VIDEO NASTY', accompanied by visuals of videos of Chucky burning in a fire. Before you could say, 'But the video was one of around two hundred rented by the Venableses,' the *Sun* had launched a campaign to get 'all other copies of *Child's Play 3* burned'.

They even had a small story from one mum, about how the 'SICK MOVIE MADE MY SON A DEMON' after she let her six-year-old watch *Child's Play 3* on repeat, after which he 'tried to kill the dog and attack me'.

MPs lined up to praise the *Sun*'s campaign to have the film destroyed, even though – by the way – there's no evidence that Jon Venables watched it at all.

'If you are going to link this murder to a film,' Inspector Ray Simpson of Merseyside Police said at the time, 'you might as well link it to *The Railway Children*.'

BLOWN AWAY FOR THIEVING? GOOD.

24 August 1999

The laws on reasonable force are actually quite straightforward and protective of people who defend themselves. You are allowed to use 'reasonable' force to protect yourself or others, or to carry out a citizen's arrest or prevent a crime. Homeowners are protected from prosecution if they acted 'honestly and instinctively' in the situation. For example, if you reasonably believed that someone who had broken into your house had a gun and smacked them around the head with a vase and then it turns out they actually had an unusually shaped potato, that's fine as far as the law is concerned.

But every now and then, tabloids will ignore what the law says and use an odd case to fight for the right to completely fucking wail on someone if they dare to trespass on your lawn. A notable example of this was in 1999, when a farmer was charged with murder simply because he shot a sixteen-year-old to death with a Winchester pump-action shotgun. PC gone mad.

OK, that was churlish. Let me give a fairer summary. Farmer Tony Martin shot dead Fred Barras and injured Brendon Fearon with an illegal gun as they broke into his home in Norfolk. When the case came to trial, his defence argued that he had shot the burglars in self-defence, while the prosecution alleged that he had been waiting for the two (he had been burgled before) and his force had been excessive, as he'd shot the burglars in the back as they tried to climb out of a window.

The jury found Martin guilty, and he was convicted of murder. This was later reduced to manslaughter after an appeal in 2001, based on evidence that he had a long-standing paranoid personality disorder.

I'm not saying it was a clear-cut case of murder/manslaughter, and who knows how any of us would act in a similar situation (my personal emergency plan is to shit myself until they give my stuff back out of pity – you've got to plan ahead for these things) but Tony Martin's case was certainly not a clear-cut case of a person defending themselves in their home either.

Yet if you read about it in the *Sun*, that might be the impression you came away with.

The day after the story broke, *Sun* columnist Richard Littlejohn (if you still don't know who that is, picture Enoch Powell animated by Aardman) wrote a column titled 'Blown away for thieving? Good.'

The piece lamented that Martin had been burgled before and the police hadn't done enough – which is fair – but also said things like Littlejohn was glad one of the men (actually a sixteen-year-old boy) was dead.

Littlejohn made his case that 'once a burglar gains entry to your property, the contract between public and police has broken down. And you should be able to take any action necessary against the intruder, up to and including shooting them dead.' Which you can: that second part is literally the law. You just can't wait for them to burgle you, then shoot them in the back as they try to flee.

The Tony Martin case, starting here, would be used by the *Sun* as a stick to beat the government with over traveller communities (whom they obviously termed gypsies) as well as self-defence becoming a major campaign for the paper.

Before that, Littlejohn would bring up a friend of his who was 'recently fined £600 – yes, **SIX HUNDRED POUNDS** – for speeding' and claim that, in contrast, the police consider stealing, brawling and public nuisance minor offences.

'It's too much trouble and far too dangerous having to deal with the scum who commit these offences. Far easier to sit outside pubs, or stick up a few more Gatso cameras, or arrest those who, horror of horror, dare to "take the law into their own hands".'

Yeah, police, a little less time [squints] policing and a little more time [squints real hard this time] allowing people to shoot people in the back as they try to flee without even a cursory investigation, please, you shits.

Unfortunately, as the *Sun* was about to prove, this was an incredibly popular opinion. They collected votes in a 'You the Jury' poll, with readers siding with Tony Martin, and demanded on 26 April 2000 (around the time of his trial) that 'when almost 250,000 *Sun* readers vote in a You the Jury Poll, MPs must listen'. In response to the perceived pressure, and probably looking to score some cheap points, Labour ministers and the Tory leader wrote for the paper, talking about just how tough they'd like to be on crime. The *Sun*'s campaign – centred around a case with many glaring problems – had worked.

On 15 October 2003, Tony Blair's government announced a crackdown on anti-social behaviour, including kids spraying graffiti, drinking in the streets and vandalism. The *Sun* was so enthusiastic about the idea that you'd have thought they'd just announced the first annual tournament of the Hunger Games.

The paper decided to launch their own 'name and shame' campaign, titled 'Shop a Yob', as a sort of fun 'play along at home' game show, but for complex and deeply private social issues.

In the accompanying Sun Says column,* of course they lamented that for years 'teachers haven't been able to cane unruly pupils' and 'the police can't deliver the old-fashioned short, sharp shock of a clip round the ear'. You know, the type that leads to kids growing up to be the well-rounded sort who fantasise about going back to a time when smacking the shit out of kids was fine in op-eds.

They went on to demand that more prisons be built, and work camps set up, but in the meantime their grass-a-neighbour campaign would have to do. The idea was that *Sun* readers would:

'Tell us about the animals who make your lives a misery and we'll name and shame the guilty ones.'

If you're a fan of hunting poor children, this was the closest you were going to get to a legal version. You could ring a hotline or email a specific address and doxx them. Then, whilst you sat back and thought about what a rat you'd been, the *Sun*'s team of investigators would 'try to catch them out'. Bearing in mind that these could be unfounded allegations, it sort of suggests that you could call in with a child's name and get them investigated for a bit in the hope they'd do something really awful, like graffiti or, I don't know, setting some hacks on unsuspecting kids.

'If we do [catch them out], we will name and shame them – and let your neighbourhoods know exactly who they are.'

To get the ball rolling, the *Sun* named and shamed eighteen people for bad behaviour. People who they deemed had been through the justice system, but they felt needed the extra punishment. They included twelve kids aged sixteen or under, with the youngest being just twelve.

I'm not sure if you're familiar with labelling theory, or just how kids work in general, but it's not classic to see social workers in schools recommending 'What this marginalised kid really needs is the psychological torture of

---

* Coincidentally, that day's Page 3 model, Michelle, informed the Sun's horny readers that she thought it was time to 'get tough on teenage tearaways', saying 'they need to be locked up to make people feel safer in the streets' and 'we're too soft on them. Enough is enough. They need a more severe punishment.'

knowing that over three million people readers know his face and think he's a real shithead. That'll sort him right out.'

The Children's Rights Alliance for England told the *Guardian* that the whole campaign 'smacks a little of lynch mob behaviour. The most important thing with young people who are getting themselves into trouble is that we do something effective to provide activities that will put them on the right track and this is not the right way to go about it. It's blatantly called "name and shame". The purpose of it isn't to help the young people in any way, it's to get vengeance and it's a very dangerous strategy.'

The campaign, which may as well have been titled 'You there, frothing at the mouth, grass someone, for fuck's sake', continued. For a completely non-Wild West/lynch mob feel, the *Sun* started printing wanted posters to be distributed across towns under the headline 'One down, who's next'.

The first 'yob' to be given the wanted poster treatment was an eighteen-year-old. Soon a fifteen-year-old was also given a full page in a national newspaper in the hope that his face would be distributed across his town, and his behaviour closely watched and monitored by strangers. Like a remake of *The Truman Show* where the whole town thinks Truman is a criminal fucking bellend.

Over the course of the campaign, the *Sun* would name and shame quite a few young people and encourage dobbing if they broke the terms of their Anti-Social Behaviour Orders. For one of the wanted, this included such things as 'associating with his yob friends' or 'being part of any group of more than three people'.

The *Sun* had been sensationalist about crime for a long time. You could argue it's not the best idea to get an audience you'd whipped up into a frenzy about 'yobs' and criminals over the course of several decades and then point them in the direction of some criminals and see what happens.

Rebekah Wade – editor of the *Sun* in 2003 – needed only to look to the *Sun*'s sister paper the *News of the World* in 2000 – under the then editor [checks notes] Rebekah Wade – to see how this could feasibly have played out. The *News of the World* had led its own name-and-shame against sex offenders, which led to: vigilante violence against sex offenders; an innocent man in a neck brace having his home attacked by a mob chanting 'paedophile' because they mistook him for an actual child abuser in a neck brace pictured by the *News of the World*; and (of course) a *paediatrician's* house getting vandalised because readers couldn't differentiate between the words paediatrician and paedophile. Why read the whole word when it's smashing time?

The actions of the paper were so abhorrent that even possessed shoe Ann Widdecombe condemned them: 'This incident shows that the *News of the World*, whatever their intentions may have been, are inciting a lynch mob mentality.'

The *Sun's* campaign thankfully didn't lead to the same kind of abuse. These were 'yobs' not nonces. But publishing the details of young people for far lesser crimes and hoping that everyone plays nice is a huge risk to take for giving the casual reader someone to scapegoat/judge.

The *Sun* celebrated what they deemed the success of the campaign (a sixteen-year-old had been 'caged' for breaching their ASBO by drinking alcohol in public, which doesn't exactly scream 'We're just happy this troubled child will get the help he needs') before quietly dropping the feature.

Before that happened, thousands of calls came in from members of the public who were willing to shame someone nationally. It was sort of like a preview of the internet.

BLOOD ON THEIR HANDS

12 November 2008

THIS HERE IS THE ROYAL COURTS OF JUSTICE, PART OF BRITAIN'S JUSTICE SYSTEM. OTHER KEY LOCATIONS INCLUDE THE SUPREME COURT AND THE SUN HEADQUARTERS, WHERE TRIAL BY MEDIA ROUTINELY TAKES PLACE.

In 2007, a seventeen-month-old boy, Peter Connelly, died following months of abuse and neglect by his mother Tracey Connelly, her boyfriend Steven Barker and Barker's brother Jason Owen. You probably know him better as Baby P. Over the course of eight months, he had been seen a number of times by the London Borough of Haringey Children's Services and health workers in the NHS.

He had sustained more than fifty injuries during this time, and serious questions needed to be asked about how his death happened, given that he was seen over sixty times by authorities in those months. In 2010, an inquiry found he was 'failed by all agencies' and his 'horrifying death could and should have been prevented'.

Criticism of the council, it's fair to say, was quite warranted.

However, the *Sun*'s coverage went 'over the top' in their attacks on the head of Haringey Children Services, Sharon Shoesmith, by the editor's own admission. Which is like a serial killer admitting, 'Yeah, OK, I stepped over the line on that last one.'

As well as genuinely heartbreaking coverage of the details of the case following the trial and conviction of Baby P's killers, the *Sun* went into campaign mode. In a series of articles over several months, they ran front-page headlines targeting the people in children's services and the medical profession who they deemed should have done more to save Baby P.

They launched a petition to have all the social workers involved in the case fired, with a cut-out petition slip to sign and return to the *Sun*. Harassing the government into firing someone before all the details came out had never been this convenient.

When it was revealed that Shoesmith could be entitled to a pension of £1.5 million, the *Sun* ran with the headline 'BLOOD MONEY' next to a picture of her and Baby P, in a layout very much in the vein of their coverage of serial killers. They had headlines such as 'GO NOW' (1 December 2008), with prominent pictures of the faces of Shoesmith and other social and healthcare workers, so you could see exactly who you were getting mad at. One person didn't have a photo, so you had to picture your own imagined face to shout with righteous anger at.

Explaining the petition, the *Sun* insisted that with 'NO SACKINGS, NO APOLOGIES, NO ONE TAKING BLAME ... ON BEHALF OF BABY P' – the *Sun* now claiming to talk on behalf of a murdered baby, as you do – '*THE SUN* DEMANDS THAT ALL OF THIS DISGUSTING LOT BE FIRED' and barred from ever holding public office again.

Below the demand, and next to the petition, they had pictures of the five women they wanted fired, along with 'Do you know [this person]?' and a number to call at the *Sun*: appeals for information if you're being kind, or begging for dirt if you're not so inclined.

The campaign was long, brutal, and it worked. Sharon Shoesmith ended up being fired live on television by notable ballroom dancer Ed Balls, who was trying to make it as Children's Minister in the Labour government at the time. He announced the decision in Parliament, before she'd been notified.

The problem is not just trial by media (although it is partly that – Sharon Shoesmith by no means had blood on her hands, and she was eventually awarded more than £600,000 in compensation for unfair dismissal) but the undue influence a tabloid would have on a government decision, without thought to the repercussions. And there would be repercussions, not just for the target of the campaign ...

THE PEOPLE HAVE SPOKEN

26 November 2008

If someone in your office maliciously fucked up a spreadsheet by putting a decimal point in the wrong place and suddenly all the size 2 screws have been sold for ten times less than they should have been (I've decided you're an accountant in a screw firm – good Lord your life sounds dull), and then Geoff from marketing ran a public campaign to have you fired for not spotting the mistake, and then you *are* fired by Mr Screws (the head of the company is called Mr Screws) in front of the whole company during the national screw conference, it's going to have a bit of an effect on the office atmosphere and morale.

In the same way, making decisions based on public demand for justice had consequences for social care in a way that could have caused other children to themselves be put in danger.

Sure enough, social service workers saw a 'Baby P effect' shortly after the live firing that the *Sun* had been cheering for for months. One measurable consequence was there was a dramatic surge in children being taken into care, a 36 per cent increase in England and Wales between April 2009 and April 2010. Social workers describe a culture of fear, and decisions being made to cover their own backs.

Children needing urgent attention became like 'needles in the haystack', as referrals to child protection shot up, one social worker told Community Care. 'Senior managers didn't want to be the next Sharon Shoesmith. Middle managers were terrified that the buck would stop with them if bad decisions were made. And the frontline staff felt like they were carrying everyone's risk and anxiety.'

This isn't the kind of atmosphere where the best decisions are made for the children.

'[Ed Balls] had no idea of the damage he was about to inflict on the social work profession and on children because of that "Baby P effect",' Sharon Shoesmith would eventually say. 'A lot of those children are still in care now. That has really troubled me for a decade.'

If Balls was influenced by the *Sun* to make that decision to fire Shoesmith – as Rebekah Wade clearly believed – then some children may not have got the care they needed, and some may have been taken into care unnecessarily and stayed there for years. All because the *Sun* seems to think social care works like vampires: you kill the head vampire and all of the rest of them crumble into dust, making everything somehow fine again.

Getting people fired might feel good, and it might be justifiable (although, again, it was deemed unfair dismissal by the courts and, as Shoesmith put it, 'doctors are not blamed when they can't cure cancer'), but if your goal is to improve care and prevent another Baby P from happening, a campaign to get someone fired that scares the shit out of the whole profession as a by-product might not be the most effective approach. This was just revenge with a side order of unintended chaos.

THE SUN SAYS SACK
THE DOCS

24 March 2016

Since the coronavirus crisis hit the UK in 2020, the *Sun* went full-throated in their support of the NHS, correctly judging the public mood. It's hard to miss that the public were fans of the people saving their lives, day in, day out, especially when they were going outside to 'clap for our carers' at eight o'clock every Thursday, like Andre the seal hearing his keeper get out a big bucket of fish.

The *Sun* have even got on the bandwagon, trying to associate the clapathon with themselves, urging readers to 'clap heroes at 8 p.m.', calling it 'the *Sun's* appeal to nation' like it was in any way their idea. They're the media equivalent of an *Apprentice* contestant trying to take credit for the whole team's idea in the hope that they don't get fired and so can unknowingly humiliate themselves for a few butt-clenchingly excruciating weeks longer.

But the paper hasn't always been so on board with the NHS. Granted, it would be weird to go around shouting out how much you love the NHS when nothing particularly out of the ordinary is happening at the time. I love *Shrek* and its superior sequel *Shrek 2*, for instance, but it's rare that I'll shout 'DONKEY IS A MORE ROUNDED CHARACTER THAN HAMLET' in the face of a stranger on the bus. But the *Sun* has at times both attacked nurses and doctors, and their favourite combo: foreign nurses and doctors.

Rather than focus on issues like underfunding to explain why the NHS might at times struggle, they've given disproportionate attention to studies that claim 'too many foreign nurses are damaging [the] NHS' and getting outraged that 'almost half of doctors at some NHS hospitals are foreign-trained' (6 April 2016), plus other articles that erode trust in foreign nurses and doctors like 'NHS probe into 3,000 foreign medics after fraudster worked as a psychiatrist for 22 YEARS on fake degree' (19 November 2019).

As well as not wanting foreign medical workers and thinking we should train up our own, it turned out the *Sun* fucking hate them too, and want to see them destitute. In one particularly infamous editorial in 2015, they wrote 'The Sun Says sack the docs' in response to junior doctors demanding better pay and more reasonable working hours through use of a strike. Of the same doctors they now claim to support, they wrote, 'if a few budding careers need to end abruptly before the rest finally understand their sworn duties as doctors, so be it'. Former editor Kelvin MacKenzie went further, writing a piece that 'junior doctors used to be saints ... now they're no better than the rail union bullies', and that all the young doctors calling for a strike should to be fired. With a dislike of foreign *and* UK doctors, it's unclear where the *Sun* would like the magical supply of life-saving medics to spring from.

Nevertheless, they have found their new line on the NHS, that they love it and have always loved it. They've also decided that their journalism during this crisis is absolutely vital.

For example, on 20 April 2020 they led with 'Pubs shut till Xmas: Boozers "will be last to open"'. How many people died from Covid-19 on 20 April 2020? Only a paltry 596, and you'll have to turn to page 4 to hear more on that, because it's more important that the front page covers the story that you'll have to wait a little longer to get shitfaced outside of your own house. My take on this is, firstly, that's the sort of person the *Sun* think their reader is: someone who cares more about getting lashed down the Dog and Rabbit than people's lives. And secondly, if Labour were in power and nurses and doctors weren't getting the PPE they needed in order to not get infected, and the prime minister had been outed as skipping Cobra meetings at the start of the pandemic like a child bunking off maths (as Boris Johnson also did), it would get a little more attention.

POLITICS

FORWARD WITH THE PEOPLE

15 November 1969

When Rupert Murdoch bought the *Sun* in 1969 it was a Labour-supporting broadsheet. Worse, he had inherited their Labour-supporting readers, and had to keep them on side. On the first day of the new *Sun*, they featured an interview with the Labour Prime Minister Harold Wilson and promised 'this newspaper will not be produced for the politicians or the pundits. It will be produced for you.'

They also made it very clear that they weren't really interested in party politics like the other papers. Their trailer for the next day promised 'adultery' and 'confession', and elsewhere they vowed to deal with taboos. It took them till day two to find a tenuous excuse to print a picture of some boobs. A few days later, they were printing stories ('GIRLS DON'T BE CAUGHT BENDING!') about a school warning its students not to bend over in miniskirts, and asking secretaries whether they would sleep with their bosses.

But, politically, a Labour paper they remained, at least for the time being. On 17 June 1970, they covered their first election, and the day before polling day explained 'WHY IT MUST BE LABOUR'. From what the *Sun* became, it's unrecognisable.

'The *Sun* deplores the fact that issues like **LAW AND ORDER** – gravely exaggerated by some Conservatives – have been thrown into the electoral arena' – fuck me, that's some heavy foreshadowing. 'Nor do we believe that **IMMIGRATION**, a very proper source of concern to a great many people, is really an election issue.'

In a piece that would be trashed by the eighties *Sun* as being written by STALIN, they praised Labour's handling of the economy, and professed to be distressed about unemployment and poverty, but on balance, '*The Sun*'s verdict is that this far, far from perfect Labour Government has just about earned the right to ask for another term of office.'

The polls had been tight, and it wasn't clear who would win. What could be construed as balance could also just be the *Sun* being careful not to piss off too many readers. They ended weakly with 'But you have a mind of your own. And it is the way you make up YOUR mind which matters.' Which is the 'can't we just hope everybody has a good time?' of political punditry.

Sure enough, when the Conservatives won, the *Sun* shamelessly spun this as a victory of sorts and did some good old-fashioned arse-kissing: 'WELL DONE, TED HEATH'.

They made their excuses and stressed how they had 'marginally' come down in favour of Labour, and even left room to make the best of the incorrect opinion polls that had so fucked their attempts to weasel themselves closer to power: 'THE BEST THING about the flood tide running for the Tories is that it has washed away the pretensions of the public opinion polls. That is a victory for the people. Which is what a General Election should be. '<u>Let's hope a Tory Government will be good for democracy, too.</u>'

It wasn't.

VOTE TORY THIS TIME

3 May 1979

In 2019, celebrating fifty years of the *Sun* as a tabloid (as if that is something innately good), the *Sun* bragged how it 'has never been shackled to a political party' and switched back and forth over the years. 'We support those most prepared to act in our readers' interests.'

The first switch came in 1974, when they changed from Labour to 'look, just vote for who you want to vote for, we don't give a shit'. I'm paraphrasing, but only slightly. The *Sun* had expressed dissatisfaction with both candidates during the second election of that year, and told their readers on 8 October 1974, 'may the best men win' – this was the seventies, when apparently nobody in newspapers had ever heard of women – 'and Heaven help us if they don't'. They urged readers to vote for whatever person they'd like to see in government, regardless of the party. Like Marge Simpson asking, 'Can't I just bet that the horses will have a nice time?', they even wrote 'every vote is a vote for Britain' (10 October 1974).

Things had changed by the end of the seventies. The paper, which had been swinging towards the Conservatives throughout the mid-decade, finally came out in favour of the Tories, whose leader was the one and only Margaret Thatcher. Following a number of industrial disputes and strikes during what was labelled the 'Winter of Discontent' in 1978–9, the paper told Labour voters to 'VOTE TORY THIS TIME IT'S THE ONLY WAY TO STOP THE ROT'.

It was a gamble for a paper with a strong working-class readership, and that was reflected in the over-explanatory and apologetic tone of their coverage, reaffirming that 'the roots of *The Sun* are planted firmly among the working class' and saying '*The Sun* is not a Tory newspaper' on a front page advising their readers to vote Tory. It was like watching a churchgoer who you've always had your suspicions about explain to the vicar why he was coming out in favour of Satan, 'just this once, mind'.

They would go on to be full-throated Maggie fans, a far cry from when they had called her 'milk snatcher' back in 1970 for taking subsidised milk away from schoolchildren, but they were right to be cautious. While the Tories were ahead in the polls – and the *Sun* love to be on the winning side – their readers weren't all that Tory at the time. Thankfully for the paper – and contrary to the narrative of how much influence they have over their readers – following the Tory win in May 1979 it turned out readers still didn't know who the hell the newspaper supported. The weekend after the paper shouted 'VOTE TORY THIS TIME' and explained 'WHY IMMIGRANTS SHOULD VOTE FOR MAGGIE', an Ipsos MORI poll found that a third of their readers thought the *Sun* supported the Conservatives, a third thought they supported Labour and a third (who I imagine, if the option was there, would think they supported breasts) *didn't know*.

The day after she was elected, the front page of the *Sun* read 'Number 10, Maggie's den'. In the election of 1983, it shouted 'THE GREAT MAGGIE MASSACRE'. The *Sun* quickly turned from apologetic 'just this once' Tory boys into a more natural role of cheerleaders who had fallen in love for the first time. They would support her pretty much without question during the Falklands War, and in facing down the unions (something they themselves were also a fan of, given their troubles with the print unions). When times were tough and Thatcher was down in the polls, of course they'd switch to giving her a kicking, because loyalty – famously without cash value – means nothing to the *Sun*.

In a remarkable coincidence, Margaret Thatcher allowed Murdoch to take over *The Times* and the *Sunday Times* in 1981 without being referred to the Monopolies and Mergers Commission, allowing his already massive media empire – and his influence – in the country to grow like a slightly more disgusting and instinctively evil version of The Blob.

HERE'S HOW PAGE 3 WILL LOOK UNDER KINNOCK

9 April 1992

In the run-up to the 1992 election, opinion polls pointed towards a tight contest between Labour and the Tories, with a likely outcome of a hung parliament. The *Sun* began to throw everything they had at attacking the Labour leader, Neil Kinnock, culminating in the infamous front page on 9 April: 'If Kinnock wins today will the last person to leave Britain please turn out the lights'. Even if they aren't powerful enough to swing whole elections, they can sure as hell swing some voters and will fight tooth and nail until you vote for the particular jerk they're cheering for this time. This is usually the Tories, but has been Labour when it was clear the Tories would be trounced anyway, and Labour had swung far enough to the right under Tony Blair that the *Sun* could make their peace with backing him.

'You know our view on the subject but we don't want to influence you in your final judgement,' the front page read on election day on 9 April 1992, next to an unflattering picture of Kinnock's disembodied head inside a light-bulb, with the role of the dying filament being portrayed by the reflection on his bald head, indicating that in fact they did want to influence your judgement somewhat.

'But if it's a bald bloke with wispy red hair and two K's in his surname,' the *Sun* continued, really helping along the stragglers with all the extra descriptors, 'we'll see you at the airport!'

The paper had not been shy about their dislike of Kinnock in the lead-up to the election. Headlines included 'DON'T SLEEPWALK TO SOCIALIST NIGHTMARE' and 'DOPEY KINNOCK IS GRIM TIM SCARY TALE' (6 April 1992). On 2 April 1992, a Sun Says column had asked, 'Are we really going barmy?' and told readers that Labour had 'NEVER worked in Britain'.

Then came a few added extras. In other years, the *Sun* had kept page 3 an 'election-free zone', and celeb stories were largely free from politics too. Not so when the polls were this close. If it was, as they would claim a few days later, the *Sun* wot won it (see page 289 for more on this), they did so by fighting dirty.

On 7 April, they gave a big splash to renowned eater of hamsters Freddie Starr, who bet £500,000 that Kinnock couldn't get the UK out of recession if he won, and also ran a piece on boxer Chris Eubank saying he'd quit Britain if Kinnock became prime minister, just in case any of their readers were waiting for people who get punched in the head for a living to weigh in before they made a final decision.

On page 3, they ran pictures of several models with gigantic rosettes (fuck you, that's not a euphemism, I'm far too classy for that) saying they were hoping for a Tory win, because nothing is sexier than a half-naked person telling you how they're 'backing Tory chairman Chris Patten'.

In a testament to how low they're willing to sink when the polls are close, they howled 'HERE'S HOW PAGE 3 WILL LOOK UNDER KINNOCK' on polling day, and published a photo of horse enthusiast and former kissogram Pat Priestman.

'Roly poly Pat Priestman would be the shape of things to come under a killjoy Labour government,' the piece read, warning that 'it's not just taxes that will be heavy' and 'it's not just the economy that will sag'.

Their reasoning was that 'lefties like Clare Short want to ban pretty girls from the nation's favourite page', which as well as being offensive to Priestman specifically and older women more generally, it's not like Clare Short had in any way suggested women in their fifties and sixties as a one for one swap. Having hired a larger and far older model than their readers were used to and photographed her in her swimming costume in order to scare their readers with the possibility that a Labour government would mean they wouldn't be able to gawp at tits any more, they then casually mentioned that 'former flab-o-gram Pat' was planning on voting Tory.

It was the saddest and most desperate bit of politics I'd seen whilst researching the book, until a few pages later, when I spotted Labour had bought ad space. Amongst all the hit pieces, about the only positive coverage in the whole of Britain's most popular newspaper was their 'Vote today to rebuild the economy' advert, which had been placed opposite an advert for a 'Bernard Matthews Golden Norfolk self-basting turkey – with giblets' and stories about a monkey that pelted police officers with jam and eggs, and a couple who got arrested for having sex on the pavement, both of which I believe to be unrelated.

WHO BLAIRS WINS

30 April 1997

Tony Blair flew out to Australia to meet Rupert Murdoch shortly before the 1997 election, which would see the *Sun* back Labour once more. We'll probably never know what was said nor which arse was kissed profusely – perhaps it was a two-man human centipede: these are the kinds of details that are lost to history – but all of a sudden the relationship of, well, an astonishingly hungry two-man human centipede began.

The *Sun* then printed the headline 'WHO BLAIRS WINS', endorsing Tony Blair; the next day Blair was pictured on a plane reading that same issue. He would write for the paper, slagging off Europe, assuring readers that 'New Labour will have no truck with a European superstate. We will fight for Britain's interests and to keep our independence every inch of the way.'

Labour were steaming ahead in the polls, appealing to former Tory voters of the type who read the *Sun* by moving towards the centre, helped in no small part by how bored and fed up the public were with John Major and the Conservatives. With or without the *Sun*, Labour were going to win, and the *Sun* knew it. It speaks volumes about the perceived influence of the *Sun* that the Labour government were willing to give away so much to the paper in order to get their endorsement in these circumstances. In terms of the effect it was going to have on the outcome of the election, it would be like Usain Bolt at the peak of his career going out of his way to get himself an endorsement from Crocs. Sure, it's a confidence boost, but this isn't going to swing it.

The benefits Labour got from the *Sun*'s backing aren't as mighty as you'd hope. In the beginning, they got friendly headlines. The hand of God touched Tony Blair's bonce on the front page under the headline 'IT MUST BE YOU' on polling day. In a particularly horny image I'd rather forget, they drew Tony Blair as a muscle man lifting weights under the Sun Says opinion 'strong man we need'.

But the relationship was uncomfortable, and the *Sun* would only give positive coverage to things it already agreed with. The government would get praise whenever they talked tough on asylum seekers, 'yobs' or 'gypsies'. By the next year, the *Sun*, paranoid that Blair would take Britain into the Euro (spoiler alert: he did not take us into the Euro) asked 'IS THIS THE MOST DANGEROUS MAN IN BRITAIN?' (24 June 1998) and branded him 'THE TONE DANGER' (24 June 1998), picturing him in a Lone Ranger mask, referencing a character so old that even back then this was only popular amongst the dead.

I can't help but feel Blair making friends with Murdoch was like offering a bully your lunch money and telling everyone how great he is in the hope that he twats you slightly less frequently on the way home from school.

'I have never met Mr Murdoch, but at times when I worked at Downing Street he seemed like the twenty-fourth member of the cabinet. His voice was rarely heard,' Lance Price, special adviser to Tony Blair, wrote in the *Guardian* years later. 'But his presence was always felt.

'No big decision could ever be made inside No. 10 without taking account of the likely reaction of three men – Gordon Brown, John Prescott and Rupert Murdoch. On all the really big decisions, anybody else could safely be ignored.'

Which seems quite a big price to pay for a(n admittedly quite fuckable) Tony Blair cartoon.

TELL US THE TRUTH TONY ARE WE BEING RUN BY A GAY MAFIA

9 November 1998

This isn't so much a headline as something you'd find your drunk grandad yelling at a pack of Frosted Flakes.

In November 1998, Nick Brown, the Minister for Agriculture in Tony Blair's government, was outed by the *News of the World*, the fourth person in his cabinet to come out in a short space of time. Naturally the *Sun* kept a level head about things and dedicated a full front page to demanding the Prime Minister answer their batshit question, 'Are we being run by a gay mafia?' On the 'are these guys OK?' scale, it's only one beneath smearing yourself in faecal matter whilst demanding the Queen announce that she's a lizard.

'The *Sun* trusts Tony Blair,' the frankly baffling article began. 'We think he is a special politician – a potentially great Prime Minister.

'But his government is going to get itself into MASSIVE trouble,' they continued, suddenly sounding like the government's mum, 'if it doesn't tell us the whole truth.'

It's at this point I imagine they started to smear the faecal matter. Try to keep in mind that this was a reaction to four people being gay.

'*Is Britain being run by a gay mafia of politicians, lawyers, Palace courtiers, TV bigwigs – or even police officers?*'

The answer to which, even without contacting the Prime Minister of the country, I can safely reveal is 'no'. They went on to say that Nick Brown admitting he was gay had set off 'alarm bells'. Presumably some kind of 'OH GOD, DIVERSITY, DIVERSITY ALERT, THERE IS DIVERSITY AND I'M SCARED' klaxon.

They explained that the alarm had gone off 'not because people despise gays, or fear them, or wish to pillory them. But the public has a right to know how many homosexuals occupy positions of high power.'

Ah yes, the reassuring 'we just want to count you is all' guarantee. 'Hands up: who's gay? Come on, we don't mind, we just want to do a completely non-sinister tally.'

The *Sun* pre-empted criticism that they were invading Brown's privacy, informing readers that they had known he was gay but chosen not to reveal that (their sister paper, not so much) and that they had a tape of Brown talking to a rent boy, but '**once again, we have chosen not to publish details**'. Which sort of sounds like asking for praise for not being a slightly bigger shit about somebody being gay.

The paper went on to outline that John Major had been warned about a 'Velvet Mafia' and they had a '**RIGHT** to know about secret sexual liaisons which might explain why certain policies are persistently pursued'.

They added, 'Their sexuality is not the problem. The worry is their membership of a closed world of men with a mutual self-interest.'

The column ended with an appeal to gay politicians, saying they had nothing to fear, and telling them to '**come out and end the doubt**'.

On page 9, they even posted a number for gay MPs to ring. 'Are you a gay MP who'd like to come out? The *Sun* has set up a hotline [...] for ministers and MPs who are secretly homosexual. Don't worry about the cost, we'll ring you back.'

A moment of self-reflection on their own stories from years past, like 'EASTBENDERS' (see page 123) and regularly calling men 'poofs' would have revealed why gay MPs might still want to keep it a secret, rather than that they were in some kind of all-powerful mafia.

BLAIR BACKS THE SUN OVER GAYS

10 November 1998

ONE DAY LATER...

THIS HEADLINE ISN'T GOING TO AGE WELL

IT'S 30 SECONDS OLD AND – HEY, I JUST GOT SUCH A STRONG FEELING OF DÉJÀ VU!

If you thought we were finished with the gay mafia story, not quite. Just when you thought we were out (I'm so sorry) I pulled you back in.

This isn't just a story of the *Sun* losing their shit in a way that's clearly quite homophobic (further apologies, but if you're worried that the gays are conspiring against you in a 'mafia', you are doing a bit of a homophobia), it's about the uncomfortable relationship between the *Sun*, the *Sun*'s idea of their readers and the government.

Whether the *Sun* did actually represent the public's views on this topic is debatable. On 9 November 1998, they had quotes from several people in Nick Brown's constituency in Newcastle saying they couldn't care less about his private life, and joking they'd only have been bothered if he'd come out as a Sunderland fan. But by the 10th they had gathered a plethora of readers who were mad about the issue, which agreed with the *Sun*'s position.

Enough readers had rung the paper in support for them to say 'SUN READERS SAY: WE HAVE A RIGHT TO KNOW'. They were self-selecting, of course, of the people who were maddest about the issue. Not many people will ring a hotline where you pay, to say 'I'M PRETTY NEUTRAL ABOUT THE WHOLE THING, NO STRONG FEELINGS'.

And yet even they were largely sympathetic to Brown. Typical quotes included that 'there is far too much secrecy' and 'they should be more open and give voters credit to accept them as they are', rather than calling him Vito fucking Corleone.

A group that wasn't self-selecting was the farmers Brown was scheduled to meet with that day, as Agriculture Minister. The *Sun* covered the meeting under the headline 'WHY NICK'S NEW LOOK IS UDDERLY RIDICULOUS', mocking him for wearing farm gear – including a hair net – on a farm. The head of the farmers' union said categorically, 'We are not interested in the Minister's private life – that's his concern.'

All in all, and even from the *Sun*'s own coverage, the public's reaction seemed to be: *meh*. As much as the *Sun* thought the public were interested, they just weren't.

'The gay mafia story felt wrong to me but I also believe it was out of step with the public, who were becoming far more tolerant and accepting of gay people,' editor David Yelland told the BBC in 2012. He added that he 'felt ashamed' that he'd let the story run, and vowed that 'in future the *Sun* would no longer invade the privacy of gay people by outing them'. Which is obviously good, but it sort of means nothing when you've just found out that your readers don't have an interest in you doing it. Bravo for vowing to never [squints] do something that is of no financial benefit to yourself whatsoever.

And yet the front page that day (10 November 1998) read 'BLAIR BACKS *THE SUN* OVER GAYS'. Whatever the actual public opinion on this was, whether through fear of the *Sun*'s audience turning against them or out of loyalty to a paper that campaigned to get them elected and they needed to keep on side, the government put out a statement in support of the press's treatment of the cabinet minister. Who had been forced to come out against his wishes.

'The papers have treated Nick Brown with sympathy and understanding,' Downing Street are quoted as saying, even though they didn't have to. 'It was perfectly fair.'

Tony Blair, for his faults, is not homophobic. And yet here was Downing Street putting out a statement of support for the press, which the *Sun* took to be a backing of them directly. Whether the *Sun* represented the public's view on this or not, and whether Blair believed them or chose to back down for other reasons, Blair chose not to fight the *Sun* on the issue.

'There is no need for regulations,' the spokesman added in one final point, starting to sound like Reek from *Game of Thrones*. 'Self-regulation of the newspapers works.'

Which is an odd comment to make when a newspaper has just turned locating gay people in politics into a fucking witch hunt.

STUR WARS A NEW HOPE

29 April 2015

In the 2015 general election, showing how much integrity they have, the *Sun* and the *Scottish Sun* backed rival parties.

In the *Scottish Sun* they Photoshopped SNP leader Nicola Sturgeon's head onto the body and hair of Princess Leia, with the title 'STUR WARS A NEW HOPE' and a caption that really screams 'look, I'm just going to level with you here, we thought the election was going to be 4 May and are making the best of a bad job':

'MAY THE 7TH BE WITH YOU: WHY IT'S TIME TO VOTE SNP'

Meanwhile, the English edition had, for some horrifying reason, David Cameron's face Photoshopped onto a baby being cradled with the headline 'IT'S A TORY'. I know you think the message (basically 'let's deliver a Tory government') might be confused somewhat by people thinking the grotesque Cameron-baby hybrid depicted one of Cameron's kids, but most people would know it couldn't be one of his kids, as it hadn't been abandoned in a pub toilet.

They listed only three reasons to vote Conservative on the Cameron baby front page, one of which was to 'stop SNP running the country'. Somewhat the opposite of their Scottish message of please make the SNP run the country.

The *Sun* had actually gone a fuck of a lot weirder than the Cameron baby Photoshop. In a piece that should have had the CEO of Adobe on the phone to his lawyers trying to forcibly revoke their licence, they had put Nicola Sturgeon's face on Miley Cyrus's body as she swung around on a wrecking ball, under the headline 'TARTAN BARMY'. The tenuous reason they gave for this was that it was their 'mock-up of how Sturgeon could demolish [the] UK'.

Yet in Scotland they refrained from the Photoshops and the policy bashing, and supported the SNP. So why the different stances?

It's perfectly reasonable to think this is some kind of genius strategy to get people in Scotland to vote for the SNP, thus depriving Labour of seats in Scotland and helping the Tories to win. But it's even more reasonable to think, 'oh right, they'll just say whatever the fuck they think people want to hear* as long as it's good for sales'.

As the editor of the *Scottish Sun* told the BBC at the time:

'We are a Scottish newspaper, run in Scotland, printed in Scotland, produced in Scotland by Scots, and it's not a surprise to anybody – least of all Rupert Murdoch – that these two papers have a diversion of view.'

Murdoch had put a left-leaning editor in charge of the *Sun* shortly before the paper backed Blair (after it looked like he was going to win easily), and now an editor was enthusiastically backing the SNP right at the time when they looked like they were going to turn the whole country yellow.

---

* Within certain boundaries: they aren't going to flip to being commie, even if it's suddenly popular.

It wasn't the only time when the contrast between the two editions was this stark. When parliament was in deadlock in 2019 and Boris Johnson (very briefly) couldn't get the election he wanted, the *Sun* in England mocked up an image of Jeremy Corbyn in a chicken costume for not agreeing to an election, whereas in Scotland they ran with the incredibly penisy headline 'Floppy Johnson can't get an election'.

When it comes to their political stance, I don't believe the *Sun* aren't blue or red or yellow: their only political belief is green.[*]

---

[*] I realise that's confusing because we have a Green Party, but I'm hoping most of you will meet me halfway and assume that I mean money. As a gesture of goodwill, in return I shall acknowledge that in this country most of our money isn't even green.

SAVE OUR BACON

6 May 2015

Over the last few years of political chaos, it's hard not to pause and think, 'all this because Ed Miliband eats bacon like a camel?'

In an infamous front page in the lead-up to the 2015 general election, the *Sun* printed a picture of Ed Miliband with the frankly baffling text 'This is the pig's ear Ed made of a helpless sarnie. In 24 hours, he could be doing the same to Britain. SAVE OUR BACON. Don't swallow his porkies and keep him OUT.'

While it's undeniable that Ed Miliband eats bacon like a camel learning how to chew from a book, or a baby duck with dry mouth attempting to choke down an entire pack of Ryvita, it's absolutely baffling how this is any way related to the job of prime minister. Perhaps the *Sun* thinks being prime minister is a lot like being some guy on a Subway poster looking happy with his purchase of a foot-long meatball marinara. Even if there was some kind of scenario where world peace relied on Miliband not looking like a tit while eating pork crackling in front of Putin, we could always just put a sack on his head. Might even look like a baller power move.

In the seventies the *Sun* may have backed some of the wrong candidates, but at least their hit pieces were in some way related to policy. By 2015 we'd sunk to a place where the front page wasn't even a vicious attack on a politician's personality, it was basically just 'this guy is shit at eating food. Vote Tory.' An analysis by the Media Standards Trust found that the *Sun* were even more anti-Labour than they had been in the infamous coverage during the 1992 election, with 95 per cent of the leader columns having an anti-Labour stance.

We could talk about how unfair it is that the right-wing media would never cover a right-wing politician like they did Ed Miliband. Cameron was pictured eating a hotdog with a knife and fork, for instance, and I remain to be convinced that Jacob Rees-Mogg has not at least considered ingesting his young. Yet neither of these two things made the front pages, despite all my emails.

But I want you to take a moment to focus on how inane their politics coverage can be. I personally don't think that the *Sun* could have swung the 2015 election enough to get the Tories into power. But I can pretty much guarantee there's at least one persuadable soul out there who looked at Ed, with his face like a Hoover nozzle on half speed attempting to suck down a pillow, and thought, 'not for me'.

BELEAVE IN BRITAIN

14 June 2016

It was a hell of a shock when a paper that had been calling the French 'frogs' and cracking garlic jokes throughout the eighties and nineties, and banging on about asylum seekers and immigration at every available opportunity, chose to back voting leave, but in the run-up to the referendum the *Sun* came out swinging.

'WE are about to make the biggest political decision of our lives. The *Sun* urges everyone to vote LEAVE. We must set ourselves free from dictatorial Brussels,' they wrote, in a piece that was pretty much verbatim the speech Nigel Farage recites alone before he comes, but without the theme tune from *Mrs Brown's Boys* playing on a loop in the background.

'Staying in will be worse for immigration, worse for jobs, worse for wages and worse for our way of life. To remain means being powerless to cut mass immigration which keeps wages low and puts catastrophic pressure on our schools, hospitals, roads and housing stock. Our country has a glorious history. This is our chance to make Britain even greater, to recapture our democracy, to preserve the values and culture we are rightly proud of.'

As much as people like to retcon it, it had a lot to do with immigration, as far as the papers were concerned. In 2013, when David Cameron had made his fabled trip to the EU to get more powers and appease the Eurosceptics in his party, they had warned 'DRAW A RED LINE ON IMMIGRATION OR ELSE!' before telling him, like Violet Beauregarde losing her shit after not being given some gum, 'FINAL WARNING TO PM WE'RE SEEING RED'.

It was also a lot to do with the media. Though readers choose the paper that suits their views, 70 per cent of *Sun* readers said they voted leave and I refuse to believe that a good chunk of them weren't swung by anti-EU headlines and scare stories from the *Sun* and the other Eurosceptic papers.

On 10 February 2013, for instance, the *Sun* had printed an article titled 'INHUMAN RIGHTS' on a Court of Appeal ruling that the system of criminal record checks requiring individuals to declare all past convictions and cautions was incompatible with the European Convention on Human Rights. Underneath, they had a gigantic bullet point quote from one of abuser and murderer Ian Huntley's victims – 'Huntley abused me when I was 11 and went on to kill' – followed by another, frankly terrifying, bullet point: 'Now EU could let fiends like him prey on your children'. It's hard to look at it without screaming 'Hard Brexit NOW!' You'd be mad not to want to leave an institution that's about to let murderers stalk your children like prey. But as the *Sun* would later admit in a clarification on 26 June 2013, 'the European Union was not responsible for the decision. The Convention is separate from the EU, and the court's decision did not concern EU law.'

Shortly before the 2016 referendum they threw every tool they had at getting the win over the line. In another article, which drew a complaint from Buckingham Palace, they wrote 'EXCLUSIVE: BOMBSHELL

OVER EUROPE VOTE, QUEEN BACKS BREXIT'. IPSO ruled this was 'significantly misleading'.

While it's nice it got clarified, it's hardly the same as millions of people seeing it on the front page of the newspaper. The audience that see a clarification is probably much smaller than the initial front page, which includes people who see it taken out of context on social media and in TV newspaper reviews. It's like you yelling out lies about your boss like 'DEREK GOT A BONER WHILST WATCHING *THE LION KING*' over a megaphone in the staff canteen, then clarifying 'in a drawing I did' under your breath at home.

Following the win, the *Sun* continued to cash in on anti-EU sentiment, really dropping their pants and waving their arse around as we left, printing headlines like 'EU DIRTY RATS' on 21 September 2018, Photoshopping Emmanuel Macron's and Donald Tusk's heads onto some mobsters with massive guns and calling them 'gangsters'. They've since moved on to screaming that Brexit – while extraordinarily hard – wasn't quite hard enough for their tastes, and got their way again. Like it or not, we're about to live through the *Sun*'s ideal vision for what the country should be.

HIJACKED LABOUR

7 December 2019

In the last few days before the 2019 general election, the *Sun* published a piece that claimed Jeremy Corbyn was 'at the centre of an extraordinary network of hard-left extremists' with a 'spider's web of extensive contacts [stretching] from Marxist intellectuals to militant groups and illegal terror organisations'.

The *Sun*'s hatred of Corbyn had been fairly well established by this point. He'd been Photoshopped into a bin under the headline 'Don't chuck Britain into the cor-bin' on 7 June 2017 after they cleverly noticed that the second half of his name sounds like 'bin'. They weren't exactly subtle.

But saying Corbyn is a bit cowardly or lives in a bin is in another league from claiming he's in a big group of buddies with terrorist extremists. As evidence, the piece pointed readers to a website 'drawn up by [...] ex-military veterans in their spare time to expose what they insist is now a party firmly in the grip of a hardline cabal'. As if that wasn't evidence enough, the *Sun* stressed that one of the makers of the website was ex-SAS, which in terms of proof is like a teenager bragging in school that he's got a friend who's a spy.

If you clicked through to the website, you were met with a web of network links that scream either Tube map or 'click away from this website quite fast now, this is definitely the kind of conspiracy-theory GeoCities that's going to get you put on a list'. Upon closer inspection it turned out that some of the sources the *Sun* cited in their piece included far-right conspiracy websites, including the relatively innocuously named The Millennium Report but also the quite Hitlery Aryan Unity.

To give you an idea of the sort of scoops hosted by those websites, at time of writing The Millennium Report is currently running stories like 'QUATERNARY WEAPON SYSTEM Activated Before Each Coronavirus Cluster Explosion' and 'THE "CASSANDRA PROPHECY": Everything Changes After Election Day 2020', as well as several more damaging anti-Semitic conspiracy theories such as 'exposing Jewish Zionism'. Aryan Unity put out exactly the kind of racist nonsense you'd expect from a group called Aryan Unity.

After the somewhat questionable sources were spotted by internet sleuths, the article was deleted by the *Sun* with no explanation whatsoever, leaving people to guess whether it was a deliberate smear on Corbyn, in which case they're shit journalists, or that the *Sun* just wanted it to be true so badly they didn't really question a batshit conspiracy citing sources that may as well have been a Hitler fan club, in which case they're shit journalists.

BABY GAVE ME WILL TO LIVE

3 May 2020

AND HERE TO UNVEIL THE OPENING OF THE BORIS JOHNSON SHRINE IS NONE OTHER THAN THE MAN HIMSELF: MR DOMINIC CUMMINGS.

In 2020, as you're probably aware (and if not, sit down, because I have some rather bad news and an explanation for why everyone is suddenly dead), the world was hit by a coronavirus pandemic.

At first, when it was less clear just how devastating the virus would be, the *Sun* and other media outlets fell back on their usual habits of sensationalist scare stories. At the end of January, when global deaths were at forty-one – a figure that would cause so much celebration and dancing in the streets that, in May, there'd be a gigantic second wave that would probably wipe out humanity – the *Sun* were writing headlines like 'KILLER BUG Coronavirus death toll soars to 41 as more than 1,200 cases of "mutating" bug confirmed' (24 January 2020) and referred to it as 'the deadly disease'.

As it happens, they and other papers were right and it did turn out to be a global nightmare, so kudos. But it's a bit like a guy who'd been pacing the high street for years with a cardboard sign saying 'The end is nigh' nodding sagely and saying 'Told you so.'

As the virus spread around the world, the *Sun* continued to report on the horror of it. When the virus hit Italy hard, they reported '"THERE ARE TOO MANY": Coronavirus leaves Italy's morgues overflowing with corpses as death toll hits 2,158' (17 March 2020) and spoke of 'coronavirus ravaged Italy', where the army had been called in to transport coffins when the death toll hit three thousand – a few months later, in the UK, this would seem very low.

Then the virus was here. Having covered the death tolls in Italy and Spain like an absolute disaster zone (which, obviously, to a certain extent they were: this virus is not pretty) you'd expect the *Sun* to pay attention to the unfolding disaster in the UK – with a steeper death curve than Italy or Spain – with the same sort of horror. Daily death tolls were soon well over five hundred. And that's when they sprang into action and sort of lost interest in the whole thing.

Sure, they'd report on the growing death toll, but it wasn't the big story. On 20 April 2020 they infamously ran with 'PUBS SHUT TILL XMAS' with just a tiny teaser of '596 DEAD see page 4' to let you know we'd had a worse day than when they'd reported that the Italian army were acting like Yodel for human corpses. They had led with 'BORIS IS OUT (Now that really is a Good Friday!)' on 10 April, when the death toll was approaching eight thousand and nearly a thousand were dying every day, which I'd argue wasn't an all-time top-ten Friday, this time with zero mentions of deaths. During Boris Johnson's recovery from coronavirus, the *Sun's* political editor tweeted that he was up and doing Sudoku puzzles whilst watching *Love Actually*, *Home Alone* and *Lord of the Rings*. Which is fine, but when over a thousand people are dying in a single day and health professionals aren't getting the equipment they need, probably the last thing I'd need to know from the people holding the government to account is things like 'BREAKING: the Prime Minister has put down the Sudoku and started playing Super Mario'.

The paper undoubtedly pulled their punches because they liked the guy in charge. It's a cliché, but it's difficult to picture a scenario where they'd have been so lenient on a Labour leader when the death toll was only second to the country where the guy in charge was casually suggesting people inject themselves with bleach to cure the virus. As much as it pains me to say it, their view was (surprise, surprise) in line with the public. Polls in mid-March, when lockdown first began, showed the Tories with 50 per cent of the vote, and nearly thirty points ahead of Labour.

So, the *Sun* focused on a ninety-nine-year-old pensioner walking endless laps around his garden to raise money for the NHS rather than ask questions of how chronic underfunding led to circumstances where that was necessary, and praised volunteers sewing makeshift scrubs for NHS staff ('DARN BUSTERS' – 22 April 2020) rather than focus on what massive incompetence of leadership led to there being a shortage in the first place. At one point, when it became apparent that nobody would be able to go abroad during the summer, they even had an opinion piece titled 'It'll do our spoiled young Remainers good to remain in Britain for the hols', clearly hating freedom of movement for Remainers so much they had begun to root for a deadly disease.

Johnson and the Brexit Tory lot were essentially getting a free pass, and he returned the favour, giving them an exclusive interview after he nearly died of the virus, in which he told them that his 'BABY GAVE ME WILL TO LIVE' (4 May 2020). Which, as well as suggesting none of the 28,446 people who'd died thus far had a baby or a will to live, was also pretty offensive to his other five to nine kids.

IT WAS THE *SUN* WOT WON IT

11 April 1992

SPOILER: THEY DIDN'T THOUGH

Of all the political headlines by the *Sun*, this is perhaps the most famous and most contentious. People hold it up as a sign of the *Sun*'s power over politics. So we're going back in time to 1992, when the election was tight and they put everything they could against Labour, before declaring it their own victory when the Tories won.

'TRIUMPHANT Tory MPs queued yesterday to say "Thank You My Sun" for helping John Major back into Number 10,' the front page read.

They had been less sure of their astonishing power the previous day, when their own exit poll showed Kinnock might have clinched it and they ran the headline 'IT'S A NEIL BITER'. In that edition, they had laid the groundwork for blaming John Major – 'It would put a massive mark over the future of John Major, who was on probation after taking over from Mrs

Thatcher as leader 17 months ago' – rather than proclaiming 'IT WAS *THE SUN* WOT FUCKED IT'.

The *Sun* has backed the party that went on to win in every election since 1979 (except for 2010, when the Tories had the largest number of seats but didn't win outright). Newspapers do influence their voters, and they know it. If they didn't, we could have had more *EastEnders* stuff and far fewer Photoshops of leaders of the opposition dressed up in chicken costumes over the years.

But how much – and whether it's enough to swing elections – is quite difficult to determine. In 1992, the *Sun* had been hammering their readers over the head with the idea that Labour were crap for a long time, which counterintuitively makes it more difficult to find out how much they'd influenced their readers by definitively coming out for the Tories prior to the election. As well as the problem of the *Sun* switching to whichever side looks like it's going to win, there's also the problem that people tend to buy papers that align with them politically anyway, making it difficult to determine cause and effect.

In order to find out how much influence papers have over their readers, Professor John Curtice, president of the British Polling Council and Senior Research Fellow at the National Centre for Social Research, looked at what happens when the *Sun* switches from backing the Tories to backing Labour. If newspapers really can sway voters enough to swing elections, this would be where you'd expect to see the biggest effect: as previously hostile papers suddenly declared their love for Tony Blair. Curtice found no real difference in voting patterns, and that support for Labour actually fell in the year leading up to the 1997 election.

'The pattern of vote switching during the campaign amongst readers of the *Sun* or any other ex-Tory newspaper proved to be much like that of those who did not read a newspaper at all,' he wrote. 'The defection of some newspapers from the Conservative camp thus failed to make any apparent positive contribution to Labour's attempts to garner the vote.'

Despite all the cheerleading from the *Sun* and other previously Tory papers, Labour went from having 57 per cent support in 1996 to 43 per cent in the actual election. The Lib Dems, meanwhile, had a surge of popularity (relatively speaking – they're still Lib Dems) despite no major newspaper backing them whatsoever.

In the 2010 election, the swing in the UK from Labour to Tory was 5 per cent, but amongst readers of the *Sun* the swing was a whopping 13.5 per cent. However, 12.5 per cent of this swing took place *before* the *Sun* explicitly endorsed Cameron, suggesting that they realised which way the wind was blowing with their readers and the country and followed suit, rather than that they have an incredible brainwashing hold over their readers.

But.

This isn't to say that the *Sun* isn't incredibly damaging. You don't have to win actual elections for the Conservatives in order to be incredibly harmful shits. In fact, their willingness to follow popular (at least amongst their target audience) opinion – and reinforce their views – is one of the things that makes them so awful.

ACTUALLY GOOD STORIES

THE DOG THAT EATS MONEY

4 November 1978

In 1978 the *Sun* ran a story about a dog that ate money. I'm not being face-tious, it's just genuinely a fun story: there's a reason people buy this paper in huge numbers, you know.

Alva, they reported on page 5 next to a picture of the dog looking guilty with a wad of cash in its mouth, is a dog that likes to eat money. I say is, I mean was. This was 4 November 1978. Unless it turns out that cash prevents dogs from ageing, this dog is definitely dead.

Her owners were fed up with her after she ate a bunch of money, and the *Sun* got some great quotes out of them, almost making the terrible paper the *Sun* would go on to become all worth it.

'She ate two tenners last Christmas and a few months later she gobbled up four quid' – that's £24, in case you're keeping track. Alva went on to eat another £32 (including £15 she ate, shat out and ate again) before they decided they might have to kill her.

'She must like the taste of money. But we cannot afford it any more and she is under a death sentence unless we can find her a good home.'

A cute story about a wacky dog turned into a sinister tale of casual dog murder. Nonsense tat doesn't get much better than this.

While I'm praising the *Sun*, I must say they do write a hell of a pun. When Inverness Caledonian Thistle beat Celtic 3–0 in 2000, somebody at the *Scottish Sun* deserves a raise for the headline 'SUPER CALEY GO BALLISTIC CELTIC ARE ATROCIOUS' (9 February 2000).

When George Michael got into a car crash they went with 'SCRAPE ME UP BEFORE YOU GO SLOW' (20 May 2013). I'm not saying it's the most appropriate thing to pun about (same with 'BIN BAGGED' (2 May 2011), when Osama bin Laden was killed, 'SHIP SHIP HOORAY' (14 January 2004) when Harold Shipman hanged himself, and 'Float like a butterfly sting like R.I.P.' when Muhammad Ali died (4 June 2016)), but if you're going to turn a car crash into a pun you could do much worse. It's a hell of a lot better than when he was found with drugs and they went for 'CARELESS SPLIFFER' (27 February 2006), or their massively homophobic puerile headline 'Elton takes David up the aisle' (22 December 2005).

But it shows that, if they put their minds to it, the *Sun* could be a better paper than they are. Tone down the xenophobia, knock off the homophobia, quit with the misogyny, lay off the asylum seekers, the puns can stay.

CONCLUSION (OF SORTS)

Look, let's be honest here and say that I came into this project with the attitude of a man who's about to watch *2 Girls 1 Cup* on repeat for six months. Don't ever tell me I'm not up to speed with current cultural references.

Just as I'd seen all the reaction videos of people being sick into buckets and knew I probably wasn't going to be watching the next *Shrek*, I'd read about the kinds of journalism the *Sun* is famed for. But just like it's not possible to guess how gross it's going to be before you watch what those two women do with that cup, there's nothing that quite prepared me for the bile the paper spewed out on a day-to-day basis in the eighties.

I began reading the *Sun* in chronological order, working my way through the early years of the paper, and for a short few years it all seemed sort of . . . not terrible. The *Sun* immediately strikes you as a paper that's desperately chasing numbers right from the off, sure. They had celeb pieces, sensationalist nonsense and weird stories designed to cater for the horny, but compared to what we see today (in no small part thanks to the *Sun*) it was all rather quaint. They introduced a topless model a year after they relaunched as a tabloid, but even that seemed to be in more of a 'we're busting taboos' kind of way than the 'here, leer at some jugs' section Page 3 would go on to become. It didn't seem like a force for evil, more like a force for just being a bit tacky and shite. Not Darth Vader but Jar Jar fucking Binks – which, let's be honest, is far worse.

This pleasant surprise was short lived, as it turned out they'd do just about anything to chase those sweet sales numbers. They were like a heroin user chasing that first high (in this case, a slight boost in sales when they started printing boobs), and in order to keep sales going they had to compete with others (like the *Star*) emulating what they did. It was a race to the bottom, which was good, because that's where you get the best upskirt shots. By the eighties, prejudice was sweating out of its pores, particularly in their coverage of AIDS and anybody who happened to be gay.

Worryingly, this coverage coincided with the *Sun*'s biggest audience share. They had found their readership, and they were shits. As Kelvin MacKenzie is quoted as saying in the eighties:

'You just don't understand the readers, do you, eh? He's the bloke you see in the pub, a right old fascist, wants to send the wogs back, buy his poxy council house, he's afraid of the unions, afraid of the Russians, hates the queers and the weirdos and drug dealers. He doesn't want to hear about that stuff [serious news].'

The *Sun* doesn't exist to tell truths their readers need to know, but to entertain them with stuff that fascists might enjoy. Less Woodward and Bernstein cracking Watergate, more Hitler's clown making amusing fart sounds. Why waste your time informing readers about the issues they're wrong about when you could make more money by giving bigots cherry-picked half-true stories about immigrants that they can take along to their next Klan meeting, for example.

If the audience really is like that – and I'd like to think that it's not (my belief is that a lot of the readers are just normal people in it for the nonsense and gossip rather than the horrifying political stances, but who get offered some terrible opinions as a side dish) – that doesn't absolve the *Sun*. You don't get brownie points for merely following the racism. I'd hazard a guess that some of the staff during the late eighties were themselves homophobic and xenophobic misogynists if they were willing to stick to the editorial line. The later writings of Kelvin MacKenzie, for instance, show a man with some deeply backwards attitudes. And if not, they were willing to write homophobic, xenophobic and sexist stuff for money, which is worse. 'I'm a nice person but for a buttload of cash I'm willing to be human garbage, officer' isn't the most robust moral code I've ever encountered. I think it's more likely

298

the MacKenzies of the writing world believed *Sun* readers are 'right old fascist[s]' to make themselves feel better about the damage they were doing by publishing things fascists would enjoy. The old 'look, they were already Nazis when I got here' defence.

The audience – fash or not fash – has been large for decades, and it's given the *Sun* leverage over politics and politicians. At the start of the book I promised I'd look at whether the *Sun* wins elections like they say they do. To which I'd say a caveated no. Their reach, though impressive, is not enough to swing elections, even the tight ones. Especially given polls showing how few of their readers seem to be able to identify who the hell the *Sun* supported at the time.

But that doesn't mean they aren't influencing their readers (and non-readers who see their headlines on newsagents' shelves, the morning news and social media) in an insidious way, nor that they haven't had a horrifying effect on politics and society for which they themselves should be fired into the actual sun.

One thing that's difficult to get across while condensing decades of the *Sun* down into ninety-nine headlines is the effect of constantly seeing negative stories about asylum seekers and immigrants. You've probably seen a quote from Donald Trump saying 'You tell people a lie three times, they will believe anything.' He didn't actually say this, but you've probably seen it three times and ironically you now believe it. Given that the majority of their readers will rarely encounter an asylum seeker, it's alarming that the *Sun* with their carefully curated, sensationalised tales of bad foreigners is the lens through which readers see people fleeing war zones. The same goes for other minorities, which the *Sun* have demonised week in, week out over the course of many years, until – I would argue – people just accept the idea that that's what the minorities in question are like.

From denigrating asylum seekers to making people eye those on benefits with the suspicion that they're cheats, the *Sun* (and other papers) have nurtured and strengthened a dark side of public opinion rather than just created it. Thanks to it being Britain's best-selling paper for quite some time, politicians have pandered to the *Sun*, believing it to be some sort of conduit of public opinion. In terms of *Star Wars*, they're not the Jedi doing mind control but more like Palpatine saying 'Good, let the hate flow through you' while you shoot electricity out your fingers at a refugee. And by you, I of course mean Tony Blair.

To be fair to Blair – who clearly did believe the *Sun* to be powerful, given how much time he spent courting it and moving policies towards their viewpoint – their hit and smear pieces on politicians have only become more honed, effective and brutal, and they've consistently backed the winning party for decades. It would be difficult to look at that and not want an easier life of having the unhinged bastards on your side in a fight.

The powerful have sucked up to the *Sun* for years, inviting them into Number 10 like Boris Johnson and someone who isn't his wife. They've also invited them for long stays as advisers to the government and to head up government comms. To lay all my cards on the table, I sort of feel like a job where you're supposed to hold politicians to account shouldn't be a well-worn path to heading up their PR team. I'd go as far as to say maybe that means your relationship is a little *too* cosy, in both directions.

And now, as if irrevocably fucking the media and politics in the UK wasn't bad enough, Rupert Murdoch has taken what he's learned and applied it to a bigger market. Here, he has the *Sun* to get him into Number 10. In the US he has Fox News, a show that can basically control what Trump is thinking or doing at any moment. It seems that there's hardly a segment, stat or opinion piece they've done in the past year or so that hasn't resulted in a deranged all-caps presidential tweet. Murdoch was also reportedly having weekly calls with the President, right from the early days of his presidency. The guy that brought you the *Sun* now has the ear of the maniac with the key to the world's biggest nuclear arsenal. Which is just swell.

I don't want to end on a bleak note, so here are some reasons to be cheerful:

Profits at the *Sun* continue to fall, as their parent company pays through the nose for hacking damages at the *News of the World*. The *Sun* itself is in decline, and Murdoch is paying dearly for the actions of his newspaper's shady pursuit of stories. Sales of the *Sun* have been falling steadily – like all newspapers – and soon Britain's number-one best-selling shitrag will become Britain's number-two selling shitrag. Before you develop anything even approaching hope, I should mention that it'll likely be the *Daily Mail* – whose readers are too old to switch from reading print to reading online – who will overtake the *Sun*. While I can't promise you things will be improved, it will be nice to gloat briefly about the decline of the *Sun* before the new racist overlords take over and see us through until we all inevitably die from climate change.

ACKNOWLEDGEMENTS

Special thanks to Emily Barrett from Little, Brown for letting me have a chance to sit here and read the *Sun* for six months, and for being a brilliant editor and reordering my howl of distressed rage from reading the *Sun* for six months until it became vaguely coherent (on a serious note, I'd never have this chance without her and I owe her a career one day). Thanks too to Zoe Gullen for further interpreting the screams. My thanks to everyone else at L, B – from design to production – for getting the book off the ground, and to Emanuel Santos for the perfect illustrations. You are all extremely talented people.

Thank you to Katie for letting me work crazy hours to get it done, and to my sons for occasionally cooperating enough to not physically slam the laptop on my hands. And to my friends and family supporting me over the years, without whom I would have given up years ago, not least my grand-parents, who I know would have loved to read it. Let's just say they were not Murdoch's biggest fans.

But mainly thanks to the *Sun* for putting enough shite out there over the years to make taking the piss out of them occasionally as simple as just writing down what they'd done. I'll say this one good thing about you: you really sped up the whole process.

ABOUT THE AUTHOR

James Felton is a writer and journalist, whose articles regularly appear in the *Guardian*, *Independent*, *Daily Mash* and *IFL Science*. As a writer for television, his work includes the BAFTA award-winning *The Dog Ate My Homework*. Through his Twitter platform of over 200,000 followers and counting, he is a well-known narrator of the Brexit crisis.

NOTES

Misogyny

4   *appeared in newspapers before:* 'Flirty not dirty at 30', BBC News, 17 November 2000, http://news.bbc.co.uk/1/hi/uk/1026989.stm.

4   *When the paper was banned:* Jessica Roy, 'A Brief History of *The Sun*'s Controversial "Page 3"', *New York Magazine*, 20 January 2015, https://nymag.com/intelligencer/2015/01/history-of-the-suns-controversial-page-3.html.

4   *Journalists allege:* Peter Chippindale and Chris Horrie, *Stick It Up Your Punter!: The Uncut Story of the* Sun *Newspaper* (London: Pocket Books, 1992), pp. 28–9.

5   *counting down the days:* Clare Hutchinson, 'Topless model's life change', Wales Online, 20 December 2009, https://www.walesonline.co.uk/news/wales-news/topless-models-life-change-2066093.

9   *'I've got a story . . .':* Chippindale and Horrie, *Stick It Up Your Punter!*, p. 214.

12   *According to the* Guardian*:* Jessica Hodgson, 'Rupert's golden girl basks in glow of brighter Sun', *Observer*, 13 July 2003, https://www.theguardian.com/business/2003/jul/13/sun.pressandpublishing.

12   *On her first day:* 'Dominic Mohan's Sun editorship starts on Page 3', *Guardian*, 2 September 2009, https://www.theguardian.com/media/mediamonkeyblog/2009/sep/02/dominic-mohan-sun-page-3.

14   *One woman:* See Emma Haslett, '11 times The Sun's Page Three girls showed how deeply they cared about the UK economy', 20 January 2015, https://www.cityam.com/times-suns-page-three-girls-cared-deepy-about-uk-economy/.

15   *'remove the degrading . . .':* 'Clare Short: My day in "The Sun" and other Page 3 stories', *Independent*, 23 October 2004, https://www.independent.co.uk/news/uk/politics/clare-short-my-day-in-the-sun-and-other-page-3-stories-535382.html.

16   *reported by the* Guardian*:* Ciar Byrne, 'Sun turns on "killjoy" Short in Page 3 row', *Guardian*, 14 January 2004, https://www.theguardian.com/media/2004/jan/14/pressandpublishing.politicsandthemedia.

19   *study by the University of Hertfordshire:* Michele Lloyd and Shula Ramon, 'Smoke and Mirrors: UK Newspaper Representations of Intimate Partner Domestic Violence', *Violence Against Women*, 23:1 (January 2017). Available at https://www.herts.ac.uk/__data/assets/pdf_file/0008/128807/violence-against-women-2016-lloyd-1077801216634468.pdf.

19   *'Lawyer Les Humes . . .':* 'Daddy's Stabbing Mummy', *The Sun*, 30 July 2002, cited in ibid, 11.

22   *'Our warmest congratulations . . .':* '"Sexist Of The Year" 2014 Award Goes To The Sun's David Dinsmore', *Huffington Post UK*, 18 December 2014, https://www.huffingtonpost.co.uk/2014/12/18/sexist-of-the-year-the-sun-david-dinsmore_n_6346190.html.

23   *'to target a newspaper . . .':* Quoted in ibid.

Celebrity

28   *'It's something I'll never forget':* See 'Goodnight Starr: Who was comedian Freddie Starr and did the I'm A Celebrity star really eat a hamster?', *The Sun*, 14 May 2019, https://www.thesun.co.uk/tvandshowbiz/9042426/freddie-starr-dead-hamster/.

28   *'I'm fed up of people shouting out . . .':* Emma Kelly, 'Freddie Starr joked "I'm a vegetarian" as he debunked hamster-eating tale on I'm A Celebrity', *Metro*, 10 May 2019, https://metro.co.uk/2019/05/10/freddie-starr-joked-im-vegetarian-debunked-hamster-eating-tale-im-celebrity-9479708/.

28   *'I have never eaten . . .':* Quoted in ibid.

29   *'There was nobody more shocked . . .':* Tom Pegden, 'Freddie Starr DIDN'T eat my hamster – Model who owned pet reveals what really happened',

Leicester Mercury, 10 May 2019, https://www.leicestermercury.co.uk/news/freddie-starr-didnt-eat-hamster-2855324.

29   *though Starr's manager:* David Hughes, '"Freddie Starr ate my hamster": What this bizarre tabloid story was all about – and if it was true', *i*, 12 May 2019, https://inews.co.uk/news/uk/freddie-starr-ate-my-hamster-true-story-max-clifford-the-sun-explained-502164.

29   *'This was the way tabloids worked . . .':* See @GMB, 9 May 2019, https://twitter.com/gmb/status/1126727754177662977.

30   *'I was gay . . .':* Elton John, *Me* (London: Pan Macmillan, 2019), p. 199.

34   *'Gay man sucks penis . . .':* Ibid., p. 202.

36   *'When I published those stories . . .':* 'Kelvin MacKenzie: Old Mac opens up', *Press Gazette*, 11 October 2006, https://www.pressgazette.co.uk/kelvin-mackenzie-old-mac-opens-up/.

40   *were also false:* David Conn, 'How the Sun's "truth" about Hillsborough unravelled', *Guardian*, 26 April 2016, https://www.theguardian.com/football/2016/apr/26/how-the-suns-truth-about-hillsborough-unravelled.

41   *Kelvin MacKenzie had apparently spent:* Peter Chippindale and Chris Horrie, *Stick It Up Your Punter!: The Uncut Story of the* Sun *Newspaper* (London: Pocket Books, 1992), p. 339.

41   *Sales in Merseyside:* Davey Brett, 'Liverpool Vs The Sun: How the City Rid Itself of the UK's Biggest Paper', *Vice*, 9 May 2017, https://www.vice.com/en_uk/article/nz8ez8/liverpool-vs-the-sun-how-the-city-rid-itself-of-the-uks-biggest-paper.

42   *'I regret Hillsborough . . .':* 'The Fourth Report from the National Heritage Committee of Session 1992–93 on Privacy and Media Intrusion', House of Commons Paper no. 294, 1993.

54   *received bids of £500,000:* Angela Balakrishnan, 'The press pack that chased Diana', *Guardian*, 7 April 2008, https://www.theguardian.com/uk/2008/apr/07/paparazzi.

55   *'But not even I could imagine . . .':* 'Brother accuses press of having blood on its hands', *Irish Times*, 1 September 1997, https://www.irishtimes.com/news/brother-accuses-press-of-having-blood-on-its-hands-1.101920.

59   *Ofcom eventually received:* Ofcom Content Sanctions Committee,

'Consideration of sanction against Channel Four Television Corporation in respect of its service Channel 4', https://www.ofcom.org.uk/__data/assets/pdf_file/0015/61404/channel4_cbb.pdf.

62   *'Meghan Markle has been subject...':* 'A Statement by the Communications Secretary to Prince Harry', 8 November 2016, https://www.royal.uk/statement-communications-secretary-prince-harry.

63   *YouGov polling:* See 'Meghan, Duchess of Sussex', YouGov, https://yougov.co.uk/topics/politics/explore/public_figure/Meghan_Duchess_of_Sussex.

76   *'the lowest form of journalism...':* Twitter statement by Ben Stokes (@benstokes38), 17 September 2019. Quoted in Jedidajah Otte, 'Ben Stokes attacks "despicable" Sun story about family tragedy', *Guardian*, 17 September 2019, https://www.theguardian.com/sport/2019/sep/17/ben-stokes-attacks-despicable-sun-story-family-tragedy.

76   *'it is only right to point out...':* Charlotte Tobitt, 'Sun defends Ben Stokes family tragedy story after cricketer slams it as "lowest form of journalism"', *Press Gazette*, 17 September 2019, https://www.pressgazette.co.uk/sun-defends-ben-stokes-family-tragedy-story-after-cricketer-slams-it-as-lowest-form-of-journalism/.

Crime

84   *A poll they conducted:* Ros Taylor, 'Hanging judgment', *Guardian*, 25 February 2008, https://www.theguardian.com/news/blog/2008/feb/25/hangingjudgment1.

86   *'If only you had done...':* Nick Cohen, 'With police and tabloids in cahoots, Colin Stagg became a sacrificial lamb', 24 June 2006, https://www.theguardian.com/commentisfree/2006/jun/25/comment.homeaffairs.

86   *'deceptive conduct of the grossest kind':* Ibid.

86   *'slowly settled into the life of a recluse':* See John Grieve, 'A fair cop?', *Guardian*, 12 January 2008, https://www.theguardian.com/books/2008/jan/12/crime.society.

87   *pieces about his intimate life:* Cohen, 'With police and tabloids in cahoots, Colin Stagg became a sacrificial lamb'.

87   *In 2011, he was informed:* James Robinson, 'Phone-hacking: Colin Stagg targeted by News of the World', *Guardian*, 5 July 2011, https://www.theguardian.com/media/2011/jul/05/phone-hacking-colin-stagg-news-of-the-world.

87   *He ended up accepting:* Justin Davenport, 'Colin Stagg "revenge" as NoW settles phone-hack case', *Evening Standard*, 20 December 2012, https://www.standard.co.uk/news/crime/colin-stagg-s-revenge-as-now-settles-phone-hack-case-8427308.html.

87   *also blagged their way:* Gordon Rayner, 'Sarah Ferguson's phone was hacked for six years by News of the World, court hears', *Telegraph*, 8 February 2013, https://www.telegraph.co.uk/news/uknews/phone-hacking/9857110/Sarah-Fergusons-phone-was-hacked-for-six-years-by-News-of-the-World-court-hears..html.

87   *'They published two pages . . .':* Davenport, 'Colin Stagg "revenge" as NoW settles phone-hack case'.

88   *'Justice has been done . . .':* Ibid.

90   *One prison officer was jailed:* 'Three men jailed for selling information to the Sun', BBC News, 27 March 2013.

90   *'to pose as a pen-pal . . .':* James Doleman, 'Phone-hacking trial: Rebekah Brooks faces Milly Dowler questions', *The Drum*, 11 March 2014, https://www.thedrum.com/opinion/2014/03/11/phone-hacking-trial-rebekah-brooks-faces-milly-dowler-questions.

93   *contacting Surrey police:* 'Police "regret" over Milly Dowler phone hacking', BBC News, 8 September 2016, https://www.bbc.co.uk/news/uk-england-surrey-37307139.

93   *the* Guardian *published an article:* Roy Greenslade, 'How News of the World's Milly Dowler stories changed between editions', 22 August 2011, https://www.theguardian.com/media/greenslade/2011/aug/22/phone-hacking-newsinternational.

93   *'a truly dreadful act . . .':* 'Milly Dowler hacking claims dreadful, Cameron says', BBC News, 5 July 2011, https://www.bbc.co.uk/news/uk-14024668.

93   *information they'd got:* Greenslade, 'How News of the World's Milly Dowler stories changed between editions'.

94   *'That was unforgivable...'*: Dominic Ponsford, '"UNFORGIVABLE":
      Andy Coulson gets 18 months for phone-hacking, Miskiw and Thurlbeck
      also jailed', *Press Gazette*, 4 July 2014, https://www.pressgazette.co.uk/
      former-news-world-editor-andy-coulson-jailed-18-months-miskiw-and-
      thurlbeck-also-sent-down/.

99   *The National Crime Survey regularly shows:* B. Duffy, R. Wake, T. Burrows
      and P. Bremner, 'Closing the gaps – crime and public perceptions',
      International Review of Law Computers & Technology, 22:1–2 (July 2008), 26.

99   *to pick 2015/16 at random:* 'Public perceptions of crime in England
      and Wales: year ending March 2016', Office for National Statistics, 7
      September 2017, https://www.ons.gov.uk/peoplepopulationandcommunity/
      crimeandjustice/articles/publicperceptionsofcrimeinenglandandwales/
      yearendingmarch2016.

101   *as measured by the police:* Tom Edgington, 'Violent crime: Is it getting worse?',
      BBC News, 7 June 2018, https://www.bbc.co.uk/news/uk-44397532.

101   *was actually falling:* Alison Walker, John Flatley, Chris Kershaw and Debbie
      Moon (eds), *Crime in England and Wales 2008/09. Volume 1: Findings from
      the British Crime Survey and police recorded crime*, Home Office Statistical
      Bulletin, July 2009, http://news.bbc.co.uk/1/shared/bsp/hi/pdfs/16_07_09_
      bcs.pdf.

101   *'a perceived threat to their way of life':* Roy Greenslade, 'The good news about
      bad news – it sells', *Guardian*, 4 September 2007, https://www.theguardian.
      com/media/greenslade/2007/sep/04/thegoodnewsaboutbadnewsi.

Prejudice

108   *'like I was some kind of rapist':* Benjamin Zephaniah, *The Life and Rhymes of
      Benjamin Zephaniah: The Autobiography* (London: Scribner, 2019).

115   *'avoid speculation of causes...':* 'Reporting on celebrity deaths', Samaritans,
      https://www.samaritans.org/about-samaritans/media-guidelines/
      reporting-celebrity-deaths/.

118   *7078 readers:* Figures quoted in *Gay Times*, December 1987. Available at
      https://gtmediawatch.org/1969/08/01/gay-times-december-1987/.

125   *'We cannot wrap . . .':* 'Scrap EastBenders', *The Sun*, 26 January 1989.

125   *The results showed:* Figures quoted in *Gay Times*, March 1989. Available at https://gtmediawatch.org/1968/08/01/gay-times-march-1989/.

126   *'I don't understand why . . .':* *Independent*, 25 November 1989.

127   *Lord Kilbracken's critics rightly said:* See David Miller, Jenny Kitzinger, Kevin Willians and Peter Beharrell, *The Circuit of Mass Communication: Media Strategies, Representation and Audience Reception in the AIDS Crisis* (London: Sage, 1988), p. 49.

129   *'There are hundreds of thousands . . .':* *The Sun*, 18 November 1989.

134   *'As an Eastern European . . .':* 'Making a meal of a myth', MediaWise, http://www.mediawise.org.uk/wp-content/uploads/2011/03/Making-a-meal-of-a-myth.pdf.

135   *The Leveson inquiry:* 'Leveson finds tabloid press reporting on asylum seekers "concerning"', 29 November 2012, https://cityofsanctuary.org/2012/11/29/leveson-finds-tabloid-press-reporting-on-asylum-seekers-concerning/.

137   *'an insult to Mr Bruno . . .':* Sue O'Reilly, 'Support floods in for boxing hero Bruno', *Irish Examiner*, 24 September 2003, https://www.irishexaminer.com/news/world/arid-10105962.html.

137   *complained about the first edition:* 'Sun back-pedals over Bruno jibe', *Guardian*, 23 September 2003, https://www.theguardian.com/media/2003/sep/23/pressandpublishing.mentalhealth1.

138   *Marjorie Wallace recalls:* Ian Cook, 'The Sun: no longer bonkers?', BBC News, 9 December 2003, http://web.archive.org/web/20040624235402/http:/www.bbc.co.uk/ouch/news/btn/bruno_sun.shtml.

138   *'I remember having the conversation . . .':* Ibid.

140   *The report the* Sun *had based the piece on:* Louis Appleby et al., 'The National Confidential Inquiry into Suicide and Homicide by People with Mental Illness. Annual Report: July 2013', University of Manchester, http://documents.manchester.ac.uk/display.aspx?DocID=37595

141   *in 2010–11:* Mona Chalabi, 'The Sun says 1,200 people have been killed by "mental patients" – is it true?', *Guardian*, 7 October 2013, https://www.theguardian.com/society/reality-check/2013/oct/07/sun-people-killed-mental-health-true#maincontent.

144   *Zeid Ra'ad Al Hussein, criticised the paper:* Sam Jones, 'UN human rights

chief denounces Sun over Katie Hopkins "cockroach" column', *Guardian*, 24 April 2015, https://www.theguardian.com/global-development/2015/apr/24/katie-hopkins-cockroach-migrants-denounced-united-nations-human-rights-commissioner.

144   *a petition signed by 315,636 people:* 'Remove Katie Hopkins as a Columnist', Change.org, https://www.change.org/p/the-sun-newspaper-remove-katie-hopkins-as-a-columnist.

146   *looked at coverage:* 'Press Coverage of the Refugee and Migrant Crisis in the EU: A Content Analysis of Five European Countries', Report prepared for the United Nations High Commission for Refugees, December 2015, https://www.unhcr.org/56bb369c9.pdf.

150   *twelve hundred complaints:* Sydney Smith, '1,200 Complaints against Sun's British Muslims Story, Sun Stands by Poll Report', iMediaEthics, 24 November 2015, https://www.imediaethics.org/1200-complaints-suns-british-muslims-poll-sympathy-for-isis/.

151   *a similar Sky News/Survation poll:* See Louis Doré, 'The Sun tried to explain the "1 in 5 Muslims" poll but only made things worse', *Independent*, 24 November 2015, https://www.indy100.com/article/the-sun-tried-to-explain-the-1-in-5-muslims-poll-but-only-made-things-worse--b1mMvXk6Yx.

152   *IPSO ruled:* Kevin Rawlinson, 'Sun ordered to admit British Muslims story was "significantly misleading"', *Guardian*, 26 March 2016, https://www.theguardian.com/media/2016/mar/26/ipso-sun-print-statement-british-muslims-headline.

154   *The Croatian authorities:* Paul Bradbury, 'Toilet Journalism, The Sun, Emile Ghessen and Croatia', Total Croatia News, 8 December 2015, https://www.total-croatia-news.com/editorial/1701-toilet-journalism-the-sun-emile-ghessen-and-croatia.

156   *'Creating a link to the faith . . .':* Sydney Smith, 'No, Train Driver didn't crash because of Ramadan Fast. UK Sun Unpublishes', iMediaEthics, 26 November 2016, https://www.imediaethics.org/no-train-driver-didnt-crash-ramadan-fast-uk-sun-unpublishes/.

158   *But Hannah said:* 'Trans newlyweds call out "offensive" Sun front page', BBC News, 27 March 2018, https://www.bbc.co.uk/news/uk-43558113.

158   *'Jake and Hannah's is a wonderful . . .':* Ibid.

161 *Within three months:* Peter Chippindale and Chris Horrie, *Stick It Up Your Punter!: The Uncut Story of the* Sun *Newspaper* (London: Pocket Books, 1992), p. 99.

161 *compete with the* Mirror: Ibid., pp. 184–5.

162 *'No, I'm not having pictures ...':* Mark Hollingsworth, 'Daylight on the Sun', *New Statesman*, 22 November 1985. Available at http://markhollingsworth. co.uk/wp-content/uploads/2018/10/Daylight-on-the-sun.pdf.

162 *When Editor MacKenzie found out:* Chippindale and Horrie, *Stick It Up Your Punter!*, p. 99.

165 *the Radio 4 programme: Punt PI*, BBC Radio 4, 8 October 2010.

166 *there are still urban legends:* 'The Crying Boy', Creepypasta Wiki, https:// creepypasta.fandom.com/wiki/The_Crying_Boy.

175 *'They didn't do anything ...': Human Rights in Northern Ireland: Promises Kept or Promises Broken? – Hearing before the Subcommittee on International Operations and Human Rights of the Committee on International Relations,* House of Representatives, One Hundred Seventh Congress, first session, 15 March 2001 (microform, 2001).

176 *She also didn't hold:* Heather Mills, 'Sudden death and the long quest for answers', *Independent*, 28 September 1995, https://www.independent.co.uk/ news/sudden-death-and-the-long-quest-for-answers-1603189.html.

176 *The* Sun *and the* Sunday Times: Duncan Lamont, 'Speaking ill of the dead', *Guardian*, 11 August 2003, https://www.theguardian.com/media/2003/ aug/11/mondaymediasection.hutton.

177 *In 1989, a mother:* Rodney Tiffen, *Rupert Murdoch: A Reassessment* (Sydney: NewSouth, 2014), p. 194.

178 *Later, Hunt would explain:* Chippindale and Horrie, *Stick It Up Your Punter!*, pp. 386–8.

179 *Finally, in 1991: Guardian*, 24 May 1991.

185 *The results have not been replicated:* Brian Deer, 'How the case against the MMR vaccine was fixed', *BMJ*, 6 January 2011, https://www.bmj.com/ content/342/bmj.c5347.

189 *countless studies:* See, for example, L. Taylor, A. Swerdfeger and G. Eslick,

'Vaccines are not associated with autism: An evidence-based meta-analysis of case-control and cohort studies', *Vaccine*, 32:29 (2014), 3623–9.

189   *no link whatsoever:* A. Jain, J. Marshall, A. Buikema, T. Bancroft, J. Kelly and C. Newschaffer, 'Autism occurrence by MMR vaccine status among US children with older siblings with and without autism', *JAMA*, 313:15 (2015), 1534.

189   *had even written about it:* 'MMR Muddle', *The Sun*, 23 January 2001.

191   *They once outed Laa Laa:* 'Telegrubbies', *The Sun*, 19 August 1997.

198   *no connection was actually ever found:* David Mikkelson, 'How Much of a Threat Is the Purported "Momo Challenge" Suicide Game?', Snopes, 26 February 2019, https://www.snopes.com/news/2019/02/26/momo-challenge-suicide-game/.

198   *'far fetched and devoid of any evidence':* 'CID: Momo invites locally generated', *The Times of India*, 29 August 2018, https://web.archive.org/web/20180830104622/https:timesofindia.indiatimes.com/city/kolkata/cid-momo-invites-locally-generated/articleshow/65591157.cms?

199   *The Police Service Northern Ireland:* 'PSNI Statement regarding Momo Challenge', Police Service of Northern Ireland, 25 February 2019, https://www.psni.police.uk/news/Latest-News/250219-psni-statement-regarding-momo-challenge/.

200   *'These stories being highly publicised . . .':* Jim Waterston, 'Viral "Momo challenge" is a malicious hoax, say charities', *Guardian*, 28 February 2019, https://www.theguardian.com/technology/2019/feb/28/viral-momo-challenge-is-a-malicious-hoax-say-charities.

Foreign Affairs

204   *'WE'LL SMASH 'EM':* Chris Horrie, 'Gotcha! How the Sun reaped spoils of war', *Observer*, 7 April 2002, https://www.theguardian.com/business/2002/apr/07/pressandpublishing.media.

206   *still include in lists of their best today:* Will Hagerty, 'No Sun No Fun: The story behind The Sun's cheekiest headlines & madcap stunts as we turn 50', *The Sun*, 18 November 2019, https://www.thesun.co.uk/news/10352474/

the-story-behind-the-suns-cheekiest-headlines-madcap-stunts-as-we-turn-50/.

208 *according to Ipsos MORI polls:* 'The Falklands War – Panel Survey', 30 June 1982. Available at https://www.ipsos.com/ipsos-mori/en-uk/falklands-war-panel-survey.

209 *'Judging by many of the comments . . .':* Hansard, 6 May 1982, vol. 23. Available at: https://hansard.parliament.uk/Commons/1982-05-06/debates/b500da24-b247-430d-81ff-0cc4e79b77ef/Engagements?highlight=%22the%20case%20for%20our%20british%20forces%22#contribution-3a8e751e-8335-4660-8486-c5291ec50e0d.

211 *According to one soldier:* See Andy Beckett, 'Belligerent Britain', *Guardian*, 28 September 2002, https://www.theguardian.com/books/2002/sep/28/featuresreviews.guardianreview1.

213 *'wholly tasteless and puerile':* 'Anti-French jokes printed in a London tabloid newspaper were . . .', UPI Archives, 18 June 1984, https://www.upi.com/Archives/1984/06/18/Anti-French-jokes-printed-in-a-London-tabloid-newspaper-were/2877456379200/.

218 *actually broke French law:* Ciar Byrne, 'Sun's French stunt branded "disgusting"', *Guardian*, 21 February 2003, https://www.theguardian.com/media/2003/feb/21/pressandpublishing.Iraqandthemedia.

222 *the Iraq Body Count project, estimates:* 'Database – Iraq Body Count', https://www.iraqbodycount.org/database/.

222 *The project has been criticised:* Amy Hagopian et al., 'How to estimate (and not to estimate) war deaths: A reply to van Weezel and Spagat', *Research & Politics*, 7 February 2018, https://journals.sagepub.com/doi/10.1177/2053168017753901.

222 *'Iraq probably has no weapons . . .':* 'Cook's resignation speech', BBC News, 18 March 2003.

222 *'Where are the Arab armies? . . .':* Matthew Tempest, 'Galloway expelled from Labour', *Guardian*, 23 October 2003, https://www.theguardian.com/politics/2003/oct/23/labour.georgegalloway.

222 *In 2016, the Chilcot inquiry published:* See 'The Report of the Iraq Inquiry', 6 July 2016, Cabinet Office and Iraq Inquiry, https://www.gov.uk/government/publications/the-report-of-the-iraq-inquiry.

225   *'aggressively investigate':* 'Pentagon vows to probe Saddam photos', CNN International, 21 May 2005, http://edition.cnn.com/2005/WORLD/meast/05/20/saddam.photos/.

225   *'military sources said ...':* Quoted in ibid.

225   *Graham Dudman soon revealed:* Ian Burrell, 'As usual, the press is hyperventilating – but this time it's out of sheer nerves', *Independent*, 26 November 2012, https://www.independent.co.uk/news/media/opinion/ian-burrell-as-usual-the-press-is-hyperventilating-but-this-time-its-out-of-sheer-nerves-8349201.html.

225   *'just a lame attempt ...':* Quoted in ibid.

229   *In defence of the article:* Michael Allen, 'Sun benefits tourism gaffe "may have resulted from subbing error"', *Guardian*, 13 November 2013, https://www.theguardian.com/media/2013/nov/13/sun-benefits-tourism-gaffe.

231   *'abnormal curvature':* Commission Regulation (EC) No. 2257/94.

231   *'came from a mate ...':* Kate Lyons, 'The 10 best Euro myths – from custard creams to condoms', *Guardian*, 23 June 2016, https://www.theguardian.com/politics/2016/jun/23/10-best-euro-myths-from-custard-creams-to-condoms.

Campaigns and Vendettas

241   *'If you are going to link ...':* 'Demon ears', *Observer*, 21 March 1999, https://www.theguardian.com/politics/1999/mar/21/uk.politicalnews2.

243   *Farmer Tony Martin:* Mark Shields, 'Tony Martin: Man who shot burglars knows he still divides opinion', 17 August 2019, https://www.bbc.co.uk/news/uk-england-norfolk-49355814.

243   *This was later reduced:* Paul Gilbert, 'Legal lessons of the Martin case', BBC News, 30 October 2001, http://news.bbc.co.uk/1/hi/uk/1628710.stm.

247   *'smacks a little of lynch mob behaviour ...':* Ciar Byrne, 'Sun's anti-yob campaign raises "lynch mob" fears', *Guardian*, 20 October 2003, https://www.theguardian.com/media/2003/oct/20/pressandpublishing.sun.

247   *an innocent man in a neck brace:* 'Vigilante attack on innocent man', BBC News, 25 July 2000, http://news.bbc.co.uk/1/hi/uk/848737.stm.

248 *a paediatrician's house:* 'Paediatrician attacks "ignorant" vandals', BBC News, 30 August 2000, http://news.bbc.co.uk/1/hi/wales/901723.stm.

248 *'This incident shows...':* 'Mob mistakes man for sex abuser', BBC News, 24 July 2000, http://news.bbc.co.uk/1/hi/uk/849098.stm.

249 *'failed by all agencies':* Katherine Sellgren, 'Baby Peter "was failed by all agencies"', BBC News, 26 October 2010, https://www.bbc.co.uk/news/education-11621391.

250 *by the editor's own admission:* Paul Cheston, 'Phone hacking trial: "Bonkers Bruno headline was one of my many mistakes at the Sun," says Rebekah Brooks', 27 February 2014, https://www.standard.co.uk/news/crime/phone-hacking-trial-bonkers-bruno-headline-was-one-of-my-many-mistakes-at-the-sun-says-rebekah-9157667.html.

251 *she was eventually awarded:* Patrick Butler, 'Sacked Baby P chief Sharon Shoesmith won payout of more than £600,000', *Guardian*, 23 July 2014, https://www.theguardian.com/society/2014/jul/23/baby-p-chief-sharon-shoesmith-won-payout-over-dismissal#maincontent.

253 *'Baby P effect':* Andy McNicoll, 'Ten years on from Baby P: social work's story', Community Care, 3 August 2017, https://www.communitycare.co.uk/2017/08/03/ten-years-baby-p-social-works-story/.

253 *One measurable consequence:* Polly Curtis, 'The long shadow of Baby P', Tortoise, 6 July 2019, https://members.tortoisemedia.com/2019/07/06/baby-p/content.html?sig=x6-yCjlmf1rAQR1rY25Rnfzu1VCuyiVAzbdW2R1erXE&utm_source=Twitter&utm_medium=Social&utm_campaign=6July2019&utm_content=family_sep_baby_p.

253 *'Senior managers didn't want to be...':* McNicoll, 'Ten years on from Baby P'.

253 *[Ed Balls] had no idea of the damage...':* Ibid.

253 *'doctors are not blamed...':* Curtis, 'The long shadow of Baby P'.

Politics

262 *an Ipsos MORI poll found:* Patrick Worrall, 'Does the Sun win elections', FactCheck, Channel 4, 30 April 2015, https://www.channel4.com/news/

factcheck/factcheck-sun-win-elections.

269 *'No big decision could ever be made . . .':* Lance Price, 'Rupert Murdoch is effectively a member of Blair's cabinet', *Guardian*, 1 July 2006, https://www.theguardian.com/commentisfree/2006/jul/01/comment.rupertmurdoch.

274 *'The gay mafia story felt wrong . . .':* Brian Wheeler, 'Gay politicians and the tabloid press', BBC News, 23 July 2012, https://www.bbc.co.uk/news/uk-politics-18709096.

277 *'We are a Scottish newspaper . . .':* 'Election 2015: The Sun and Scottish Sun endorse rival parties', BBC News, 30 April 2015, https://www.bbc.co.uk/news/election-2015-scotland-32523804.

280 *An analysis by the Media Standards Trust:* John Plunkett and Ami Sedghi, 'Sun has torn into Miliband even more viciously than it hit Neil Kinnock', *Guardian*, 6 May 2015, https://www.theguardian.com/media/2015/may/06/sun-ed-miliband-neil-kinnock-murdoch-labour.

282 *70 per cent of* Sun *readers:* Tom Newton Dunn, 'IT'S THE SUN WOT BREXIT: The Sun had the highest percentage of Brexit voters than any other newspaper, new research says', *The Sun*, 7 December 2016, https://www.thesun.co.uk/news/2346308/the-sun-had-the-highest-percentage-of-brexit-voters-than-any-other-newspaper-new-research-says/.

283 *'significantly misleading':* 'Sun's Queen Brexit headline ruled "misleading"', BBC News, 18 May 2016, https://www.bbc.co.uk/news/uk-36319085.

290 *'The pattern of vote switching . . .':* Quoted in Patrick Worrall, 'Does the Sun win elections', FactCheck, Channel 4, 30 April 2015, https://www.channel4.com/news/factcheck/factcheck-sun-win-elections.

Conclusion (of sorts)

298 *'You just don't understand the readers . . .':* Peter Chippindale and Chris Horrie, *Stick It Up Your Punter!: The Uncut Story of the* Sun *Newspaper* (London: Pocket Books, 1992), pp. 176–7.